Royalist, But ...

Royalist, But ...

Herefordshire in the English Civil War,
1640–51

by
David Ross

LOGASTON PRESS

LOGASTON PRESS
Little Logaston Woonton Almeley
Herefordshire HR3 6QH
logastonpress.co.uk

First published by Logaston Press 2012
Copyright © David Ross 2012

ISBN 978 1 906663 63 6

Typeset by Logaston Press
and printed and bound in printed in Spain
by Graphy Cems

For Isabel and Miranda

And the face of the King's Servants grew greater than the King:
He tricked them, and they trapped him, and stood round him in a ring.
The new grave lords closed round him, that had eaten the abbey's fruits,
And the men of the new religion, with their bibles in their boots.
We saw their shoulders moving, to menace or discuss,
And some were pure and some were vile; but none took heed of us.
We saw the King as they killed him, and his face was proud and pale;
And a few men talked of freedom, while England talked of ale.

G.K. Chesterton, *The Secret People*

We are all cousins in Herefordshire.

Old local saying

Contents

Acknowledgements

Students of the Civil War in Herefordshire are fortunate to have a number of good books on the period. The prime one is the two-volume *Memorials of the Civil War Between King Charles I and the Parliament of England, as it Affected Herefordshire and the Adjacent Counties,* by John Webb and completed by his son T.W. Webb. Its ambit ranges beyond the borders implied by the title, and its scholarship and judgement were of assistance to Samuel Rawson Gardiner in his magisterial *History of the Great Civil War.* The Webbs' account was published in the 1870s, since when the causes and events of the Civil War have been the subject of much further research and thought, most significantly in the past forty years. Detailed information on the leading men of both sides was collected by Geoffrey McParlin for a University of Wales PhD thesis in 1981, 'The Herefordshire Gentry in County Government, 1625-1661'. Two of these men have been scrutinised in Jacqueline Eales's *Puritans and Roundheads: The Harleys of Brampton Bryan and the Outbreak of the English Civil War,* and Ian Atherton's study of Viscount Scudamore, *Ambition and Failure in Stuart England.* Dr Atherton has made other valuable contributions to Herefordshire's history in the Civil War period. Events in Herefordshire are also treated in Anthony Fletcher's *The Outbreak of the English Civil War,* John Morrill's *Revolt in the Provinces* and Ronald Hutton's *The Royalist War Effort, 1642-1646,* among others, and in numerous contributions to books and journals by G.E. Aylmer (see Bibliography). Another great asset to students of Herefordshire's past is provided by the papers and reports in the Proceedings of the Woolhope Naturalists' Field Club.

Other sources of contemporary information are the British Library, the National Archives, the Bodleian Library, and the London Library. Closer to home, the Herefordshire County Records Office, the Hereford Reference Library, the Hereford Cathedral Library and the Woolhope Club Library have all been extremely helpful. I am grateful to have been able to discuss aspects of the subject with Ron Shoesmith, author of *Herefordshire in the Civil War* (1992). Thanks are also due to Edward Harley for an instructive visit to Brampton Bryan, to Dr Howard Tomlinson for his helpful interest, and to Lawrence Barroll Christmas of Oak Park, Illinois, USA, for use of his Barroll family research. For assistance with picture research I am grateful to Andy Johnson of Logaston Press, Lauren Price and other staff at Hereford City Library, Catherine Willson at Herefordshire Museums, and Edward Harley.

Foreword

In Herefordshire a sense of historic continuity is threaded into the fabric of daily life, sustained by the age-long patterns and processes of the land – the breeding of sheep and cattle, the yearly harvest, the use and conservation of woods and water-meadows, the management of rivers. Ancient buildings survive, intact or as evocative ruins. Local surnames testify to successive generations of family life in the county. Its pattern of settlement is still that of four hundred years ago, with the same distribution of towns and villages, though Hereford city now holds over a third of the county's population rather than one tenth. But the boundaries of the old walled town are still clear. Twice taken and twice reclaimed before its final capitulation, it was the last place to give the ill-fated King Charles I a 'victory' in the Civil War.

Eleven or so generations separate us from the people who lived through that war. To visit the period requires a journey in time, into a countryside that would be immediately recognisable through familiar landmarks, and yet disconcertingly different, with far greater expanses of open ground, more pools, streams and marshland, denser woodlands, and occasional pockets of industry. But it also needs a leap in imaginative sympathy. The disturbances and troubles of the mid-17th century forced people to think very seriously about personal choice in national issues, about the nature of government, and about even vaster considerations. When two warring factions each claim divine authority, whose side is God on? Profound differences in attitudes and values between the people of then and of now have to be borne in mind if we want not only to know what happened, but to get a sense of how and why events fell out in the way they did. The people of Herefordshire were facing an altogether new and deeply alarming situation. No wonder the Vicar of Clun, speaking at Brampton Bryan in Herefordshire, cried out, 'Oh! what comfortable times we had (through God's mercy) before the wars!'[1]

Note. In the 17th century, the official year was dated from 25 March to 24 March, and as a result, 'January 1643' in documents of the time often means January 1644. Dates have been adjusted to modern usage. Money values, of course, were very different. There were 240 pennies to a pound. A labouring man earned around six pence (6d) for each day that he worked. Most of his reckonings would be in farthings, worth a quarter-penny.

Herefordshire in the Civil War – a Timeline, 1640-49

(Key national events in italics)

1640

January	Grand Jury draws up list of grievances
	300 men sent to participate in the second 'Bishops' War'
March and October	Parliamentary elections
November	Sixth writ for Ship Money

1641

May	Protestation against papist conspiracy
August	Bishop Coke impeached
November	Fitzwilliam Coningsby loses seat in Parliament; his son Humphrey elected
November 19	Panic over Catholic attack
December	Bishop Coke imprisoned

1642

January	*King Charles quits London, January*
	Pro-Bishops petition
Feb-March	Attempt to impose Protestation oath is generally ignored
March-April	Exchange of letters between the 'Nine Worthies' and county Members of Parliament
May	Pro-Parliamentary petition
	Commissioners of array appointed to raise forces for the King
June	Anti-Roundhead demonstrations
July	'Declaration of the County of Hereford' (pro-King)
July 14	Muster of Royalist forces
July 26	James Scudamore elected to Parliament
August 22	*King Charles raises royal standard at Nottingham*
Sept-October	Charles I at Shrewsbury
September 23	Fight at Powick Bridge, Worcester, Royalist victory
October 1	Lord Stamford's force occupies Hereford
October 23	*Battle of Edgehill*

November 12	*Battle of Brentford*
November 13	Skirmish at Ewyas Lacy
December 14	Stamford evacuates Hereford. Royalists resume control with Fitzwilliam Coningsby as Governor

1643

January	Grand Jury sends 'Humble Petition' to Parliament
Feb-March	Lord Herbert's attack on Gloucester fails. Royalists surrender at Highnam, 24 February
March	First attempt against Brampton Bryan
April 18	Royalist muster at Hereford
April 25	Parliamentary force under General Waller captures Hereford. Several Royalist leaders imprisoned
May 20	Waller evacuates Hereford. Royalists resume control. Sir Henry Lingen appointed Sheriff; Sir William Vavasour appointed Governor
July 24	*Prince Rupert captures Bristol*
September 25	*Solemn League and Covenant ratified by Parliament*
September 27	*First Battle of Newbury; Royalists fail to stop Parliamentary army's return to London*
July-September	Siege of Brampton Bryan
October 31	Brilliana Harley dies
November	Hereford forces join in blockade of Gloucester. The deception of Vavasour Sir Michael Woodhouse appointed Governor of Ludlow

1644

January	*King Charles's Parliament at Oxford*
	Prince Rupert named as Captain General
February	Royalists fail to capture Gloucester
March 13	Massacre at Hopton Castle
April	Siege of Brampton Bryan resumes
April 17	Surrender of Brampton Bryan Castle
April	Colonel Massey advances to Ledbury. Shooting of Rev. John Pralph, Stoke Edith
May	Parliamentary forces occupy Ross-on-Wye and storm Wilton Castle
June	Nicholas Mynne appointed Governor of Hereford
June 29	*Royalist victory at Cropredy Down*
July 2	*Parliamentary victory at Marston Moor*
August 3	Fight at Redmarley, death of Nicholas Mynne
August	Col. Barnold made temporary Governor of Hereford until appointment of Barnabas Scudamore on 10 September
	Herbert Croft appointed Dean of Hereford
October 27	*Second Battle of Newbury, inconclusive*
November 6	Prince Maurice named as Major-General of Worcester, Shropshire, Herefordshire, and Monmouthshire

| November 19 | Robert Kyrle defects back to Parliament, captures Monmouth |
| December 2 | Barnabas Scudamore appointed Sheriff of Herefordshire |

1645

January	Association of Worcestershire, Herefordshire and Shropshire formed
February	Skirmish at Eastnor, Richard Hopton captured
March	Rising of the 'clubmen' in Broxash Hundred. Fighting at the Lugg Bridge, 18 March
March 29	Prince Rupert defeats the clubmen at Ledbury
April 23	Fight at Ledbury, Prince Rupert defeats Col. Massey Col. Thomas Morgan is made Governor of Gloucester
June 8	Fight at Stokesay, Royalists defeated
June 14	*Battle of Naseby, major victory for Parliament*
June 19-1 July	King Charles I in Hereford
July	Canon Frome stormed by Scottish force
July 30	Scottish army lays siege to Hereford
August 7	Scottish cavalry depart
August *c.*14	Shooting of the Rev. Rowland Scudamore
September 2	Scottish siege is lifted on the approach of Charles I and a cavalry force
September 3-17	King Charles I's second visit to Hereford
September 10	*Prince Rupert surrenders Bristol*
October 9 and 5 November	Scudamore's failed attacks on Canon Frome
November 12	Skirmish at Ledbury
December 18	Colonels Birch and Morgan capture Hereford for Parliament, Birch appointed Governor

1646

January	Ambrose Elton, Jr, appointed Sheriff
March 9	Birch attempts to capture Goodrich Castle
March 21	Hereford forces participate in battle at Stow on the Wold, Royalist defeat
March	Sir Henry Lingen's demonstration in Hereford
March 28	Puritan ministers appointed to Hereford
April	Birch lays siege to Ludlow
May 5	*King Charles I surrenders himself to Scots at Newark*
end of May	Ludlow surrenders to Birch
June	Birch resumes siege of Goodrich
June 24	*Oxford surrenders to Parliament*
July 19	Worcester surrenders to Parliament
July 31	Lingen surrenders Goodrich Castle
August 19	Surrender of Raglan Castle
October 5	Royalist fracas in Hereford
November	John Birch and Edward Harley elected to Parliament

1647

March	Outbreak of violence at Ewyas Lacy
June 15	Col. Samuel More appointed Governor of Hereford Castle
mid-July	Parliamentary troops at Hereford mutiny; Birch temporarily imprisoned

1648

February	*Fighting in south Wales, as 'Second Civil War' opens*
May	Militia Committee formed in Hereford
July	Lingen raises a Royalist force
late August	Lingen defeated by Col. Thomas Horton and Maj. Robert Harley
October	Birch's regiment at Hereford is finally disbanded
November	Major Wroth Rogers replaces More as Governor
December 6	Sir Robert and Edward Harley arrested in 'Pride's Purge'
	Presbyterians excluded from Parliament, which sits as the 'Rump'

1649

January 30	*Trial of King Charles I; his execution*

Introduction: What was Royalism?

The English Civil War was a national catastrophe. Those who lived through it mourned the fact that it was happening. No place, however small or remote, escaped its impact. Tax collectors knocked on every door, and the appearance of the military press-gang was feared. Thousands were killed in battles, skirmishes and sieges, desolating families on a scale not matched until 1914-18. Many thousands more suffered privation, loss, or financial ruin. These were years of deep anxiety, grief and worry, felt by individuals not only on a personal or family basis, but for their stricken nation. No one knew when, or how, the conflict would be brought to an end. Yet through it all, like a detailed picture defaced by rips and scribbles, the underlying normalities of life remained. Crops were harvested, business went on, communities held together, and the sense of national unity survived. As desperate times do, the war had its moments of heroism and altruism as well as brutality and terror; of endurance as well as destruction.

Though the war was a national, indeed pan-British, conflict, it was mostly waged in a series of local and regional campaigns, each with its own dynamics, triumphs and disasters. Both Royalist and Parliamentarian commands strove with fluctuating degrees of success to provide overall strategic direction to their dispersed forces and supporters. The nature and extent of 'localism' and how it affected the war's events and outcome is still a current topic for historians. In tracing the involvement of individuals, this book tries to establish what the war meant to Herefordshire and how its people viewed and reacted to the struggle. All writers on the war agree that Hereford and its county were a Royalist area. But what did 'Royalism' mean in terms of opinions, behaviour and activity? Before and even during the Civil War period, the overwhelming majority of the English people were Royalists: '... in a real sense everyone was a Royalist in 1641',[2] with a belief in the institution of monarchy and in the king's right and duty to lead the country's government. There had for centuries been one England, an ancient and established nation rich in traditions and with its own distinctive ways of managing its affairs. Now, in the early 1640s, two or more views of England were emerging in public discourse. The King presented himself, and was widely seen, as the crucial component in the English state and polity, established and sanctified by God, of unassailable integrity and authority. To govern the nation was both his right and his duty. The person of the King and the institution of monarchy were inseparable from each other, or at least it was in the King's interest to insist that this was so. The Parliament, by contrast, was not a divinely-ordained institution, but plainly man-made and man-changeable. But in its proceedings it invoked concepts and general ideas that could be seen as God-given and requiring defence if put under threat. On a mundane level it stood for the provision and protection of laws and rights which underpinned everyone's lives. Perhaps also it was, as the elected assembly of the nation, a more important component of national identity than was realised at the time. Well into the 1640s, Parliament fully accepted the King's right to govern, taking 'King and Parliament' as its slogan. During that decade, however, another idea gained strength: that Parliament had the right, even the duty, to make national policy, if the King should be seriously misguided. This took it beyond its historic role of approving taxes and making laws to maintain civic order, and encouraged some people to see in Parliament the supreme element of national authority. At this time the notion of 'political parties' did not exist. Previous history and experience offered no tools or techniques to resolve the hardening deadlock. Only when the English were faced with having to fight one another for alternative forms of monarchy did 'Royalist' become a really meaningful word, identifying someone who chose to express loyalty to the King, against any other considera-tion. Though it now stood for something definite, it still embraced a wide range of opinion and commitment.

Another large and related question is how deeply the issues of the war reached into the hearts and minds of the common people, particularly of rural England (almost all of the country outside London). One historian went so far as to say, '... it is becoming obvious that there were two civil wars, the formal struggle between the rival partisans, and the struggle between these partisans and the bulk of the population, whose support they attempted to enlist for their war effort'.[3] Did the war erupt from deep and no longer containable contra-dictions within a many-layered social fabric, or did it flame from the competition of two power-groups, neither of which could tolerate the other's supremacy? It hardly needs to be said that a full answer will not be found in any one county. But every county's experience reflected the wider issues of the time, and every county's actions contributed to the fluid and unpredictable swirl of events during the war years.

The English people did not want what was called an 'intestine war'. The last great outburst of civil strife had been the Wars of the Roses, far beyond living memory. That conflict could be readily understood as a struggle between rival dynasties for the crown. In 1642, the situation was very different. No-one disputed that Charles Stuart was England's legitimate king. Activists on the Parliamentary side insisted that they were fighting for the King, or at least for his best interests, to rescue him from mistaken or evil-purposed advisers. Equally, the King would repeatedly stress his acceptance of the role of Parliament in the governance of the country, though he meant a Parliament more subservient to his wishes than the one elected in October 1640, which was dominated by members whom he regarded as rebels. The inhabitants of Herefordshire could take their own views of what each really meant, views that might wax and wane in strength and expression, or change. They could be kept quiet or freely expressed. But with the outbreak of war, private opinions became public confrontation. English one-ness had ceased to exist.

Commenting in 2007 on how little is known about the motivations and intentions of those who took the King's side, two scholars wrote that '... we need to begin to consider the extent and composition of the water in which those who actually fought for the King were nourished and protected'.[4] Royalist Herefordshire is surely a good place to start.

Part One

City and County

1

City and County

Hereford in the mid-17th century was a walled city, with gatehouses to control entry and exit. Around five thousand people lived within the walls, and another several hundred beyond them, in houses built along the access roads. The city was divided into six parishes: All Saints, St John Baptist, St Martin, St Nicholas, St Owen and St Peter. St Martin and St Owen extended beyond the walls, to the south and east, and their churches were just outside the walled area. For civic administration, the town was divided into five wards: Wyebridge, St Owen's, Bye-Street, Eigne and Widemarsh. The street pattern had scarcely changed since medieval times.

It was a flourishing town, however, with many new and fine buildings. An authority on the period singled it out, with York, for the elaborate carvings on its guild and market halls and private homes.[1] But along with the steeples of All Saints and St Peter's churches, three buildings in particular stood out. The cathedral had its original arcaded nave, ending in a western tower. A chapter house with fine fan-vaulting around a central pillar opened off the cloister on the south side. On the central tower, a lofty wooden-framed spire was mounted, rising to the highest point in the city at 230ft; a landmark visible from far off. Close by, set on a mound above the River Wye, was the castle keep, with its own outer walls. Though still intact, and formidable in appearance, Hereford Castle had seen better days. It had been in a state of comparative neglect since the 13th century, when the subjection of Wales by Edward I had reduced its strategic importance, though some work had been done to strengthen it during Owen Glyndwr's raids in the early 1400s.[2] Since the political unification of Wales and England under Henry VIII, it had not been manned. As a royal castle, it was nominally the responsibility of the county's High Sheriff, but little had been done by successive sheriffs to maintain it. In a manner still familiar today, the government, looking for assets it could privatise for cash, 'granted' it in 1630 to a courtier, Sir Gilbert North, who in turn conveyed it to William Page, a Baron of Exchequer, and his son Edward 'who held it by feudal tenure from the manor of East Greenwich'.[3] Why the Pages should have wished to be proprietors of a crumbling castle a long way from London is unknown, but they retained ownership until 1646. A local man, John Mason, paid them £1 a year to graze cattle inside the castle walls and for the fishing rights by the river-bank.

In the centre, in what is now the open space of High Town, rose the third outstanding building. Hereford's Market Hall was a two-storey wooden structure set on 27 massive chestnut-wood pillars,[4] with much carving round the eaves and gables. Built in 1576, it was still referred to as 'the new market hall'; the 'old' market hall, on a site closer to St Peter's

Church, may still have existed in 1640.[5] On the first floor was a civic hall where the Assizes and Quarter Sessions were held, and on the floor above, fourteen city guilds had their own rooms for meetings, keeping records, and equipment.[6]

Of these dominant buildings, only the cathedral survives, but castle, cathedral and market hall together stated what Hereford was for – the city provided authority, security, and trade, the essentials for an agricultural region to survive and prosper. Through its pattern of narrow streets, along with the bustle of pedestrians, carts and horses ran also the invisible currents of commercial dealings, official business, personal relationships, news and gossip. Almost all its trade and activities were linked to agricultural produce and the agricultural calendar. Then as now it lay at the centre of a region of farms, orchards and grazing land, traversed by the rivers Lugg and Frome on their way to join the meandering Wye. By the 1640s, Hereford's functions were taken for granted, coded and regulated by royal charter, city by-laws, guild rules and time-honoured practices.

The city's administration had been renewed and confirmed by a royal ordinance as recently as 1620.[7] The Mayor and six aldermen led a common council made up of thirty-one of the 'better and more approved citizens', elected by the burgesses in each ward. It nominated a Mayor each year. Mayor, aldermen and council could elect a High Steward of the city. This would be a nobleman of influence at court, able to speak for the city's and its citizens' rights or needs. The High Steward would also appoint a deputy or deputies, to act as Justices, along with the civic dignitaries. The city maintained a proper style, with a sword bearer preceding the Mayor, and four serjeants carrying maces and the official 'hat of maintenance'.[8] It was required to maintain a gaol, appoint a coroner, and erect a gallows for the execution of criminals. The main gaol was a building to the right (looking outwards) of the Bye Street Gate, but there was also a 'Freemen's Prison', in the Booth Hall.[9] The civic authorities could impose fees and taxes on traders, and were responsible for framing and enforcing a range of by-laws. Each year the merchants and traders of each ward had to present their weights and measures, to be examined against those of 'His Majesty's standard' kept in the market house. Perhaps the most important by-laws related to fires and hygiene. In a town of mostly wooden houses, the fear of fire was always present, and the bakers in particular were regularly fined for keeping piles of firewood and gorse outside their shops.[10] Water supplies came from wells and pumps, and the wards were supposed to keep these clean and scoured. Plague was a constant peril at this time – a virulent outbreak had killed 600 people (around a third of the population) of Ross-on-Wye as recently as 1637. Many households kept a pig or two, and their roaming was a daily source of annoyance. Civic discipline was not tight. Perusal of the Mayor's and Ward records shows the same defaultings recorded year by year: the 'chain causeway' at Drybridge over the Rowditch remains in a state of decrepitude; the privy built on one of the Wye Bridge buttresses is dangerously dilapidated; St Martin's parish fails to maintain its stocks in usable condition; certain people persist in failing to clean up their rubbish, in obstructing the highway with shop counters, in piling faggots on the pavement; Eign Ward never seems to mend its faulty pump; the 'barginhams' or washing place on the road leading towards Barr's bridge[11] is in a state of decay. For these and many other cases of misappropriation of funds, fines were regularly issued but perhaps less often paid.

The cathedral, then as now, was the seat of the bishop, administered by a dean and canons. Music was an integral part of its services and it maintained a residential college of vicars choral, with a library of its own. In 1637 there were twelve vicars, with four sub-canons, sub-deacons and deacons, who took it in turns to say matins at 5 a.m. between the Feast of the Annunciation (25 March) and 1 September, and at 6.30 a.m. in winter.[12] The bishop was George Coke, who had been appointed to Hereford from the see of Bristol in 1636. An elder brother was one of the King's joint Secretaries of State from 1625 to 1640. Coke, a vigorous nepotist, had had his son Richard appointed as chancellor of the cathedral, and another son, John, was a prebendary. Yet another Coke, Francis, was precentor.[13] The bishop was a churchman of moderate views, 'one of the few remaining Calvinist bishops',[14] and not a follower of Archbishop Laud's 'Arminian' policies, which emphasised the priesthood and sacraments rather than divine grace and predestination. But as the political situation deteriorated, he would still get into trouble. As bishop, he had temporal powers in the area close to the cathedral and palace, and to back these up, and for cases of ecclesiastical offences, he had a small prison in the cathedral precincts. The dean was Dr Jonathan Browne, 'a good Preacher and much respected',[15] succeeded in 1644 by Herbert Croft, one of the brothers of Sir William Croft of Croft Castle, who married Browne's daughter, Anne.[16] Among the cathedral clergy were two or three who strongly supported Laud's reforms, but the general tenor of the chapter was to maintain the form of

Hereford Cathedral as it would have looked at the time of the Civil War,
before the collapse of the west front, by an unknown artist
(Hereford Museum & Art Gallery)

worship and procedure that had been established in the previous century. A boys' choir was maintained; of the seven boy choristers, five were paid for by the Chapter and two by the vicars choral.[17] The dean also had responsibility for the free grammar school in the cathedral precincts. In 1636, following a visit of inspection by Archbishop Laud in 1634, King Charles I had granted a new set of statutes to the cathedral, including the school. Clement Barksdale was appointed as its master in 1637, at a salary of £20 a year. He was also a vicar choral and vicar of St Nicholas and All Saints.[18]

Around 60,000 people lived in Herefordshire,[19] only a quarter of them in towns. The other towns of the county, Bromyard, Kington, Ledbury, Leominster and Ross, were much smaller than Hereford, and open to the countryside. They too had their markets, fairs, free schools, and local customs, along with the usual apparatus of justice: stocks, whipping post and ducking stool. A bailiff presided over civic affairs and held regular manor courts. The rest of the population were distributed in villages, hamlets and farms across the countryside. City and county had separate administrations, but naturally they were interlinked, with some individuals involved in both. Local government in England, tightened up and clarified from 1631 when the Government's Book of Orders was introduced, was heavily dependent on the gentry families who owned most of the land. For a country squire, it was part of the established order of things that he should select the vicar of the parish, act as a justice of the peace, and be an officer in the 'trained band' or local militia. In a more general way, he would also expect his opinions on all matters to be shared, or at least deferred to, by the 'inferior' inhabitants, especially if they were his tenants. Herefordshire's administration had one unusual aspect, shared with the other border counties, Shropshire, Gloucestershire and Cheshire, and even Worcester.[20] They came partly under the authority of the Council of Wales and the Marches. This body, part-administrative, part-legal, with its headquarters in Ludlow Castle, was the relic of earlier times. As a tribunal created under the royal prerogative, it was to be terminated with other such bodies by Parliament in May 1642. Its president was John Egerton, Earl of Bridgewater, who was also Lord Lieutenant of Herefordshire until February 1642. Though active in Ludlow (he commissioned John Milton's masque *Comus* which was first performed in Ludlow Castle, in 1634), he was not prominent in Herefordshire, where he had no property or links. Most important, in terms of running county affairs, were the Deputy Lieutenants, who, like the Lord Lieutenant, were appointed by royal authority. Their prime role was as leading members of the county's Commission of the Peace. The Justices of the Peace formed the basis of local administration, described as 'the effective voice of the county', and even as 'the conscience of the elite' since they administered the Poor Law and enforced the statutes governing minimum pay rates for labourers.[21] They also granted official licences, such as for alehouses. JPs were appointed under the Great Seal of England, and so by the Lord Chancellor, acting on advice from assize judges, Deputy Lieutenants, and other consequential persons with local knowledge. The Commission of the Peace met four times a year at the Hereford Quarter Sessions. These three-day sessions were important occasions, though not all Justices attended each time. In addition, a conscientious Justice would be kept busy in his own district or division by the need to deal with local problems or disputes, and to represent the demands of central authority. Neighbouring JPs could meet in what effectively were local 'petty sessions'.

The other senior royal appointee in the county was the High Sheriff, appointed for a year at a time. His role, once primal in the shire as the name suggests, had been overtaken by the Lieutenancy, but in Charles I's reign it had been given a new and undesirable distinction – the Sheriff was the official required to collect a new impost, the Ship Money tax. There will be more to say about Herefordshire's reaction to this. Other shrieval functions included the enforcement of legal decisions: the hangman and his helpers were under the Sheriff's orders.

Most crime was of a petty nature, usually fuelled by cheap ale or cider. Beyond the decorum of the cathedral precincts, Hereford was a lively and sometimes quite rough place. For those who found country life too quiet, its taverns, like that kept by 'the Widow Seaborne' in Bye Street, provided entertainment and company, and the city magistrates found it hard to enforce laws against such gambling games as shuffleboard, dicing and cards. People who stayed overnight in such places kept their purses under their pillows and even then might find them missing.[22] Some of the population were robust flouters of law and authority. At the Mayor's court, witnesses confirmed that one Blanche Philpotts, summonsed for selling ale without a licence, said, 'turd in Mr Mayor's teeth' and 'she would sell ale or beare in despite of Mr Mayor's nose'.[23] Cases of minor assault and petty theft were frequent, and some serve up ripe samples of 17th-century abuse, as when one John Holt called Mrs John Cutler 'ye filthy sott and a spawne of a bastard', and as for her husband, 'he did not care a fart or a turd for him'. He also called Thomas Lowe 'cuckholde and whitewall [wittol; one who has knowledge of or even condones his wife's unfaithfulness] fellow and a number of such filthy terms'.[24] But to have a rowdy element typified a town just as much as a market or fair, and indeed these aspects were inseparable.

Cases beyond the powers of the justices to handle were held over for the regular assizes, held twice a year in Hereford and sometimes in Leominster, presided over by a royally-appointed judge, with the assistance of jurymen sworn in for the occasion. The county also had a Grand Jury composed of some twenty-three freemen, whose prime legal purpose was to initiate and evaluate criminal indictments before a trial was held, but which had also acquired the function of a tribune to express the generally-held feelings, especially the grievances, of the citizens. The authority and control of the Lieutenancy and the Justices extended down into the old land divisions of hundreds and parishes. Herefordshire was divided into eleven hundreds: Broxash, Ewyas Lacy, Greytree, Grimsworth, Huntington, Radlow, Stretford, Webtree, Wigmore, Wolphey and Wormelow, each of which had a high constable (sometimes more than one), appointed by the Justices. He might be a member of the minor gentry or a substantial yeoman farmer. Within his area, he was responsible for the rule of law. He had to maintain the watch (surveillance of the ways in and out of his group of parishes) to ensure that local roads and bridges remained passable, and to enforce the agreed wage scales for labourers within the county. He called local sessions of masters and servants if there were disputes over wages, boundaries, or other local issues, and reported any breach to the Quarter Sessions. The high constable of Radlow hundred was also required to maintain the fire-signal on Hereford Beacon, the southernmost peak of the Malvern Hills.[25] There were other beacon sites, including Aconbury Hill south of Hereford, and Croft Ambrey by Croft Castle.[26] He controlled a team of petty constables, elected in each manor or appointed by its squire or steward. A last clawing fingernail at the end of the long arm of demand and enforcement stretching right back to Whitehall, the petty constable was responsible for keeping order locally, and for collecting taxes. He was immediately answerable to his high constable and through him to the local Justice or Deputy Lieutenant. But he was also the vehicle of 'yeoman opinion'; he could pass feelings of protest back up the line, and if enough of his fellows did likewise the results could shake men in high places.[27] Within the parish the other key figures, aside from the rector or vicar, were the churchwardens, elected annually. Their prime responsibility, apart from ensuring church attendance and suitable behaviour, and the payment of tithes, was administration of the Poor Law within the parish. Often the same man might be both petty constable and churchwarden. Both roles, of course, offered their perquisites. The constables could claim a twentieth part of what they collected, and took small payments or 'compliments' in cash or kind to ensure their goodwill or as thanks for assistance.

The county was also divided into military districts, each with a muster commission, formed of JPs and perhaps a Deputy Lieutenant. From these musters of able-bodied men and youths, their names recorded on the muster-rolls, came the trained bands who could be called out in emergency. Usually trained and run by men of some military experience, often Dutchmen or Scots, the bands were officered by members of the gentry. Arms and ammunition were held in the county magazine, at St Owen's Gate in Hereford. Unlike modern territorials, the trained band was recruited only for service within its own county. England had a professional Navy but no regular army.

Eight Members of Parliament represented the county and its towns, two each for Herefordshire, the city of Hereford, the borough of Leominster, and Weobley (a tribute to past importance in the latter case; Weobley's ancient franchise had been restored in 1628 through the efforts of the Tomkins family).[28] They were elected by tiny constituencies of freemen and usually, though not invariably, the result was fixed in advance.

It was not a tightly structured, unified system, more a framework formed at different times, parts of it new or restored, parts crumbling. It worked because it dealt largely with routine and familiar matters, but its effectiveness was dependent on the co-operation, energy, zeal and ability of a handful of men whose functions as civic councillors, Justices and trained-band officers often overlapped. Most of them had long-established family roots in the county, with consequent links, rivalries, friendships and feuds going back for generations.

2

Family and Other Networks

In a provincial area, at a time when communications were poor and when the economy was based on agriculture, continuity of families in the same place from generation to generation was to be expected, and Herefordshire was certainly no exception. Most of its leading families in the 1640s had been established in the county for several hundred years. Place-related surnames like Hereford, Lingen, Wigmore, Bodenham, and Croft attested the connection. Many names were Welsh or of Welsh origin, indicating both the fluidity of the ancient border and the influx of immigrants since the political unification of England and Wales in 1536 (until then the hundreds of Wigmore, Huntington and Ewyas Lacy had been part of Wales). A complex and layered range of relationships had developed. Intermarriage was frequent and though this implied friendship, it could also give rise to disputes and lawsuits, especially to do with wills, dowries and other aspects of finance and land tenure. In general, it seems that the Hereford gentry were not a band of brotherly cousins and far from being a mutual admiration society. Dislikes and feuds were frequent, but they could generally co-operate in their common interest. It might be tempting to label them as backwoodsmen, big fish in a small and remote pool, but it would not be altogether true. Most had family and business links in other counties and with the political and financial world centred in London. At least three owned houses in London.

There was no Earl of Hereford, though there was a Viscount Hereford, this being the secondary title of Thomas Devereux, Earl of Essex, who owned some tracts of land in the county, at Fownhope, but had no domicile there. The Earl of Kent was lord of the manor of Archenfield, and the Duke of Buckingham possessed a large estate around Leominster, but these magnates owned land in many areas and their Herefordshire properties were managed by stewards. The leading personage in city and county was John, Viscount Scudamore of Sligo, aged 41 in 1642. He was indeed the only peer living in the county, though his title was a recent one, being one of a batch of viscountcies in the peerage of Ireland put on sale by King Charles I in the 1630s (they cost £1,500, though Scudamore may have been awarded his for 'outspoken loyalty'[1]). The Viscount's seat was at Holme Lacy, a few miles east of Hereford. Through his marriage, he was also the owner of Llanthony 'Secunda', the former abbey and its grounds just south of the city of Gloucester. Other branches of the numerous Scudamore family were established at Ballingham, further down the Wye, Kentchurch and Treworgan. A relative, Rowland Scudamore, was Vicar of Fownhope. Viscount Scudamore had been Ambassador to France from 1635 to 1639, and in the years prior to the War, lived mostly at his London house, hoping and angling for some prestig-

John, Viscount Scudamore

ious and lucrative post from the King, whom he most loyally served. But further preferment did not come his way. At heart he was a countryman, interested in cider apple-trees and cider-making, also in cows and horses, and the intricacies of crossbreeding. He took his local responsibilities and powers seriously, having accepted the roles of High Steward both of Hereford City and its cathedral, and of *Custos Rotulorum*, keeper of the records and head of the Commission of the Peace.[2] A churchman, friend and keen disciple of Archbishop Laud, he had paid for and supervised the renovation of Dore Abbey with new carvings and stained glass. He had established, at his own expense, a troop of horse, 92-strong, as part of the county's military structure. His biographer describes him as cautious and timid by nature,[3] but he was not unwilling to make a splash on occasion, having thrown a memorable 19-days long Christmas house-party at Holme Lacy for a large assemblage of guests at the end of 1639 to celebrate his return from his ambassadorship.[4]

Hardly beneath Scudamore in prestige was Sir William Croft, of Croft Castle. Sir William, 49 in 1642, had been a courtier, a Gentleman of the Bedchamber to Charles I, and so a member of an inner, confidential circle. In the furore after the murder of the Duke of Buckingham, Charles's close favourite and in effect the country's chief minister, in 1628, he had lost the position, having been one of Buckingham's many critics, but remained a loyal supporter of the King. One of several brothers who, apart from the dean, would also be active Cavaliers, Sir William was a man of intellect and culture, and a shrewd observer saw him as the brains among Hereford's royalist activists: 'Sr William Crof gouerns all of them'.[5] Among the Crofts' highly-placed friends were the Earl and Countess of Leicester. Sir William rented lands from them, and the Countess wrote to her husband from Penshurst on 1 December 1636: 'Herbert Croft went from heere but two daies agoe. Sir William intends not to visitt me for he has been at my Lord of Barkshires and is retired to Herefordshire. He write me a letter to excuse his not paieing my monie at Michaellmas according to his promise, and saies I shall have it in Candlemas term.'[6] Leicester, who had also been a diplomatic representative in Paris, was no friend of Viscount Scudamore.

The third dominant family were the Coningsbys of Hampton Court, under Dinmore Hill. Originally from Lincolnshire, they had been established in Herefordshire for more than a century. Fitzwilliam Coningsby was aged 49 in 1642, and his eldest son Humphrey was 22. Two other sons, Robert and Thomas, would fight in the King's army.[7] Their influence was strongest in Leominster,[8] but they had clout in Hereford too, where Fitzwilliam's father had endowed Coningsby's Hospital, on the road outside Widemarsh Gate, in 1617. Coningsby appears to have been a pushy and perhaps impulsive character. In October 1640

Coningsby's Hospital as drawn by G.R. Gill (1827-1904)
(Hereford Museum & Art Gallery)

he was elected as one of the county Members of Parliament. He was involved in early forms of capitalism, as a member of a combine which purchased a national monopoly in the manufacture of soap.[9] But he was not a successful businessman; his kinswoman Joyce Jeffreys noted that even before the war he was encumbered by debts of £20,000.[10] The hospital was re-endowed with a new Act on 28 May 1641, when Fitzwilliam Coningsby settled £200 a year on it, as part of a mortgage arrangement to manage his debts. The other county and town Members of Parliament were included in a committee for 'the new Settling of the Estate of the said *Fitzwilliam Coningsby*'.[11]

Herefordshire was sprinkled with castles and fortified houses (Robinson lists 42 in *A History of the Castles of Herefordshire*), large and small, all testifying to warlike times in the past. In the extreme north-west of the county was the old castle of Brampton Bryan, seat of the Harley family for some three hundred years. Sir Robert Harley, aged 63 in 1642, was the odd man out in the upper echelon of Hereford life. Unlike any of the others, he was a politician of national stature, one of those leading figures in the House of Commons who were willing to confront the King to the point of military resistance. Sir Robert was the senior Member of Parliament

Sir Robert Harley

13

for the county, reflecting his local prestige as the proprietor of a large estate with further possessions extending into Radnorshire. As a young widower in 1605, he had sought to marry Fitzwilliam Coningsby's sister, Ann, but had withdrawn his suit as a result of what he considered 'scornful usage' by her father, Sir Thomas, over the size of her dowry.[12] One of his local responsibilities in the 1620s was to be Master of the Game in the Royal Forest of Deerfold.[13] From 1626 to 1635 he had been Master of the Mint in London, a post of major importance (there was as yet no Bank of England). The chief difference between the Harleys and the other leading landed families of the county was that Sir Robert and his wife Brilliana were wholehearted 'Puritans' – members of the wing of the Anglican Church which clung to the Calvinist doctrine of predestination, grace and the personal relationship of the individual Christian with God. While Viscount Scudamore erected altars and crosses, and commissioned stained glass, Sir Robert Harley was a determined iconoclast

Map of Herefordshire showing the location of many of the places mentioned in the text

who tore them down. Harley's elder sons Edward and Robert would both hold commissions in the Parliamentary army. Puritans were not necessarily joyless, but Sir Robert himself was earnest, industrious, and devoid of humour. His wife was altogether a more lively and human character.

Numerous other families were prominent in the county, less wealthy perhaps, but equally conscious of a long history and dominant status within local communities. There were the Pyes of the Mynde (Pye was an anglicised form of apHuw): Sir Walter Pye's father had held the lucrative post of Attorney of the Court of Wards and Liveries, and his uncle (a Parliamentarian whose daughter was married to the Parliamentary leader John Hampden) was Auditor of the Exchequer. Sir Walter himself was steward of the Duke of Buckingham's estates around Leominster and High Steward of the borough. He also owned land in Bedfordshire.[14] There were also the Kyrles, with several households on the Wye between Hereford and Ross; the Brabazons of Eaton Gamage; the Hoptons of Canon Frome; the Herefords of Sufton (Mordiford); the Lingens of Sutton Frene; the Whitneys of Whitney; the Rudhalls of Rudhall; the Bridges of Wilton Castle; the Skipps; Halls and Eltons of Ledbury; the Walwyns of Hellens; the Aubreys of Clehonger; the Baskervilles of Eardisley and Canon Pyon; the Lochards of The Leen and Byletts, close to Pembridge; the Barnebys of Brockhampton; the Danseys of Brinsop; the Hoskinses of Morehampton; the Smallmans of Kinnersley; the Vaughans of Hergest and Bredwardine; the Tomkins of Monnington; the Unetts of Castle Frome; the Wigmores of Shobdon; the Powells of Pengethley; and the Prices of Marden. Sir Edward Powell, an official of the Court of Requests in London, was at least a nominal supporter of Parliament, and the Eltons and Hoskinses were also Parliamentarians, as was Roger Hereford of Sufton;[15] but most of these families would support the King, to varying degrees. Several, including the Scudamores, Hoptons, Vaughans and Kyrles, were of split loyalties, and sometimes individuals switched sides. Walter Baskerville of Canon Pyon earned some notoriety by changing sides three times: 'first for the Parliament, then for the King, then theirs, then taken prisoner by us and [with] much adow gott his pardon and now, *pro Rege*, God wott.'[16] Many of these families were interrelated. Sir Walter Pye, Henry Lingen and Fulke Walwyn were Royalist brothers-in-law, their estates lying close to one another across the centre of the county. Ambrose Elton Sr of Ledbury and John Scudamore of Kentchurch were Parliamentarian cousins.[17]

A third and broader tier comprised a range of extended and interrelated families in both county and city, which included the Aldernes, Barrolls, Berringtons, Bodenhams, Boyles, Carwardines, Clarkes, Herrings, Howarths, Masons, Philpotts, Rodds, Seabornes, Trahernes or Trehearnes, Westfalings and many others. The heads of these family groups were usually armigerous, while some were placed more ambiguously between gentry and yeoman status. G.E. Aylmer noted that Hereford had 'a very numerous gentry class, stratified into many different gradations of wealth, culture, interest, outlook … not very many wealthy yeomen, or non-gentry townsmen of real substance,' but 'a relatively prosperous class of farmers and husbandmen, agricultural improvers and exploiters of economic change'.[18] A gentleman was someone who did not have to earn his living by manual work, though this alone did not suffice: in the last resort, a gentleman was a man recognised as such by other gentlemen. A contemporary account of Cheshire observed: '… you shall have in this country, six men of one surname (and peradventure of one house) whereof the first shall be called a Knight, the second an Esquire, the third a Gentleman, the fourth a Freeholder, the fifth a Yeoman, and the sixth a husbandman'.[19] The same was true of Herefordshire. Within and among these families, intertwined personal relationships and business dealings gave elasticity and cohesion to a shared way of life. In a county more than self-sufficient in basic foodstuffs, good cheer was not lacking. The New Year feast given by the Westfalings at Rudhall to their tenants was probably matched by other landowning families. It encompassed fowls, large mince pies shaped like hearts and stars, vegetables, baked currant bread pudding, mutton pasties, gammon of bacon, loin of veal, roast goose, apple pie, pigeon pie, sirloin of beef, legs of mutton, boiled rump of beef and a large boiled plum suet pudding.[20] Though the account does not say so, the feast was doubtless helped down by copious draughts of cider.

Aylmer also notes that the county had 'numerous very poor people for whom life had extremely little to offer'.[21] Wealthy families formed a small minority of the population. The real social bar, set quite high up on the social-financial scale, was that of the 'forty-shilling freeholder'. Someone with land, held as freehold under a tenant-in-chief, which provided an income of £2 (40 shillings) a year or more, was a freeman, eligible to vote in elections and in a position to advance socially if he could increase his wealth. For most of the inhabitants of Hereford and its county, the idea of land-owning even on the most modest scale was a wild dream. They were 'the multitude' – servants, peasants, brewers, artisans, wood-choppers, charcoal burners, quarrymen, porters, and labourers of all kinds in tanneries, forges, mills, brickfields, pottery kilns, dyeworks and woodyards. Wage-labourers, even if skilled, were regarded as unfree, not in control of their own lives, and they had no say in public affairs. 'Their poverty and helplessness was accompanied, as cause and effect, by an unfree status.'[22] Historians once tended to discount the interest and influence of the common people in national politics: 'As a factor in the religious and political disputes of the time the agricultural labourer counted for nothing. No evidence exists to show that he cared for either King or Parliament.'[23] This dismissive view of a silent and supposedly unthinking majority has been eroded by greater understanding both of the events of the time and of the ways in which ideas and attitudes are acquired within a rural and largely illiterate community. The intensive propaganda campaigns of both sides in the Civil War show that they knew the common people had to be wooed.[24] What the 'multitude' lacked was power to influence their individual lives, and the ability to record their individual views and feelings. Illiteracy was normal and their children were put to work from as early an age as possible. Their homes were farmyard or village hovels, or they lived on the masters' premises. Some preferred a precarious freedom squatting on patches of heath or in forest clearings. At the least fortunate level were the unemployed or unemployable: paupers, beggars, itinerants, misfits of all kinds, disabled or disordered, dependent on begging, charity or petty crime. Only a few gained refuge in almshouses. Serfdom had withered away two centuries before, but the multitude remained trapped within a strongly hierarchic social system. The arrangement was seen as divinely ordained, and acceptance of it was imbued from the earliest age. Parish clergy had the duty to teach all children the Church of England's catechism of 1549, including the injunctions 'to submit myself to all my governors, teachers, spiritual pastors and masters; to order myself lowly and reverently to all my betters … to do my duty in that state of life unto which it shall please God to call me.' To challenge the way in which society was ordered was getting dangerously close to treason and blasphemy. Property-owning Puritans were no less keen than the Cavaliers on maintaining this attitude. When the repeated calls for foot-soldiers came to be made, it was among the 'unfree' that the constables and ward officers looked for fresh cannon-fodder.

In some parts of the country, the concepts of 'freedom' and 'birthright' were being keenly discussed. Notions of civil or natural rights for everyone were in their infancy. Could you be free if you lived on a wage? What, if anything, was an Englishman's birthright? Radical views on equality and freedom were being voiced in the early 1640s and beginning to fuel protest movements which would increase dramatically in influence before the end of the decade. In counties such as Somerset and the West Riding of Yorkshire, 'groups of peasants and craftsmen were perfectly capable of forming political opinions and expressing them forcibly in action',[25] but no hints of such debates can be gleaned from Herefordshire. Its multitude, distributed in small groups across a community still largely given over to a land- and farming-based economy, and dominated by the network of gentry and sub-gentry families, had few opportunities to combine or agitate for betterment of their status, even if they thought of doing so. When Herefordians were finally goaded into forceful protest, it was in the hope of restoring traditional forms, not of establishing a new order.

Women do not find it easy to get adequate recognition in a male-oriented, male-dominated society, and the importance of their role is easier to assume than to define. Wives tended to play a secondary or purely domestic role except when compelled by circumstances, like Brilliana Harley, to take the lead. If Sir Robert had stayed at home, we would know much less about her. He was a two-times widower, and she was his third wife and mother of seven children, almost 20 years younger than her husband, having been born in 1598 (at Brill in the Netherlands where her father, later Viscount Conway, was lieutenant-governor of an English garrison). Her spirited defence of the family home (and the preservation of some 400 of her letters) were to make her famous. But she was standing in for her absent men-folk. Widows and unmarried women had to make their own way, and parish records of the time show that independent spinsters were far from uncommon. A strong-minded woman could make an impact on the community, if circumstances offered the chance. One such was Mary Croft, sister of Sir William, who had married the Royalist Richard Tomkins of Monnington. Lady Harley makes several references to 'my cosen Tomkins', and wrote to her son Edward that 'many thinke that her very words is in the Heariford resolution' (a Royalist proclamation of summer 1642), and again later, 'my cosen Tomkins is as violent as ever'.[26] Theodosia Mynors, although married to the Catholic and Royalist Rowland Mynors of Treago Castle, was a Protestant, and their son Robert would be a Puritan member of county committees in the 1650s. Another contemporary of Brilliana Harley's, Joyce Jeffreys, a half-sister of Humphrey Coningsby, never married. She not only effectively managed her own estate, at Broadward, south of Leominster, but provided a kind of banking service, as a money-lender, lending amounts from £3 to £800 to around a hundred clients. She employed a man of business, Matthias Rufford, at £51 16s a year plus a horse, and her preserved account books show not only her financial transactions, at 8%

interest (the official rate for the time), but also a lively and generous character. They also shed some valuable light on domestic affairs in the county during the 1640s.[27] At a lower social level, the Hereford civic records are not short of evidence of outspoken or truculent women holding their own in the rough and tough environment of the town's alehouses and labourers' lodging places.

Since religion and Church organisation were vital issues in the dissensions which culminated in the Civil War, the clergy were very much in the firing line, figuratively and on occasion literally. Religious belief and practice were central to public and private life. The role of God in human life and events was accepted without question by almost everyone, and atheism was regarded as deeply anti-social and depraved. Since the reign of Henry VIII more than a century before, the Anglican Church had been a department of state, with the monarch as supreme governor and its hierarchy of bishops, deans, rectors and vicars financed by tithes levied on every household. It was, of course, a reformed Church, its theology based on the teachings of Calvin, but expressed in a wide range of local practices depending on the ideas of individual bishops and parish incumbents. Viscount Scudamore and Sir Robert Harley could both consider themselves faithful adherents of the Church of England. (Harley, incidentally, despite his anti-episcopal views, was a good friend of Bishop Coke, to whom he passed on newsletters from London. While imprisoned in the Tower of London, Coke wrote to Harley: 'I have to move for your assistance in this present danger. You can testify better than anyone what my life and carriage has been in this diocese.'[28]) English society accepted that there was a range of religious belief and observance, just as nowadays it accommodates a broad range of political beliefs. Church and secular society were also interlocked through the ownership, by many of the gentry, of parish tithes and the advowson, or right to appoint the clergyman. Bishop Coke complained of these lay patrons who employed ill-paid curates 'reading prayers once a month or perhaps not so oft'.[29]

During the reign of Charles I, two contrary trends disrupted this pattern. One was Archbishop Laud's royally-backed 'Arminianism'. The other was unofficial but widespread, reflecting the desire for a more personal form of Christianity, sticking closely to the Calvinist doctrine of grace by election, and generally labelled 'Puritan', though their own word was 'godly'. Most of the godly also believed that the organisation of the Church should be radically changed, with the abolition of bishops and the replacement of the diocesan structure by a Presbyterian one. The divergence was not just a question of theology and church government, but ran deep into social behaviour. Most people joined in the still-rich pattern of seasonal celebrations and pastimes, many based on saints' days, and going back to medieval times; others, like November 5 and its bonfire, of recent origin. Sports, games and entertainments were often rough and, to modern eyes, cruel. Cock-fights, dog-fights, bull- and badger-baiting, and bare-knuckle bouts between men, all provided spectacle, excitement and opportunities for gambling. Not least because they usually happened on Sunday (the only non-working day), these activities, along with old-style mummers' shows, dancing, inter-parish ball games, and most other forms of popular entertainment, were condemned by Puritans. The 'Book of Sports' published by King James I and reissued by Charles I, with its list of approved Sunday games, was especially detested. Even in the late 16th century, 'there were towns in the Welsh Marches (Worcester, Hereford, Shrewsbury,

Chester) in which Puritans were to be found, and from which Puritan ideas infiltrated'.[30] But apart from Brampton Bryan, Herefordshire did not offer opportunities for religious radicals to impose themselves.

In this broad Church, Dr Coke was no more able than any other bishop to achieve unanimity among his clergy. Among his canons and prebendaries were some, like Dr Rogers, also Rector of Stoke Edith, who were strongly Laudian, but they were a small minority. Certain parish clergy, like Dr Swift, rector of Goodrich, and Dr Sherburn of Pembridge, would also be outspoken for the King. Puritan clergy were far fewer. The minister of Brampton Bryan, Stanley Gower, installed by Harley, was ardent for the 'Root and Branch' campaign which demanded the abolition of bishoprics. In December 1641 he wrote to his patron: 'The Atheists, papists and prelats, our common enemys, are now to be scoured and swept away … our Land hath bene long sick and yow [Harley and his fellow MPs] are the physicians.'[31]

Sometimes a vicar might change his views, like John Tombes of Leominster who became increasingly Puritan and had angry confrontations with Wallop Brabazon in December 1640 when he reversed Brabazon's rearrangement of the communion table in Leominster church.[32] Gower, Tombes and another outspoken Puritan, Mr Green of Pencombe, were all forced to leave Herefordshire, and until 1646 there were few Puritan ministers in the county, whose lack of 'sufficient' clergy was to the godly a sign of its being one of 'the dark corners of the land'.[33] It seems that the great majority of the county's clergy followed the path of discretion, like the Rev. Henry Page, vicar of Ledbury through successive crises of Church and State from 1631 to 1663;[34] '… in some parishes the clergy must have conformed to all the successive changes, from the fall of Laudianism in 1640-41 through the innovations of the 1640s and 1650s, to the restoration of episcopacy and the Book of Common Prayer in the early 1660s'.[35] Parish clergy often had useful local rights and privileges, like the Rector of Eaton Bishop who had 'ye right shoulder of every calf yt any Parishioner kills in his own house of his own herd',[36] and might well be reluctant to lose them.

Catholicism as an aspect of Herefordshire life at this time is hard to evaluate, but one thing is clear: the Civil War gave England's Catholics something to fight for. More than a hundred years after the formation of the Anglican Church, Catholicism was far from extinct, despite drastic penal laws against it. In 1610 a secular priest, Roger Cadwallader, born at Stretton Sugwas, had been executed at Leominster in the horrible way prescribed for traitors: hanged, drawn, and quartered. His head was placed on the Town Hall, and his divided body hung up at the four entrances to the town. He had been offered a pardon if he would take the oath of allegiance to the King as supreme head of the Church, but refused to do so, although he acknowledged him as lawful head of the State.[37] These laws had not been enforced in Charles I's reign, but were not repealed. To right-thinking Anglicans, Catholics were 'malignants', and contemporary references to Herefordshire as one of their strongholds are borne out by the surviving parish records which list the names of recusants. In some parishes, especially in the south-west, they number hundreds: Garway had 163 recusants, excluding children, in the 17th century.[38] A recusant was someone who refused to attend Church of England services, but was not overtly Catholic, and most are noted as 'gent.' or 'yeoman', though weavers and even the occasional labourer are found, as well as many single women. To be officially recorded as a recusant meant both exclusion from public office and the incurring of fines for non-attendance at church, and some persons of Catholic sympathies adopted a superficial Anglicanism, including Sir Walter Pye of the Mynde and his brother-in-law Fulke Walwyn at Hellens.[39] One historian puts Catholics in Herefordshire as 1 in 20 of the population, but this may be a conservative estimate.[40] Even Sir Robert Harley had relatives who were Catholics,[41] and among prominent families who were wholly or partly Catholic were the Bodenhams of Rotherwas and Bryngwyn, the Wigmores of Fownhope and other places, the Berringtons of Bishopston and Cowarne, the Mynors and Merediths of Garway, the Vaughans of Welsh Bicknor, the Kembles of Welsh Newton, and the Scudamores of Treworgan. Eclipsing them all and powerfully influential were the Somersets at Raglan Castle, not far away over the Monmouthshire border, whose head, the Earl of Worcester, was perhaps the richest man in the entire realm. He had given a house and land in Herefordshire, Cwm in Llanrothal parish, for an establishment run by Jesuits, a combination of college and mission station. In 1644 it was reported to comprise 27 priests and two lay brothers.[42] Although of course it had to be clandestine, its existence was probably well-known locally.

If Catholics were suspect, Jesuits were regarded not only by the Puritans as sinister and ruthless enemy agents.[43] Orthodox Anglicans were brought up to regard Catholicism as a depraved cult, undermining the integrity of the state as well as teaching a fatally misleading, perverted Christianity. But although most of Herefordshire's leading Royalists made all the customary anti-papist remarks, and there is no reason to suppose these were not sincerely meant,[44] they did not consider their long-established neighbours to be actively plotting the overthrow of the English state, and there was little in the way of anti-Catholic activism. Only Sir Robert Harley, perhaps influenced by some of his Westminster colleagues, believed that a deep Catholic conspiracy existed, intending to put England under Papal subjection. In fact, his Hereford neighbours may have been more concerned about Harley's icon-breaking Puritanism – '… conformist Calvinists often saw Puritanism as a greater danger than popery'[45] than about any Catholic threat. Herefordshire's Catholics, however, knew they had nothing to expect from Parliament other than re-enforcement of the penal laws. From the King, they could look for more consideration. His Queen, Henrietta Maria, was openly Catholic, and his Church reforms seemed to hark back to a pre-Reformation theology. But the Catholics had learned to keep a low profile; in 1640 and later, troops would be reluctant to serve under officers known to be Catholic, and might even mutiny.[46] For King Charles, the support of the Catholics of England was of tremendous importance, and yet, in order to allay suspicions – always blown hot by Puritan speeches and writings – of a Roman plot to reinstate Catholicism as the national religion, he had to act exceedingly warily, or run the risk of a catastrophic loss of support. It was 'a serious and embarrassing contradiction in the king's recruiting campaign' that while Charles was promising to defend the Protestant religion, so many Catholics were coming out in his support.[47] But not all of Herefordshire's Catholic or recusant squires joined in the struggle. Thomas Blount of Orleton, a lawyer who practised at the Inner Temple in London, took no part. Fulke Walwyn, at Hellens, went 'underground … to all strange comers, the master was busy "farming"'.[48]

3

What Herefordshire Did for a Living

Within the national community, local identity was far stronger than it is nowadays. While in rural areas there was much movement among adjacent settlements and parishes,[1] most of the Herefordshire population hardly travelled at all. To go more than half a day's journey was out of the question for the great majority. Even the well-off did not travel unless they had to. Money, contacts, route knowledge and, not least, physical stamina were needed by the merchants and men of substance whose business, private or public, required them to travel to Worcester, Gloucester, Bristol or London. Patriotically English as they certainly were, when the people of Herefordshire thought of 'England', they thought of their city or county. But they understood themselves as part of a national structure, taking in both past and present. Englishness and the English inheritance were common property. When in 1641 the Herefordshire Grand Jury petitioned Parliament about weirs blocking the Wye, they based their complaint on 'the statute of Magna Carta'.[2] Commercial links extended beyond the county. Hereford Cathedral drew some of its income from ownership of a tavern, the Labour in Vain, in the City of London, as well as from tenements in London suburbs and in Worcester. Merchants traded with London, Bristol, Birmingham and other places for quality fabrics, materials, metal articles, glassware, spices, wine and everything else which could not be produced locally. In 1634 the council received a petition from 'foreign tanners' for 'a safe and sufficient place in which they may keep and sell their goods'.[3] 'Foreign' means from outside the county, rather than abroad. And to pay for its imports, Herefordshire exported.

The land was the thing. Herefordshire's soil provided rich nourishment for both plants and animals. From the Bromyard Downs to the Lugg watermeadows, rich grassland nourished sheep and cows. From north to south, grain was planted and harvested: wheat on the better ground, also rye, oats and barley: 'Rye is the best grayne growes generally in the county, and oates and pease'.[4] Hops were being cultivated, though not on a large scale.[5] The cattle, very numerous, were native red longhorns. Breeding of the Hereford stock did not begin until shortly after the Civil War; its origins are not documented, but, given his known interest in such matters, it is likely that the traditional credit given to Viscount Scudamore is correct.[6] From the Middle Ages, Herefordshire wool had been famous for its high quality – an important consideration when bulk transport was difficult. 'Lemster ore' was acclaimed as the finest wool in England from the 15th to the 18th centuries.[7] For the central and southern March sheep districts, Leominster was a convenient centre, surrounded by the natural sheeplands, hills and downlands providing 'the same scanty grazing in a not too unkindly environment, which was ideal for the growing of a wool of the finest staple'.[8] Pigs and poultry were kept in large numbers and most manors had a pigeon house, pigeon pie being a popular dish. In the south-east and north-west, dense deciduous forest covered much of the landscape. In all these different areas, there was abundance of game from rabbits to partridges. Skins and feathers were used or sold on; nothing was wasted. Around the towns, market gardens grew beans, cabbages and other greens. Some enterprising farmers were trying out new crops like potatoes and turnips. A Ross-on-Wye by-law of 1651 specified that 'Neeps, Cabbages and all other garden stuffe shall stand for sale under the Market Hall stayers and not elsewhere'.[9] In some parts of the country, notably the Archenfield district, land inheritance may still have been on the old Welsh basis of 'gavelkind', whereby a property was divided among all the heirs, resulting in tiny farms, with families struggling to live off their holdings. But mostly the aim was to produce a crop, or to breed animals to sell, live or dead. Some of Herefordshire's corn farmers were wealthy men.[10] Dead animals yielded not only meat, but bone meal, hides, and horns. Sheep, of course, gave their annual contribution of wool. Farming also supported significant industrial activity in the form of grain mills (mostly water-powered), tanneries, leather-works, shoe-making (a speciality of Ross-on-Wye), gloves (Hereford gloves were well-known[11]), and all the stages of cloth preparation (Hereford again, and Ledbury). Hereford is named in an Act of Parliament of 1552, with Worcester and Coventry, as a town permitted to make cloth,[12] and from the references to clothworkers in the city records, this was still going on in the 1640s, though not on the scale of Worcester, to which city much wool was carried in bales.[13] In the late 1630s, the wool industry was suffering from Spanish competition; cheaper but good quality 'Segovia wool' was coming into England and spoiling the market, bringing a united chorus of protest from Hereford.[14]

Among the few occupations considered suitable for gentlemen, apart from the Church, were those of lawyer and physician, both of which required intimate and confidential knowledge, whether of the family affairs or bodily problems, of others. Some knowledge of law was essential. Every manor held its own 'court baron' in which tenancy agreements were made and reviewed. The sons of the Herefordshire gentry, if intelligent enough, went to Oxford University, often to Brasenose College, or to the Inns of Court in London, most usually the Middle and Inner Temples. Dr Edward Alderne, a doctor of civil law, would be an active Royalist in the city. Francis Geers, of Garnons, was a 'Batchelor of Physick'; one of his sons would take holy orders and another became an Inner Temple lawyer.[15] Hereford had at least one physician, Dr Bridstock Harford, who was 'violently in favour of the Parliament' and would be accused, after the Restoration, of having passed on information to Parliament.[16] Another medical man was Dr Nathaniel Wright, originally from Shrewsbury, one of the Puritan community at Brampton Bryan. Such men, university graduates, were in a much higher social bracket than the barber-surgeons who trimmed beards and hair, dressed wounds, and pulled teeth.

Modern writers on the period are apt to stress the difficulty of communication and transport in the 17th century, but these can be overstated, if only because people at the time did not anticipate later technologies. Though some complained, they accepted their mudbound roads and lurching coaches and carts as normal. Surprising distances on horseback and even on foot could be covered by individuals within a day. Joyce Jeffreys owned a coach, pulled by two bay mares,[17] to visit her estate at Broadward and her friends at Garnons, and many others of her income and class must have done the same. There was a national postal system, and Hereford was a mail-exchange point, where letters destined for as far as St David's were passed on to carriers who would take them across Wales.[18] It had a postmaster, who in 1640 was Christopher Dewe, who had paid 'above £40' for the position, and kept horses for the king's service. In addition he was authorised to commandeer horses, and he protested directly to the Secretary of State when the innkeeper John Rogers, with a stable of 16 or 17 horses, tried to prevent him from doing so. Dewe had something of a persecution complex, regarding himself as 'so much envied at for his proceedings as postmaster, that the mayor, justices, and common council have joined in an information against him, pretending that he is a man of evil life and conversation'.[19] In other towns the local carriers were the letter- and parcel-bearers, along with bulkier goods, in their stage-waggons. Passed on at staging points, a letter would normally get to its destination, eventually. Viscount Scudamore in London could send and receive letters via the Leominster carrier at 8d a time. Dobbs, the Ross carrier, could make it to London in six days.[20] Though she thought it unreliable, Brilliana Harley sometimes used the post of Ludlow to send boxes of pies and cheeses and cider, to her husband and son.[21] Traditional drove roads for Welsh cattle also crossed the county[22] to the market at Gloucester (900 head of cattle were seized by Parliamentary forces from 18 Welsh drovers at Gloucester in 1644). Although the River Wye was navigable for shallow-draught vessels, the frequency of weirs and the long-established rights of salmon fishing, with nets staked out on posts, restricted its usability, as did seasonal spates and droughts. Complaints about obstructions to navigability were frequent.

Hereford's markets and fairs drew people from all over the county, bringing money into the town and helping to account for the splendour of the market hall. The autumn fair in particular was a great one, with large numbers of livestock being sold before the winter. Joyce Jeffreys gave money to street fiddlers, a man exhibiting an ape, and another with a 'dancing horse' on one fair day.[23] The general prosperity of the pre-Civil War decades is also shown by the building of fine new houses and new market halls at Ledbury, Leominster and Ross, the latter of stone rather than timber, though still built over an open selling-area at ground level. Ledbury's hall had been begun in 1617 but it is unlikely that much work was done on it during the period of the Civil War, and in 1650 it was recorded as 'erected and built, but not complete'.[24]

Not much that Nature had to offer went unused. The trees and bushes, apart from their value in harbouring game, were an important resource. Fruits and nuts, wild or cultivated, were harvested. The town bakers used furze and gorse to fire their ovens, and everyone needed firewood for cooking and winter warmth. Wood had many other uses, and pollarding, felling and cutting were closely controlled. Unauthorised wood-choppers would be prosecuted, like Francis Wright, denounced before the city magistrates in 1642 as a 'devourer of young Elmes to make ox bowes'.[25] But the forests were also being increasingly exploited by industry. On its south-east border the county abutted the Forest of Dean, where coal seams had been dug into for centuries, and which by the previous century had begun the smelting of iron. Ironworks needed hammering power which could be supplied by water wheels, and high sustained heat which was provided by burning charcoal. The process of turning wood into charcoal was an industry in itself. In 1640 Dean's entire coal and iron industry was in the possession of one man, Sir John Winter or Wintour, Secretary to Queen Henrietta Maria, who had paid handsomely for his monopoly. The example of Dean was not lost on Herefordshire landowners who happened to have woodlands and water-power. Viscount Scudamore, Sir John Kyrle and Sir Robert Harley all invested in this very up-to-date industry.[26] By 1640 there were ironworks at Carey Mill on the Wye below Fownhope, site of a water-powered grain mill since medieval times, on estates owned by the Earl of Essex. Further downriver at Whitchurch, just below Goodrich Castle, rent-money for ironworks, successively at Old Forge and New Mill, went to the coffers of the Earl of Kent. Others were at Pontrilas and St Weonards[27] and at Downton in the Teme Gorge by Bringewood Chase. At this latter site Clee Hill ironstone was smelted using local limestone. Cannon used in the Civil War were cast here.[28] An undated 17th-century plan exists of a mill and ironworks, Strangeward Forge, on the River Arrow near Pembridge.[29] As a lessee of the royal forests in this area and extending into Radnor, Sir Robert Harley appears to have assumed the power to have great extents of woodland cut down to be sold for charcoal-burning. Sampson Eure, one of the Leominster MPs and a landowner in this area, was also involved in the timber trade.[30] Iron-making was a significant industry in the county, and the appetite of the ironworks for wood was such that the towns regularly protested about the difficulties of obtaining firewood.[31] But wood prices at Pontrilas, Goodrich and Carey were lower than at almost all ironworking sites in other counties,[32] which offers an economic reason for Herefordshire's ironworks and suggests that the townsfolk were used to getting their wood on the cheap. Herefordshire iron, supplied in slab form, had a ready market in Bristol, England's second-largest city.

Pottery, of a basic household and farmhouse kind, was being made in several places where suitable clay and fuel were available, including Whitney, Brilley and Lingen, probably for sale within the region.[33] As the habit of tobacco-smoking spread, perhaps encouraged by wartime conditions in which bands of soldiers often sat around with little to do, a community of clay-pipe makers flourished in the parish of Aston, possibly prompting a name-change to Pipe Aston, and 'intermarriage between the pipemaking families ensured a tight-knit community with links from Cleobury Mortimer … to Kington.'[34] Other clay articles were made, including wig-curlers. A more unexpected industry was the manufacture of saltpetre, a prime constituent of gunpowder, set up by John Giffard in Hereford in 1637, on the basis of a contract to supply the Admiralty,[35] with an auxiliary works at Bishopstone, close to woodlands a few miles west of the city. Again, cheap firewood for the boiling process may have been the key, though availability of quantities of human urine was also a necessity.

Though localised, this evidence of industry shows that Herefordshire cannot be regarded as a wholly agricultural county. On a modest scale, groups and communities of industrial artisans evidently existed, though many fewer than in Gloucestershire and Warwickshire. Herefordshire was essentially a primary producer area, from which wool and slab iron were transported elsewhere to be fashioned into products whose added value created larger incomes further down the line. The effect of this on the county's social make-up has already been noted. With only a small proportion of craftspeople – a group whose incomes and sense of skill encouraged them to be aspirational both in living standards and in political ideas – there was a clear and deep gulf between rich and poor.

Even in 1640, in this busy, workaday community, the idea that in less than two years the nation would be at war with itself, and Hereford captured by the 'enemy', would have been incredible to almost everyone.

Part Two

The Years of War

4

The Slide to War

Until the prospect of war became plain, there was no Royalist party in Herefordshire. There was no need for one; the King's role as supreme governor of State and Church was accepted by everybody. That did not mean liking, or accepting without complaint, everything he did. In 1629 Charles I had dismissed Parliament and embarked on a twelve-year spell of personal rule. With no Parliament to vote him a regular income, he found it necessary to raise money in other ways in order to maintain his government, including the sale of 'monopolies' on certain products or services. Wealthy men were required to lend him large sums.[1] The King's various forms of taxation were all resented, but things came to a head in the 1630s with the yearly series of assessments for 'Ship Money', ostensibly to finance the Navy, then seen as England's essential means of defence. Collection being the personal responsibility of the Sheriff, he in turn leaned heavily on the constables. In the first assessment in 1635, the county was required to raise £3,780 and the city £210. This was paid up fairly promptly. A second writ was issued in 1636 for £3,130 and £185. The collectors found much more reluctance to pay up this time. The third writ, in 1637, was for a total of £3,500, and it provoked a stream of complaints about inability to pay, on grounds of localities being impoverished or badly hit by the prevalent plague. A petition was raised in 1638, signed by Bishop Coke, Sir Robert Harley, and many others, attesting to the county's difficulties in finding the money. The Sheriff at this time was Henry Lingen, and his collection was still well in arrears when the fourth writ for Ship Money was issued in 1638-39. Lingen's successor as Sheriff, Sir Robert Whitney, found it very difficult to get the high constables to enforce collection. Long before this, protest had reached a national scale. On 10 November 1640 a fifth writ was issued. Sheriff Thomas Alderne had an even more difficult task than Whitney, failing to raise more than a small proportion of the required sum. In a somewhat murky episode, he was imprisoned in May 1640 by the Privy Council for giving false information about the murder of an under-sheriff who had been collecting Ship Money, then released on a bond of £3,000.[2] In his appeal for release, Alderne claimed that his appointment was contrary to precedent, 'he being only a Proctor in the diocesan court and chapter clerk to the Dean and Canons'.[3] It would seem that it was difficult to find a willing candidate for Sheriff in 1640.

Other demands were being made from 1638. King Charles's attempts to reform Protestant worship in Scotland brought about what was in effect a revolution there, and the royal government was ignored. To re-establish his authority, the King set about raising an army to force the Scots into submission. Each county was laid under assessment for

King Charles I

the collection of a 'coat-and-conduct' money tax for the equipping of troops. In Herefordshire, 200 men, not proud volunteers but 'a naked, poor-conditioned people of the meanest sort,'[4] were pressed into armed service to join the King's expedition against the Scots in 1638-39, which was a failure; and in 1640 another 300 were impressed, provided with coats, and sent with three drummers to join the royal army in the second, even more ill-fated 'Bishops' War',[5] which ended with a Scottish army occupying north-eastern England.

At the Epiphany sessions, on 12 January 1640, the Grand Jury of the County of Hereford drew up a list of local grievances. They included protests against the existence of weirs on the Wye, 'a greate Nusance and greevance to this County, so far as they hinder navigation … ,' and against the importation of 'sigovia' wool, as 'the native wooll of this Countie of Hereford is made of less value and reputation then otherwise it would bee'. It asks for Herefordshire to be removed from the jurisdiction of the Council of Wales and the Marches, and complains of the Ship Money tax as 'a great chardge greevance and Impoverishinge' of the county, as well as of 'the unlawfull taxe of Coate and Conduct money within this County'. It concludes with the claim that the existence of iron mills in the county had resulted in the general destruction of trees, timber and coppice wood around Hereford so that wood had become scarce and expensive 'to the great impoverishinge of the Inhabitants of the said citty'.[6] To draw up such a 'presentment' was a typical action at this time, and shows the Grand Jury fulfilling one of its functions in representing the views and needs of the inhabitants to the government, particularly since no Parliament had been called for over a decade. The signatories included men who would later be on opposing sides but who were united on these local issues.

Herefordshire had much to complain about. But when the opportunity came to elect members to the nation's forum, it did not send a band of radical reformists. Parliaments were rare in Charles I's reign, but two were summoned in the course of 1640. The first had only a brief session, from March to April, before the irate King dissolved it. But in October, with a Scottish army occupying the north-eastern counties, he found it necessary to summon another. This became the Long Parliament, the King's corporate opponent in the Civil Wars. Sir Robert Harley and Fitzwilliam Coningsby were returned to it as the county members. Hereford city was represented by Richard Seaborne (who was also Lord Scudamore's deputy as Steward) and Richard Weaver; Leominster by Sampson Eure, an eminent lawyer, knighted in 1641, and Walter Kyrle; and Weobley by Arthur Jones and

William Tomkins. Probably all of them shared to some degree in the desire for change, if only to the extent of securing the King's income in a different way. Harley was the only one who would later oppose the King, though Kyrle, who did not attend Parliament between July 1642 and October 1646, was also reputed to support the Parliamentary cause.[7] But at Westminster, Harley was part of the majority. The Weobley member Arthur Jones became Viscount Ranelagh in June 1643 (by which time he was with the army in Ireland). His colleague William Tomkins died at the end of 1641 and was succeeded by his brother Thomas Tomkins.[8] The Hereford members of October 1640 were from a thoroughly conventional cadre, expected to look after the traditional and established interests of city and county, and certainly not to turn the world upside down. Even Sir Robert Harley was returned, not because of his views on church government but because he was a county magnate.

But for Sir Robert, as for many other members, the new Parliament offered the opportunity to press forward a range of policies and Acts which were abhorrent to the King and increasingly discomfiting to Sir Robert's Herefordshire colleagues. To the 'godly', ministers who did not preach were considered 'insufficient' and often 'scandalous', and Parliament quickly appointed a committee to inquire into the lack of preaching ministers and how the insufficient might be removed from their livings. One of its members was Sir Robert Harley. In 1641 it reported that in Herefordshire there were 'but twenty constant preachers' in 225 churches and chapels.[9] In September of that same year, Sir Robert supervised the breaking-up of the church cross at Wigmore and smashed the stained glass windows at Leintwardine (he was patron of both livings).[10]

In March 1641 Parliament had the Archbishop of Canterbury committed to the Tower of London for high treason. Viscount Scudamore, Fitzwilliam Coningsby and Wallop Brabazon had all publicly supported Laud's policies.[11] Brabazon had had the church in Leominster altered and Coningsby had installed stained glass in the chapel at Hampton Court. Through 1641, as Parliament pushed through measures which bolstered its power and authority against the King's, there was growing anxiety in Herefordshire, as elsewhere, about the way things were heading. Almost everyone had supported the initial reforms, which included the abolition of Ship Money, but many felt that as the reformists' agenda became longer, it was going far beyond what was necessary or desirable. Parliament's assumption of authority to shut the Archbishop of Canterbury in the Tower of London, and to execute the King's prime counsellor, the Earl of Strafford, was disturbing. Unified rule by the monarch over his three kingdoms and one principality seemed to be breaking up. Rumours were rife of papist plots and a French invasion. The House of Commons drew up a Protestation against papist conspiracy, which all right-thinking persons were expected to sign, and Sir Robert Harley sent a copy to the Herefordshire Justices on 8 May.[12] But it was ignored except in his own corner of the county.[13] On 15 June the Commons passed a resolution calling for the abolition of deans, chapters, archdeacons, prebendaries, canons and petty canons, with all lands taken from them to be employed for the advancement of learning and piety.[14] Even in Herefordshire there was a small element of Puritan extremism. Gower wrote to Sir Robert Harley in August 1641 complaining of the activities of Brownists, people who believed in no church structure at all, spreading 'anarchy and confusion'.[15]

There is a tiny indication here of what would later become a fatal division among the godly, separating those who wanted free, independent congregations from those who wanted to see a single national Church. On 17 August the Commons declared the soap-making monopoly to be illegal, and anyone sharing in it was to be considered a delinquent.[16] As a consequence Fitzwilliam Coningsby, a part-owner of the monopoly, was ousted from Parliament on 30 October, but in the resultant by-election in November, the Herefordshire electors responded by sending his son Humphrey, a Middle Temple law student aged barely 20, in his place. Other concerns were overshadowed when in October the Catholic population of Ulster broke out in revolt, and news speedily reached England of atrocities and large-scale massacres of the Protestant settlers. Though greatly exaggerated, these reports gave the Catholic Irish a reputation for extreme brutality, and there would later be ugly repercussions close to Hereford. Fears of a general rising and Catholic invasion reached new heights. Herefordshire was named in Parliament as one county where the recusants were ready for action.[17] A pamphlet published late in the year told how in November the ostler of an inn in Ross-on-Wye was hired to guide a mysterious stranger to Raglan Castle, where he saw scores of horses and a huge armoury.[18] Sir Robert Harley wrote to his wife to put Brampton Bryan Castle into a state of defence, and on 19 November a sudden panic fear of imminent attack spread from Brampton Bryan through Ludlow and Kidderminster to Bridgnorth, keeping people up in arms all night.[19] Any speculation about warfare at this time probably supposed a conflict between a Parliament-led England and Catholic forces both internal and from abroad, rather than what was actually to happen.

Towards the end of the year stormy debates were held on whether Episcopacy should be abolished in England, as it had already been in Scotland. Bishop Coke of Hereford was one of twelve prelates, led by the Archbishop of York, who during this political rage signed a document intended to affirm their right to sit as members of the House of Lords. By suggesting that any Acts passed without the presence of the bishops would be null and void, they inflamed popular fury against themselves. Coke spent 18 weeks under arrest in the Tower of London before being allowed to return to Hereford, two wealthy Londoners having put up bail of £5,000 on his behalf.[20] For having been a member of a Church Synod which brought forward new Canons, or church laws, in 1640, he had already been impeached in August 1641, though not put on trial. When the Commons finally deprived the bishops of voting rights on 7 February 1642, Sir Robert Harley bore a message from the Commons to the House of Lords, asking them to send the Bill to the King for his (most reluctantly given) assent.[21] Harley was also chairing a Committee of both Houses for Irish Affairs, in effect supervising the rather ineffective efforts to set up a military campaign against the rebellion.[22]

Bishop Coke was not a resistance leader, and has been described, rather unkindly, as 'a minnow among sharks',[23] but two of his clergy rallied to his support with a petition which was presented to the county Justices and Grand Jury at the January 1642 Quarter Sessions in Hereford. They were Mr Mason, vicar of Yazor, and Dr Sherburn, rector of Pembridge, and their petition was addressed to the two Houses of Parliament as coming from the High Sheriff, Isaac Seward, 'and divers of the Gentry, Ministers, Freeholders and Inhabitants of the Countie of Hereford', signed by 3,826 persons altogether.[24] It was a brief document, 'in

The memorial to Bishop George Coke in Hereford Cathedral

the behalf of Episcopacy, Liturgies, and Supportation of Church Revenues, and Suppression of Schismaticks', pleading for the retention of bishops, as the ancient and primitive government of the Church, and the best protection against schism and heresy, especially 'that Hydra of Heresies, the Roman Papacy'.[25] Petitions, protestations and declarations were flooding into Parliament from all corners of the kingdom on this subject. It was suggested that this Hereford petition 'shows little doubt that the ecclesiastical question restored the loyalty of the county which the exaction of Ship Money had shaken',[26] but the King is not even mentioned and the document is addressed exclusively to the Lords and Commons. It is not a testament of loyalty but a single-issue petition to those in effective power.

The High Sheriff for 1642, Isaac Seward, was the recipient of instructions both from the King and from the Parliament. Seward, who was from Leominster and had made his money in trade,[27] is a rather shadowy figure, but clearly he was unwilling to show support for one side or the other, though his sympathies were on the Parliamentary side. Pressed from London by letters from Harley, faced at home with a largely anti-Parliament set of county magnates, he tried the expedient of passing on both sets of orders. Both sides wanted a signed declaration of loyalty from every citizen of substance. The Speaker of the Commons had written to all Sheriffs on 20 January 1642, ordering that the Protestation oath of the previous year should be administered to all adult males by 12 March, and in

February Seward summoned the Justices to begin the process by signing their own names. Few turned up, and even fewer were prepared to sign.[28] Seward had also distributed copies of the King's 'Declaration', and in a somewhat ambiguous phrase, he had written to Harley that he wanted 'to be found as ready to serve his Majesty and Parliament, as any other man'.[29] Seward may have hoped that matters would be quickly resolved, but the temper of the Herefordshire Royalists was sharpening.

Anthony Fletcher's study of the war's outbreak notes that 'Whereas in the summer of 1641 there was a gulf in understanding between the Parliamentary leadership and the leaders of county communities, by early 1642 that gulf had closed.'[30] In this assessment, Herefordshire should not be included. Their bishop's ordeal, and the demand for signing of the Protestation, helped prompt nine Herefordshire gentlemen, all of them JPs, to write a letter on 5 March 1642 to Harley and Humphrey Coningsby, for presentation to Parliament. They were Wallop Brabazon, Fitzwilliam Coningsby, Sir William Croft, Henry Lingen, Thomas Price, William Rudhall, John Scudamore of Ballingham, William Smallman of Kinnersley, and Thomas Wigmore of Shobdon. Their letter took an unmilitant tone, setting out moderately-stated though firmly-grounded views, protesting against ordinances from Parliament which did not have the royal assent. To emphasise that they were not Laudian extremists, they commended the way in which Hereford Cathedral had been purged of papist-leaning practices – 'Copes, Candlesticks, Basons, Altar with Bowing and other Reuerence unto it' – but made clear their support for the continuation of episcopacy and the use of the Book of Common Prayer.[31] Claiming to be ignorant of the extent of Parliament's 'power and privilege', they pointed out that there was dispute on this question both within and between the Houses, as well as between Parliament and the King. The two members sent a joint reply which survives as a draft, and reflects Harley's views. He was very much involved in pushing for more of these objected-to changes, and had nominated his parish minister, Gower, to serve in a national synod which would consider 'the due and necessary reformation of the Government and the Liturgy of the Church'.[32] They had not presented the JPs' letter to Parliament because it might be regarded as a sign of 'disaffection'. Harley insisted that Parliament was the supreme source of power, with the King's role as one element in that source, along with the authority of the two Houses, and thus Parliament's ordinances were not to be refused by those in official positions.

The Justices sent a reply on 18 April, which made it clear that they were not to be fobbed off by Harley. They reproved the members for not presenting their first letter to Parliament, and went on to explain their views in some detail. For them, the King was at the head of affairs and only he had the right to govern. As free subjects they would not give their obedience 'to any authority which is not derived from his Majesty … you tell us truly that the constitution of this kingdom is composed of three estates, King, Lords and Commons. It is a triple cord, and it would be dangerous to untwist it.' Accepting that there could be disagreement, they insist that 'if any should have the power of binding it should rather be thought the King, than the Commons, for we find in the statute books those charters and other acts (which story tells us, cost our ancestors much blood) are yet there entered as proceeding from the free grace and favour of the Prince'. They remind their MPs that 'we send you' and, emphasising a point which Harley's letter had evaded, 'we send you, not with the authority to govern us or others (for who can give that to another that is not in himself) but with our consent for making or altering laws as to his Majesty, the Lords and Commons shall seem good'.[33]

This exchange of letters is of great interest. First of all it shows the Herefordshire magnates as thoughtful men, taking a non-aggressive stance. If among the King's adherents there was a Cavalier faction hell-bent on a showdown, they were not members of it. They are well-informed on the issues, have an awareness of history, and articulate a key constitutional point – Parliament had no intrinsic or historic right to govern the realm, but merely to make and amend laws. They take a level-headed view against Harley's somewhat hysterical fears of a papist conspiracy: 'with us they are so quiet we have found no cause hitherto to apprehend any danger from them'. The correspondence also exposes the difficulties and frustrations which arose when an MP's opinions were radically different to those of his leading and most vocal constituents. Harley's refusal to represent their point of view imposed a blockage in the system of information exchange between Parliament and county. (He had also refused to present the pro-Episcopacy petition to Parliament, in January.) The effect was to make the Justices abandon further communication with Harley and concentrate their attention on fulfilling requests from the royal headquarters. But if Harley's intransigence helped to consolidate Royalist engagement among those in Herefordshire who were already favourably disposed to the King's cause, it may also have stiffened the resolve of those who shared his views.

The Justices' second letter makes reference to a petition then being circulated for signatures in the county, and warns the two members not to tender it to the House. This was a very different document to Herefordshire's pro-Episcopacy petition. Addressed only to the House of Commons, it opens with a fulsome tribute to that House's wisdom, pains and patience. Although it also expresses concern for 'the Kings Royall Person', its commendation of Parliament's 'pious care to settle a Government in the Church according to the word of God' (i.e. without bishops), and its praise of Parliament's 'prudent care in disposing the Militia, Navie, and places of Importance of this Kingdome, to such persons of Trust, as may (by Gods Blessing) give assurance of Safety to the Kings Royall Person, and good Subjects of all his Majesties Dominions' show its sympathies are not with the King's policies. It records the county as 'now abounding with insufficient, Idle and Scandalous Ministers, whereby the people generally are continued in Ignorance, Superstition and prophaneness, and are ready to become a prey to popish seducers, which Idolatrous profession hath of late yeares with much boldnesse appeared in this county'.[34] This was not an isolated effort from Herefordshire; godly groups in numerous counties sent similar petitions in what was clearly an organised national campaign.[35] Inclusion of a plea, echoing the 'Grievances' of 1640, against the excessive importation of Spanish wool, undercutting the home-grown product 'to our great impoverishing' seems something of an afterthought, though it shows how important that topic remained locally. It may have been intended to encourage signatures from those who might balk at the rest. Evidently the petition was meant to show that in Herefordshire too there was a body of opinion to back the reformists. It does not seem that Sir Robert Harley, still in London, was involved with it. His wife considered it to be the work of 'Mr Kirll and some other gentellmen' (presumably James Kyrle of Walford), though the principal hands behind it seem to have been the Puritan clergymen Tombes, Gower, and John Green, rector of Pencombe. Sheriff Seward was also noted as among the planners.[36] The whole thing was apparently much mocked at locally.[37] Delivered to the House of Commons at the beginning of May 1642 by a delegation of Hereford gentlemen probably led by Kyrle (Brilliana Harley wrote to her son Edward that 'Mr Kyrle and some other gentlemen intend to set forward with the petition, which I hope will be well taken'), the petition was favourably received by the Commons, but nothing was done about wool imports. Parliament had other things on its mind.

5

The Muster

On 10 January 1642 the King had left London, fearing for his and his family's security. In March, he established his court at York, and among the gentry who joined him there were 'some from the county of Hereford'. In that month, he sent Sir Walter Pye on a secret mission to the Pope in Rome, its purpose unclear.[1] But the King had perhaps already realised that he would need the active support of English Catholics. By now, people were beginning to see armed confrontation as a real possibility, and the King's Council and Parliament vied to secure control of the counties' trained soldiers and ammunition magazines. Both acted as though they were in control of the entire country, making dispositions and sending orders whose effect depended entirely on who was actually in charge of affairs at a local level. Parliament attempted to assume control of the militia, but could only do so where it had enough support. County militias were under the control of the Lord Lieutenant, and Parliament nominated first Lord Dacre, who was unable to act because of illness, then the Earl of Essex, as Lord Lieutenant of Herefordshire. But Essex, despite his landholdings in the county, had no influence among the leaders of society; they waited on the King's orders. Charles responded to Parliament's efforts to mobilise the militias by appointing commissioners of array with responsibility to muster forces on his behalf, an ancient but long disused method of raising troops. Named persons in each county were instructed, in the King's name, to recruit, arm and equip men. A useful aspect of this method was that, unlike troops raised under the Lord Lieutenant, these men could be required to campaign outside their county (though in practice the Royalists would find it hard to persuade them to do so).

In early summer, Brilliana Harley had been worried by demonstrations at Ludlow and Croft, where people shot at a head on a may-pole 'in derision of roundheads'.[2] At Brampton's traditional Horse Fair, held on 11 June 1642, a man was arrested for disorderly behaviour. Sent to the stocks by order of Edward Broughton, an associate of Sir Robert Harley's, 'All night he swore against the Roundheads'. Incidentally, Brilliana Harley notes that Broughton was a man of little estate and that his appointment as a JP had made him 'odious to the country'.[3] Also in June, in response to a Parliamentary call for raising funds 'for the defence of the King and both Houses of Parliament', Harley arranged for his wife to send up two horses and some of the family's silver plate (she rather unwillingly complied). She was still anxious about her security but Sir Robert was adamant that she should stay, and she wrote to her eldest son: 'Since your father thinkes Hearfordsheare as safe as any other country, I will thinke so too.'[4]

Through the first half of 1642, many counties and boroughs had addressed petitions either to the King or to Parliament, in approval or disapproval of what was being done, and mostly pleading for a peaceful solution. Neutralism, or non-participation in the anticipated struggle, was widely proposed, with attempted neutrality pacts in 22 counties,[5] but Herefordshire was not among them. Early in July, when things were already critical, both Houses of Parliament were presented with a printed document which had also been sent to the King, 'A Declaration or Resolution of the Countie of Hereford'. It was unsigned but supported by the Grand Jury,[6] and the authors, 'as faithfull Subjects to his Majesty, as free-borne English-men', joined in a unanimous resolution to maintain: 1. The Protestant Religion; 2. The King's just power; 3. The Laws of the Land; 4. The Liberty of the Subject. Acknowledging that there had been wrongs which needed curing, it claimed the cure had gone much too far under 'an Arbitrary Government, and a high stretcht Prerogative'. It complained about Parliament's interference with free speech and its reliance on the London mob, and observed that Parliament itself was far from unanimous. The declaration proudly announces:

> Nor shall we ever yeeld ourselves such Slaves, or so betray the liberty purchased by our Forefathers blood and bequeathed unto us as to suffer our selves to be swayed by an Arbitrary Government whatsoever, nor stand with too much contention of Spirit to cast off the Yoake of one Tyranny to endure many worse.
> And seeing his Majestie is graciously pleased to maintain the true Protestant Religion; his owne just Power; the Lawes of the Land, the Liberty of the Subjects, and that these waters of Reformation, having long been stirred; we want onely the favour of his Princely Majesty to let us in and heale us; So we doe reciprocally declare that we conceive our selves bound to maintain him in all the Premisses with our Lives and Fortunes.[7]

Such trumpeted defiance to Parliament from his own county was a profound embarrassment to Sir Robert Harley. He denounced it to a committee of both Houses as a 'scandalous and infamous Libel', and wanted the authors to be prosecuted 'to the utmost'.[8] The (London-based) distributors were arrested, but the actual authors of the declaration were never identified. It is likely that some and probably all of the Justices – locally hailed as the 'Nine Worthies'– who had written to Harley and the younger Coningsby earlier in the year were behind it. But things had moved on, and the unmilitant tone of their letters is entirely lacking. Despite the Declaration's anonymity, no-one doubted, probably least of all Harley, that it expressed a genuine and majority feeling. Not only that, it shows, according to one scholar, 'a lofty strain of Royalist sentiment that had not at that stage been heard from any other county'.[9] Herefordshire was nailing its colours to the mast. It was hardly surprising that when Parliament tried to raise the vast sum of £1,000,000 to fund the military campaign in Ireland, on the basis of contributors acquiring land to be confiscated from the Catholic rebels there, Herefordshire collected under £100.[10]

Dr Rogers, in the cathedral, was busy raising the temperature with vigorously anti-Parliamentarian sermons. Hereford's Puritans were being insulted and molested, and felt seriously alarmed. One of them, John Wanklyn, wrote to Harley on 1 July to complain of Rogers's activities, and hoped Harley could get the fiery cleric arrested: 'I pray you have Dr

Rogers sent for, that the rest may take warning by him'.[11] Wanklyn said he was in fear of his life. Later that month Lady Harley reported that another of the godly persuasion, Mr Herring of Holmer, had been driven from his home and 'Mr Crowden, I mean the honest Mr Crowden' feared the same would happen to him.[12]

The MP Richard Weaver had died in May 1642 and was replaced in a classic piece of fixing. Several members of leading families aspired to the vacant seat, including Edward Harley, eldest son of Sir Robert, and, like his father, of a godly turn of mind. Sir William Croft was also said to be interested, as was Thomas Price of Wisterton. But all stepped back when Viscount Scudamore proposed his 17-year-old son, James. A city member had to be a freeman and James could not become a freeman, or burgess, of Hereford until he was 18; but (just over three weeks after his birthday), he was elected as second member for the city on 26 July.[13] This action would seem to stress Scudamore's dominant position, yet during these months he is a largely absent figure. There is no indication that he participated in any way in the plans and declarations of the King's supporters in Herefordshire, apart from signing the pro-episcopacy petition of January 1642. John Webb wrote that he was 'probably in daily intercourse with members of both Houses', but no contemporary account suggests that Scudamore was involved in discussions, whether to prevent war or to build support for the King. Foreseeing troubles ahead, he was busy arranging his own affairs. His landholdings were extensive quite apart from Holme Lacy and Llanthony, and he drew up a deed which assigned various estates to trustees, sometimes against payment of debts, but also securing the positions of his wife, elder son and his daughter. He was by no means the only wealthy Royalist landowner to take this precaution, but it was Scudamore's ill luck that 'it was signed and delivered just ten days too late to invest it with all the security that was intended'.[14] Several years later the Viscount would have to compound with a Parliamentary committee to regain the rights to his properties.

Writing to her son Edward on 5 July, Brilliana Harley noted that a commission of array had been issued for the county by the King.[15] She hoped that Parliament would send down men to take charge of the militia, but there was no likelihood of the Parliamentary ordinance being put into effect here. Though named as a member of the commission of array for Herefordshire, and picked out as one of three members who could form a quorum,[16] along with Wallop Brabazon and the nominal inclusion of the Prince of Wales, the Viscount played no part at all in its proceedings. Altogether some twenty commissioners had been named, including two, Francis Kyrle, a son of Sir James Kyrle, and Bennet Hoskins, who were, or would become, Parliamentarians[17], but the 'Nine Worthies' took the initiative, summoning the trained bands and taking control of the county magazine at St Owen's Gate without any opposition. They set about raising and equipping a troop of 200 horse for six months, and collecting money for the King's war chest.[18] On 14 July, they organised a muster of forces outside the city walls. James Barroll, who had been Mayor in 1639, was at the head of 150 city volunteers, and Sir William Croft's youngest brother Robert was appointed to lead a cavalry troop, when raised, to join the King, who was then still at York. Naturally none of the Harleys was present (Sir Robert and his eldest son Edward were in London), though sixty of Sir Robert's trained-band troop of around 100 appeared, and his captaincy was transferred to Fitzwilliam Coningsby, who had also recruited 100 volunteers

*Two views of St Owen's Gate,
site of the county magazine in 1642.
Above: a late 18th-century watercolour
depicting the outside of the gate.
Left: a drawing of 1784*

on his own.[19] Richard Wigmore, John Scudamore of Ballingham and Edward Slaughter of Cheney Court, Bishop's Frome, were also troop captains. The spirit of the occasion was vociferously anti-Parliament and an observer, sent by Lady Harley, reported that 'a great many cried out and wished you [Sir Robert Harley] were there that they might tear you in pieces'.[20] Viscount Scudamore was also absent. Only a third of his cavalry troop appeared at the muster, and Fitzwilliam Coningsby noted 'his too apparent Absense'.[21]

Why, at this critical moment, the county's most prominent and wealthy Royalist should have failed to appear has been much debated. Ian Atherton discounts any suggestion that Scudamore hung back because he was a 'moderate' or neutral, and provides evidence to show the Viscount's attachment to the King's cause, including a cash donation of £225, sent probably during that summer.[22] However, such a sum was hardly more than a token of support, from a man whose income was around £2,500 a year.[23] Atherton ascribes Scudamore's absence to pique or jealousy at the prominent role that Fitzwilliam Coningsby had taken. But with his personal resources, and his well-stocked armoury at Holme Lacy,[24] the Viscount could have put on a strong show, even if during his years in Paris the proud troop of horse had been neglected, and there seems no reason to suppose he could not have asserted his position among the commissioners of array, just as he had done in the by-election. Despite a taste for the trappings of chivalry, however, Lord Scudamore did not have the qualities of a military leader. His posture in these pre-war months suggests someone battening down the hatches to survive the coming storm rather than be preparing for combat. Many others avoided involvement: an example close to home was Lord Bridgewater at Ludlow, who after a couple of years of increasingly apathetic co-operation with the Royalist side, opted out, with 'his focus on keeping his lands, family and communities intact'.[25] It would seem that Scudamore shared a widespread reluctance to countenance a struggle that would tear his country apart, whether 'timidity'[26] played a part or not. In a society accustomed to take its cue from the top, he completely failed to give the expected leadership.

The Nine Worthies, however, busied themselves to help the King's affairs, and old animosities among Coningsbys, Crofts and Scudamore of Ballingham were put aside for the time being at least, though there were occasional spats, as when Richard Wigmore refused to take orders from Brabazon without seeing his commission. Brabazon, as a recent incomer, may have been regarded as something of an upstart.[27] Brilliana Harley, watching from Brampton Bryan, noted that 'Sir William Croft whoo once did not loue Mr Cunnisbe nor Mr Scidmore is now theire mighty frinde'.[28] Writing to Sir Robert Harley on 19 July, Stanley Gower reported that Coningsby had set up a room in Leominster for people to come forward with contributions of horses and money for the King, 'But no man would propound'.[29] Coningsby, 'diligent in his Majesties Service', as he later said of himself,[30] was appointed High Sheriff by the King on 18 August, replacing Isaac Seward whose attempts to obey both King and Parliament had discredited him with both sides, and who seems to have withdrawn from public life until the end of hostilities.

Hereford's Royalists were very much in the ascendant, and ready to show it. Weekly meetings of males aged 16 upwards were convened in the city wards with the intention of showing loyalty to the King and decrying the Roundheads. Richard Taylor, a tobacco-seller and vociferous supporter of the King, mounted an effigy on his counter of the Parliamentarian Earl of Essex with horns fitted to the head (Essex's marital difficulties were common knowledge), and was reported to have pasted his privy walls with pictures of nobles who agreed with the Parliament. To a Puritan observer, Taylor was 'a lewd seditious fellow'.[31] John Tombes, the Puritan vicar of Leominster, fled the town in August because of the 'barbarous rage and impetuous violence' he and his family were experiencing.[32] Lady Harley, alarmed by rumours of Catholic plots and foreign landings on the King's behalf, again wanted to leave Brampton Bryan, but her husband's response was that she should stay.[33] She had already been gathering in stocks of arms and ammunition, though her main expenditure around this time was with a Worcester contractor who was repairing and releading the castle roofs. She also ordered '50 waight of shot' from Worcester, not because it could not be provided in Herefordshire, but 'because I would not haue it knowne'.[34]

Soon after the muster a Gloucestershire gentleman, Sir Ralph Dutton, arrived at Hereford claiming royal authority to receive the men assembled by the commissioners. Through a piece of malice on the part of his 'host', one John Barnett, Dutton was lodged with Roger

Seaborne, a prominent citizen in his own right, foreman of the Grand Jury. No Royalist, he had already persuaded his fellow jurymen that they need not subscribe to the 'Declaration'. Seaborne appears to have bad-mouthed the county's resources and the Declaration to such a degree that his lodger complained about being put in a Roundhead's house and refused to pay for his lodging.[35] Dutton was a freelance hoping to gain credit with the King, and Hereford's commissioners had no intention of letting him be rewarded for their efforts. He moved on to Shropshire.

The county Assizes were held in the normal way at the end of August. The circuit judge, Sir Edward Hendon, was instructed by Parliament to inquire as to who were responsible for the Declaration. This prompted a noisy Royalist show of force led by William Cater (a wine-merchant, Mayor in 1645) and Richard Taylor, vehement enough to make numerous county gentlemen, including James and Walter Kyrle and Henry Vaughan of Bredwardine, in town for the occasion and known to be Puritans or Parliamentarians, to take refuge in Roger Seaborne's house. Evidently Seaborne continued to be under pressure to show loyalty to the King by paying £9 10s towards a horse and arms for the royal cause,[36] though he did not pay up. Prompted by Croft and Brabazon, Judge Hendon replaced some members of the Grand Jury, including Harley's associate Edward Broughton, and Martin Husbands of Wormbridge, who would later figure on county Parliamentary committees.[37] Two of the county Justices, Ambrose Elton Sr, of Ledbury, and John Scudamore of Kentchurch, denounced the commission of array as illegal and lost their places on the Preace Commission.

The final breakdown of relations between King and Parliament came as no surprise. When news came to Hereford that King Charles I had on 22 August called on all loyal citizens to support and join his cause, nothing much happened at first. People carried on their normal activities. But there must have been plenty of excitement and speculation. Men who knew each other's opinions and personal qualities also knew that the time had come when they might meet as enemies. Others were in no hurry to declare for one side or the other. Arrangements were being pressed ahead to muster fighting men, but they were to be sent elsewhere. Perhaps, on Ledbury's main street, Ambrose Elton and the Royalist John Skipp might prefer to avoid each other, but both were still concerned with the town's everyday affairs. The War, by a general consensus, was going to be a trial of strength between armies in the field – wherever that might be – and not a carnival of blood among neighbours.

6

Opening Shots

To the Royalist leadership, Hereford was an important place. It had made itself a vocal centre of support for King Charles, and it was a strong point: a walled town with a castle guarding one of the county's two bridges over the Wye. Although its walls dated from the late 13th century, they seem to have been in good condition, though at many points shacks and lean-tos had been built against them, on the berm or bank. The county magazine, a store of gunpowder, lead for bullets, and match for firing the various types of gun, was held in the upper chamber of St Owen's Gate.[1] To the strategists of the Parliament side, it was less promising, seen as a refuge for 'malignants', a place which could only be held by force rather than consent, but still a prize worth trying for. The Anglican preacher Richard Baxter noted that Herefordshire was wholly for the King at the start, '… none, to any purpose, moved for the Parliament'.[2] But while the Royalists certainly seized the initiative, there were clearly more than a few pro-Parliamentarians, though they kept their heads down. Among the county JPs in 1642, fifteen were for the King, three were of uncertain loyalty, and ten could be regarded as Parliamentary supporters of varying degrees of warmth.[3] Five of the latter were only appointed to the Commission of the Peace in 1642, at Sir Robert Harley's instigation and seemingly unopposed by Lord Scudamore. While Harley was backing his own friends, it is also an indication that even at that point there was little sense of two opposing 'parties' in the county. In 1643 the Parliamentarians would be removed.[4]

In the vocabulary of confrontation, the terms 'Cavalier' and 'Roundhead' quickly became current. Writing to her husband in June 1642, Brilliana Harley recorded that, 'Every Thursday some of Ludlow, as they go through the towne, wish all the Puritans of Brampton hanged, and, as I was walking one day in the garden … they looked upon mee and wished all the Puritans and Roundheads at Bramton hanged'.[5] Ludlovian sympathies were strongly Royalist and they had a grudge against Harley and Parliament for cutting away the powers of the Council of Wales and the Marches, reducing their town's importance; but evidently attitudes were hardening.

Herefordshire was one of only eleven counties to execute a commission of array for the King between July and October 1642.[6] Its commissioners installed an organiser in each city ward, Cater for Wyebridge, his brother-in-law Edward Cockram for Widemarsh, David Bowen for Bye Street, Joseph Bowcott or Boulcott for Eigne, James Barroll, 'ever since a mischievous fellow',[7] for St Owen, to drum up support. By 5 August they had sent a contribution of £3,000 to the royal funds and could announce that the county had fitted out a troop of 200 horse and undertaken to support it for six months. One man summoned to the muster, Priamus Davies, refused to appear, and it was clear that his refusal was based on opposition to the royal cause. When the commissioners of array issued a warrant for his arrest, he left the county and turned up in London, where the House of Commons found time on 24 September to listen to his story.[8] The House responded by ordering that Brabazon, Croft, Coningsby, Lingen, Price and Rudhall should be brought to London to be tried as delinquents, though even if a messenger were sent to Hereford, his chance of enforcing the order was non-existent. Parliament acted as if its writ ran everywhere in the country, primarily to assert its national role but also in case, by some change of events, its friends might gain power in Royalist places and enforce its ordinances.

Early in August, Sir William Croft paid a visit to Brampton Bryan Castle. The Crofts and the Harleys were related by marriage,[9] but it was more than a social call. Like many other people, Croft was preoccupied by the need to find some means of reconciling the hostile sides. His solution was that the forces now being raised should be diverted to Ireland, in support of the Protestants and loyal subjects there.[10] Sir William hoped to bring Harley into line with the other leaders of Hereford society by dropping his support for the Parliamentary cause, but this notion was as illusory as his hopes for peace. Croft also warned Lady Brilliana that whatever his private feelings, in his public duty as a commissioner of array he could show the Harleys no favour.[11] Sir Robert was also proprietor of the castle at Wigmore, entire but probably unoccupied, and he appears to have had it destroyed at this time, presumably feeling that he could not defend both it and the nearby Brampton Bryan, if war should come.[12]

The ruins of Wigmore Castle from a drawing by Thomas Hearne in 1806 (Hereford Library)

War quickly began to have an effect on commerce. A Bristol customer of the ironworks at Carey wrote in September 1642 to William Scudamore of Ballingham that he was not in a position to place further orders, and could not send a due payment of £148 15s 2d because of the Marquess of Hertford's soldiers at Sherborne, but offered to pay it in London 'in few weeks' to anyone designated by Scudamore.[13] But though Webb says trade was at a standstill, this was not generally the case. Perhaps the worst affected were cattle dealers. In autumn 1642 the price of Welsh cattle fell by half at Border fairs,[14] because of the difficulty of getting them to the London markets. Following many protests, in December 1642 the King issued a proclamation that no stop or interruption should be made by his troops or agents to those travelling from the Western Counties to London with goods to sell. Seven months later he rescinded the order, as a reprisal for London's opposition to him, and renewed the rescindment in October 1643.[15] Later in the war, bearing in mind the royalism of most Welshmen, the Commons empowered the Speaker in July 1645 to grant passes 'to whom he thought fit' to buy cattle in Wales and drive them across country to London.[16] Cross-country travellers throughout the war years had to look out for who controlled the territory they would traverse, and ensure that they had a valid pass or safe-conduct (which would rarely be issued without some payment being made). Nevertheless, hindering and inconveniencing as it did in many ways, it is unlikely that the Civil War diminished the level of trade to any great extent. There has been scant research into the economic history of the war years, but it is likely that some forms of commerce may even have increased, along with industrial production. Iron was needed for cannon, balls, pikes and other military equipment. Gunpowder, barrels, and digging tools were in constant demand. Large quantities of cloth, leather and canvas for uniforms, boots, bags, cart-covers and tents were needed. Since very many families, like those of the Hereford guildsmen and their employees, lived on the proceeds of trade, they had to make every effort to keep up business. The effects of war were generally sporadic and localised, and though trade in some places could be paralysed by sieges or disrupted by passing armies, outside the affected areas life and commerce went on as normally as possible.

As autumn approached, it seemed that the war was drawing close to Hereford. By 20 September the King had moved his headquarters to Shrewsbury. The Earl of Essex, Lord General of the Parliament's field army, recruited largely in London, was leading his forces from London, at first towards Coventry, then swinging south towards Worcester, held by Royalist sympathisers. With Essex's army reported to be closing in on Worcester, Mayor David Bowen of Hereford sent around 30 men and half a dozen barrels of gunpowder from the county magazine, under the command of James Barroll, in support. At this juncture, a military convoy commanded by Sir John Byron, escorting cartloads of gold and silver plate from Oxford colleges as contributions to the King's treasury at Shrewsbury, had reached Worcester, and a detachment of the Parliamentary army, under Colonel Brown, was sent forward in the hope of capturing this treasure. The King's Anglo-German nephew, Prince Rupert, came with 1,000 horse to help in its defence, and, by resourceful generalship, he scattered the Parliamentary force at Powick Bridge on the Teme just east of the city, on 23 September. A skirmish rather than a battle, it was the first field encounter between the two sides, and a Royalist victory. Byron's wagons moved on safely, but Rupert considered that

Worcester could not be defended. The Royalist forces withdrew, leaving the city open to their opponents, who moved in without delay.

Herefordshire's Royalists had taken command in the summer, but now there was a chance for the supporters of Parliament to rally. A group were named as Deputy Lieutenants in September, including Sir Robert Harley, Sir John Kyrle, James and Walter Kyrle, Sir Richard Hopton, Ambrose Elton Sr, John Scudamore of Kentchurch, and Bennet Hoskins. Some of these attended on the Earl of Essex at Worcester at the end of September, and requested military aid.[17] Among the signatories were Sir Robert Harley, Sir Richard Hopton, Henry Vaughan, Edward Broughton, James Kyrle and John Flackett. Harley had come to Worcester with other local MPs, bringing instructions to Essex from Parliament,[18] but took the opportunity to visit his home and family. His eldest son Edward was also at Brampton Bryan at that time. It was hoped to form an association of Herefordshire, Shropshire, Cheshire and Gloucestershire to combine in action on Parliament's behalf, while Richard Hopton Jr helped to raise the temperature by making a plundering raid on Brabazon's estate.[19]

Charles remained at Shrewsbury until October 12, and the Royalists of Monmouth and south Wales were busy mustering men to reinforce him. Two thousand Welsh recruits appeared at Hereford around 20 September on their way to Shrewsbury, and were admitted to the city but expelled on the following day because they 'used themselves so inhumanly towards the townsmen and attempted to disarm them'.[20] It was clearly an unpleasant revelation of the realities of life on a war footing. For the Parliamentarians, to block the route between Raglan and Shrewsbury was an obvious move. Essex's decision to attempt the capture of Hereford was a sound piece of strategy, and undoubtedly he was well-informed about the state of the city's defences.

With a large Parliamentary army in Worcester from 24 September, 'many of the people with their children fled' from Hereford.[21] One of those who left town was Joyce Jeffreys who went to Kilkington, near Staunton-on-Wye, to stay with relatives, then moved to live with the Geers family at nearby Garnons. Nevertheless, when it became known that Essex had directed a subsidiary force under Henry Grey, Earl of Stamford, to take Hereford, a robust opposition might have been expected from the city of the Nine Worthies. News would certainly have come of the Parliamentary troops' behaviour in Worcester, where the homes of known Royalists were looted, the Mayor and other magistrates were imprisoned, the cathedral was turned by the troops into a stable, and its ornaments, books, stained glass and records destroyed.[22] If occupied, Hereford could no doubt expect similar treatment.

7

The First Surrender

Hereford had six road gates and three or more postern gates.[1] All were closed when Stamford appeared before the walls on 1 October with 900 men, three troops of horse (one commanded by Robert Kyrle, son of James Kyrle of Walford), and two light field guns. The weather was vile, with both rain and snow. A junior officer in Stamford's force, Nehemiah Wharton, wrote to a friend:

> After we had marched 10 miles, we came to Bromyard, the weather wet, and the way very foul. Here we got a little refreshment, and from hence marched 10 miles further to Hereford. But very late before we got thither; and by reason of the rain and snow, and extremity of cold, one of our soldiers died by the way; and it is wonderful we did not all perish, for the cowardly Cavaliers were within a few miles of us. In this poor condition coming to Hereford, the gates were shut against us, and for two hours we stood in dirt and water up to the mid-leg, for the city were all malignants, save three which were Roundheads, and the Marquess of Hertford had sent them word the day before that they should in no wise let us in, or if they did, we would plunder their houses, murder their children, burn their Bibles and utterly ruinate all, and promised he would relieve them himself with all speed, for which cause the citizens were resolved to oppose us unto the death, and having in the city three pieces of ordnance charged them with stones, nails, &c., and placed them against us, and we against them, resolving either to enter the city or die before it. But the Roundheads in the city, one of them an alderman, surnamed Lane, persuaded the silly Mayor, for so he is indeed, that his Excellency and all his forces were at hand, whereupon he opened unto us and we entered the city at Byster's gate, but found the doors shut, many of the people with their children fled, and had enough to do to get a little quarter.[2]

The Roundhead troops were admitted without a shot being fired. How could a stalwart Royalist city submit so tamely? The yielding of Hereford in October 1642 has never been satisfactorily explained. Viscount Scudamore had been in the town on 28 September, when he gave dinner at mid-day to the Common Council,[3] but left for his Llanthony home on the same day. The commissioners of array left also. John Scudamore of Ballingham, Henry Lingen, Thomas Price, Sir Walter Pye and Sir William Croft went to join the King at Shrewsbury, and Fitzwilliam Coningsby went to Raglan Castle, stronghold of the Earl of Worcester.[4].One explanation for their defection is that, having sent men to the royal army and men and material to the defence of Worcester, they had insufficient troops and ammunition to mount a defence. Wharton noted that there were only three pieces of ordnance in the city, loaded with stones and nails. Since the outbreak of hostilities, there had been little time to improve the city's defences, but it does not seem that any work had been done at all. In their defence, it can be said no-one had been appointed as Governor or military commander of the city. Lord Scudamore, as Steward, was the senior figure, but after his inaction during the summer it seems unlikely that he would have taken any initiative. The Mayor and his council were left to confront the enemy, and though Bowen was reported as saying he would be hanged before surrendering the city,[5] he evidently consulted Parliamentarians like Lane and Seaborne and decided that it was better to yield on agreed terms.

With a Parliamentary army at the gate, and no royal garrison inside, it is probable that negotiations between the Herefordians accompanying Stamford, and the Hereford city councillors (some of whom, including the incoming mayor, William Price, favoured Parliament), achieved an agreement to surrender on assurance of protection for people and property, including the cathedral. Some such arrangement may have been made even before Stamford left Worcester. Certainly Hereford's cathedral was not desecrated as Worcester's had been[6] and there was no looting. After the Royalist sentiments and the Roundhead-baiting of the summer it was a humiliating come-down, which suggests that there had been a febrile quality about that earlier enthusiasm. For the wider Royalist cause it was an early blow, and a propaganda coup for their opponents.

Military occupation was a new experience for everyone, including the occupiers. Nehemiah Wharton, despite being a Londoner, was impressed by Hereford:

> Saturday our squadron watched at St. Owen's gate, which day I took an opportunity to view the city, which is well situate, and seated upon the river Wye, environed with a strong wall, better than any I have seen before, with five gates and a strong stone bridge of six arches, surpassing Worcester. In this city is the stateliest market-place in the kingdom, built with columns after the manner of the Exchange; the Minster every way exceeding that at Worcester; but the city in circuit not so large. The inhabitants are totally ignorant in the ways of God, and much addicted to drunkenness and other vices, but principally to swearing, so that the children that have scarce learned to speak do universally swear stoutly. Many here speak Welsh.[7]

Unlike the situation in London,[8] the Parliamentary troops behaved peaceably, but made their presence felt. On Sunday 7 October, Wharton recorded that, 'about the time of morning prayer, we went to the Minster, where the pipes played and the puppets sang so sweetly, that some of our soldiers could not forbeare dauncing in the holy quire; whereat the Baalists were sore displeased'. The 'pipes' were the organ and the 'puppets' (poppets, meaning dolls) the surpliced choristers. Plenty of bravery was displayed in Hereford during the war, by children as well as adults, but perhaps this was the most courageous action of all, for the boys to sing on in the face of the mockery and derisive prancings of these armed strangers with their flapping bandoliers and heavy boots. The service continued and the clergy 'prayed devoutly for the kings, the bisshops, etc., and one of our soldiers, with a loud voice, said, "What! neiver a bit for the Parliament?" which offended them much more'. Dean Jonathan Browne had to vacate the pulpit for the lengthy sermons and adjurations of the Rev. John Sedgwick, Stamford's chaplain. Tougher actions by the occupying troops were also recorded. It was claimed that some individuals were hanged without proper trial, and others punished by being dragged behind horses. Stamford also opened up the prisons and allowed the convicts to go free, presumably requiring Hereford's limited prison accommodation for 'such Roman Catholics and others as he thought unfit to be at large'.[9]

Stamford took up residence in the Bishop's Palace. Dr Coke was not in Hereford; probably he was at the bishop's country house, the old moated manor of Whitbourne, on the Worcestershire border.[10] Stamford's regiment was quartered in the town, with Mayor Price and Sir Robert Harley active in helping with the billeting arrangements. In the (usual) absence of cash reserves, troops of both sides were billeted on what was known as 'free quarter', in which the soldiers received food and accommodation in exchange for promissory notes which could be exchanged for cash at some later date. Needless to say, these pieces of paper were not received with any enthusiasm. Commanders also managed to extort money for upkeep of their troops, and some receipts are preserved in Hereford's County Records Office.[11]

At this time, Hereford was drawn into a novel aspect of warfare, one that was only possible in a country with good communications and a relatively high rate of literacy. It was the war of propaganda, waged at least as energetically as the military campaign. There was good reason for this: both sides knew that a large proportion of the population, perhaps the majority, were against the war, and many were uncommitted to either side. Through exaggerated or misleading reports, and downright falsehoods, published in an unending

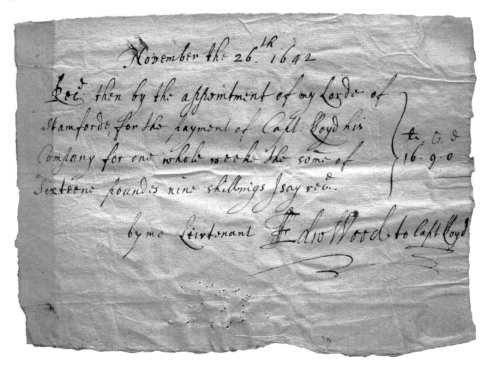

'November 26th 1642
Received then by the appointment of my Lord of Stamford, for the payment of Capt. Lloyd his
Company for one whole week the sum of sixteen pounds nine shillings. I say received by me
Lieutenant Edward Wood to Capt. Lloyd' (HCRO CF 50/278)

Extract from a book of receipts and disbursements of William Price during his Mayoralty, 1642-43, including entertainment of the Marquess of Hertford and the Earl of Stamford, and payments for gunpowder, match and bullet (HCRO CF 50/278) flow of newsletters and pamphlets, each camp denigrated the other and tried to convey the sense that they were the God-favoured and winning side and thus the safe one to join. 'Disinformation' is not a 20th-century invention. While Stamford was already in Hereford, London printers produced news reports so wide of the truth that they must be regarded as deliberate lies rather than hyped-up rumours. 'A Wonderful Deliverance', supposedly written by 'Mr Thomas Kittermaster of Hereford' and dated 21 October, told how a thousand parliamentary dragoons saved 'the Town of Draiton in the County of Hereford' from plundering by the cavaliers under 'Prince Robert'. Drayton was and is a farmstead and there was no such incident. Another pamphlet, 'A True Relation of the Proceedings at Hereford', invented an account of how on 7 October Lord St John and his Parliamentary regiment were welcomed into Hereford. On the 8th, the King appeared and requested admission to the city, to be informed that he would be let in only if he would return to his Parliament, and listen to their faithful counsel, whereupon he rode off to Chester in a passion. Equally fictitious, 'True Newes out of Hereford' described Stamford's victory in a wholly imaginary battle with a Royalist army led by Lords Hertford and Herbert.[12]

On 23 October, Charles's army, marching from Shrewsbury in the direction of London, and Essex's army, which had left Worcester to intercept the King, met at Edgehill in Warwickshire. This first major battle of the war was inconclusive. Many on the Royalist side were that summer's levies from Herefordshire, the Marches and south Wales, and among the Royalist officers was James Croft, in the Gentlemen Pensioners' troop. Tradition has it that Sir William Croft, as a colonel in the King's service, also fought in the battle.[13]

Once the main Parliamentary army had left Worcester, Stamford at Hereford was out on a limb. Scouting parties, or others engaged on raids and money collection, were sent out to the edges of the county. Some supporters, like Thomas Blayney, Sir Robert Harley's neighbour, joined in the collection of levies.[14] Joyce Jeffreys found that her refuge at Garnons was not secure: 'On Tewsday morning, October 4, captain Harmon and his barbarous company plundered Mr Geereses house at Garnons, both them and me of much Goods, toke away my 2 bay coach mares and som money, and much Linen.'[15] In January she had to pay out 21s to retrieve two black beaver hats and two gold bands, which the raiders had presumably sold in the city. The vicarage of Goodrich, just across the Wye from James Kyrle's fortified house at Walford, was a particular target. Thomas Swift, the incumbent, had built it as recently as 1636 to house his large family of ten children. His wife was sister to the poet John Dryden and they were grandparents of the author of *Gulliver's Travels*.[16] Swift, an ardent Royalist, who was also Rector of Bridstow, owned an estate by the castle, and clung on to his house and livings despite hostile new neighbours. Goodrich Castle was described by Stamford as 'a Place of infinite Importance',[17] and 100 soldiers sent from Hereford to garrison the castle (its owner, the Earl of Kent, was a strong Parliamentarian) had no compunction about maintaining themselves by plundering the vicar's property. With a 900-strong Royalist garrison at Monmouth, a few miles down the river, they were probably insecure and edgy, aware of being in unfriendly country. Some others of Hereford's 'worthies' were not far away. A detachment sent from Hereford to Presteigne, under Robert Kyrle and including Edward Harley, captured some Royalists who had been meeting earlier that day to plan the retaking of Hereford for the King; Fitzwilliam Coningsby and Lord Herbert of Raglan, son of the Earl of Worcester, had been there but left before the attack.[18]

Messengers came to Stamford from far-off Pembrokeshire, where local Parliamentarians were holding out against the Marquess of Hertford who was busy raising troops for the King in south Wales. If Stamford could help them with 2,000 foot and 300 horse, they reckoned they could drive the Marquess right out of Wales. If they got no help, Hertford would defeat them and then turn on Hereford. Whether this reading was correct or not, Stamford was in no position to offer such assistance. His military stores were running low and his men had not been paid. Meanwhile Lord Hertford's recruiting bands were building up a substantial Royalist force in Monmouthshire, from where raiding parties pushed far into Herefordshire, focusing their attentions on the properties of those known to be sympathetic to Parliament.[19]

Essex, as Lord Lieutenant, issued a commission on 30 September to Sir John Kyrle, the two Harleys, and Sir Richard Hopton of Canon Frome, to raise troops for Parliament, but if they tried, it was a failure. Herefordshire was not to be a recruiting ground for the Roundheads. Though Stamford sent hopeful messages to the House of Lords about his ability to recruit up to 500 dragoons in the county,[20] it was evident that this was implausible, just as John Sedgwick's sermons in Hereford Cathedral failed to win converts from episcopal Anglicanism. A meeting of county gentry and freeholders was called by Stamford in mid-November in the hope of finding local support, but he was silent about its outcome. Perhaps no-one turned up.[21] Early in December Sir Richard Hopton, 'who had promised the Earl of Stamford that he had 1,000 dragoons at four days' warning to be ready for his service, came into Ledbury with his colours and his drum, and there, in a commanding manner, called all the countrymen in order to bring in their dragonnes'. No-one came forward.[22] Unless there should be a dramatic fall in the King's fortunes, Stamford and his troops were in Hereford on borrowed time.

Something of a game of challenge was being played in the south of the county, where Royalist troops came and went, drawing support from those who were sympathetic and plundering those who were not. Some of the latter who had suffered wrote a petition of complaint to Stamford, claiming that 'since the Beginning of this present Month of November' they had had 'to flee, with our Wives and Children, for our Lives and Safety' while their houses were rifled, their cattle taken away, their corn and grain threshed and removed 'by the barbarous Cavaliers of the Welsh Parts, who are under the Command of a dangerous Papist, the Lord Herbert'.[23] By mid-November an advance party of Royalists had established themselves at Ewyas Harold, only ten miles from Hereford. Captain Robert Kyrle, who had been sent out to intercept a raiding force of 350 Cavalier troops who had ventured within five miles of the city, found that the Royalists, warned by local supporters, had drawn back to Ewyas Harold. Kyrle pushed on and found six men blocking the way at 'the town's end'. Challenged as to who they were for, they replied 'For the King, and the Plague take the Parliament'. They were shot dead, and another nine were also killed, while the rest fled into the hills around.[24] This was the first fight between the two sides in Herefordshire. It has been dated as 16 November, though it is likely to be the occasion laconically referred to on the 13th in the diary of Walter Powell of Llantilio Crosseny: 'the men slayne at Pontrylas'.[25] Despite this setback, the Royalists appear to have established themselves at the Pyes' fortified mansion, The Mynde, in Much Dewchurch parish, only five miles from Hereford,[26] and from there a Royalist officer, Sir Richard Lawdey, wrote to a former comrade-in-arms, now Sergeant-Major of Stamford's regiment, to try to get him to change sides, advising that 'We shall suddenly approach to Hereford with such Forces as will (God willing) soon reduce the Rebels in it to the King's Mercy', and offering a bribe of £500 for his assistance. The offer was refused.[27]

On 12 November Prince Rupert's troops stormed Brentford, just outside London, and rumours of a Parliamentary defeat, spreading westwards, helped to depress the spirits of Stamford's men. Despite the raising of a loan among those in the city and county who were willing to be supportive, or to chance their money, they were out of funds, out of credit, and receiving beady-eyed looks from a citizenry who surmised they would not be there much longer. Stamford was already thinking in terms of departure.[28] A more stalwart commander might have toughed it out, but he had given up hope: 'the Country, as well as this vile city, are so base and malignant …' that they preferred being raided and robbed by 'Welch Papists, and other Vagabonds', the post-Edgehill remnants of Lord Herbert's army, than 'to be rescued and relieved by us'. The Parliamentary garrison at Worcester had already left that city, leaving it to Royalist control, and on 3 December Stamford withdrew the garrison from Goodrich. Abandoning Hereford was not part of Parliament's plans, and certainly not something Harley wanted. With the member for Tewkesbury, Sir Robert Cooke, he had written to London on 22 November to propose that Stamford be confirmed as military commander of the four Marcher counties. But on 7 December Stamford wrote to Harley

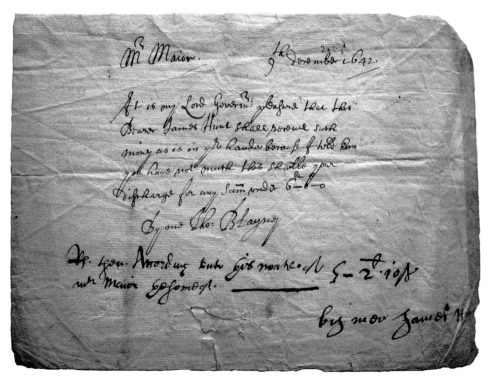

A demand made on 9 December 1642, just before Stamford's departure, from Thomas Blayney to the Mayor, requiring 'such money as is in your hands', although he appreciates it is 'not much'; to be paid to James Hunt (HCRO CF 54/56 p.34A)

that he had received 'His Excellency's [Essex's] commands to march away to my government of Gloucester and Bristol',[29] and though the role proposed by Harley was confirmed by Parliament on 13 December, Stamford was already preparing to leave. On the 14th he evacuated Hereford with all his men, animals and remaining stores, though it was reported that 'privately many had gotten arms from his own soldiers'.[30] These presumably were Parliamentarians, feeling an imminent need for self-defence. As the Earl was preparing to move, he called up the Mayor and aldermen, and obtained from them an undertaking that the city would admit no force (except by force) other than a Parliament one. Leaving three houses on fire to keep the inhabitants occupied and prevent pursuit,[31] the former garrison made their way to Gloucester, and from there Stamford went on to join the Parliamentary forces in the south-west, leaving his regiment of foot under Colonel Edward Massey to hold Gloucester; while such Herefordshire Parliamentarians as Thomas Blayney and Edward Broughton, whose names appear on receipts for sums of money unlikely to have been willingly donated by their fellow-citizens,[32] must have had an uneasy time.

On the departure of Stamford's men, Royalist enthusiasm was immediately rekindled and some of his more laggard troopers were attacked as they tried to leave. An entry in the churchwardens' accounts for All Saints parish notes that three soldiers had been buried at the Mayor's order around this time, although no date is given.[33] Charles Booth, a member of a Royalist family at Breinton, was despatched to Hereford on the next day, a Sunday, and 'rode up and down the town informing the mayor and others that Mr Fitzwilliam Coningsby was appointed governor, and all should be well'.[34] The Mayor and aldermen went to hear prayers at St Martin's church, at the far side of the Wye bridge, and while they were outside the walls, 'the damndest crew of rakehells as ever passed any port' entered the city. As the civic leaders were outside the walls, the gates could not be shut and these new arrivals, Lord Herbert's men under Colonel Lawdey, possessed themselves of the place, mounting guards on the gates and 'crying in Welsh and English, "The town is our own"'.[35]

Was the absence of the Mayor, following his undertaking to Lord Stamford, intentional? Not to be on hand when the Cavaliers returned may have seemed the most sensible option. Yet if he had colluded with the Royalists, the indignities which followed would hardly have occurred. Having sat up until midnight assisting with the business of finding lodgings for the troops, he had then to provide a meal for the officers, while his house and his mercer's (cloth and clothing) shop were searched and looted, though the commanders 'relieved and rescued all'. There were threats to hang him at his door. He was blamed for the surrender to Stamford: a Royalist pamphlet said that 'Hereford was sold by that perfidious mayor Price' and claimed that he wanted to name his newborn son 'Parliament'.[36] Price appears to have been so affected as to succumb to a mental breakdown in which, while under house arrest, he smeared his face with his filth.[37] David Bowen, the former Mayor, a Royalist, was made acting Mayor. Alderman Lane, being taken before the new Mayor, had the discomfiting sight of a noose dangling from a window of the market house, while Richard Taylor, vocal again, tried to rouse up a lynch mob to hang him. Other known Roundheads had their houses plundered and were themselves subjected to insult. For several hours things threatened to get completely out of control before the Royalist officers, Major Drury and Captain Adams (Catholics from Monmouthshire) got their troops and the civilians under restored order.

8

Coningsby Triumphant

Four days later, Fitzwilliam Coningsby arrived to exercise his role as Governor. He had a commission from the Marquess of Hertford, conveyed to him by Lord Herbert, styling him as 'Gouernor of the Cittie and Garrison of Hereford as touchinge the Militia', and also bore a commission to raise a regiment of which he would be colonel. He ascribed his appointment to '… it being supposed that a Native Gentleman would be most tender of the Countrey & most able to enlist them to ready Service & to raise a considerable Garrison'.[1] For a time the city was packed with troops. Apart from those already in possession, another 1,500 came, both horse and foot, all on free quarter. Two wagon-loads of muskets were sent by Lord Herbert. The Parliamentarians might have gone, but no-one could say the city was not now well-guarded.

Now a county-wide purge began, investigating all those who had backed or given any support to the Parliamentarian forces, and exacting penalties.[2] The vicar of Kilpeck, Mr Greenleaf, who had complained to Stamford about the incursions of Royalist troops, was put, with his wife Joan and one of his sons, in the bishop's prison. It was probably the last use of this gaol. Joan Greenleaf and her son were claimed to be intelligencers (spies) for the Parliamentary forces.[3] A vengeful expedition was mounted against Canon Frome and the house was stripped, with Sir Richard Hopton's moveable property divided among his opponents. Among those who managed to switch sides was John Abrahall, of Mountbury Court in Yarkhill parish, a high constable of the hundred of Radlow, who had joined with Hopton in escorting Stamford to Hereford. The wrathful Hopton watched as Abrahall took a share of the spoils, a table-board, chairs and a pack of wool,[4] and later prosecuted him for his looting (Abrahall paid him off with 20 marks). For some days there was a disturbed and virtually anarchic situation, until the Marquess of Hertford appeared, on his way to join the King with 2,000 Welsh recruits he had gathered. Hertford's stay was brief – he moved on towards Oxford shortly after 20 December. The commissioners of array were empowered to restore the trained bands and replenish the store of weapons and ammunition.

Coningsby's post as Governor of the city was a military one, without civil powers, but he was already High Sheriff of Herefordshire. For the citizens, the fact that they had given contributions, forced or not, to Stamford, made no difference when collection was made for the King. There was a new garrison to feed and pay, as well as the need to raise contributions for the King's campaign. The commission of array was revised in January 1643 to ensure that assessments were made and payments received. Herefordshire was required to find £3,000 a month, though this was reduced to £1,200 from April.[5] In addition, the gentry, clergy and freeholders were 'encouraged' to make loans to the King. On the whole, the citizens appear to have borne the burden with resignation. The Parliamentary *Perfect Diurnall* observed that Coningsby 'doth lay great taxes upon the County and those that refuse to pay … or to bring in such men or provision which is required of them, are forced to leave their habitations and fly to Gloucester or some other place of safety; yet such a mist is upon the peoples understandings, that they (for the most part) doe rather submit to any thing then to seeke their owne freedom'.[6] People paid the more willingly because the Royalists seemed to be getting the upper hand that winter in Gloucestershire, where Tewkesbury was in Royalist hands, and the Parliamentary commander Colonel Massey, having for a time controlled most of the county, was forced to concentrate his troops in Gloucester city. Parliament itself imposed a national weekly levy for maintenance of the army, in an Ordinance of 24 February,[7] requiring £437 10s from Herefordshire, which it was in no position to collect.

When the county Justices assembled for the Epiphany Quarter Sessions in January 1643, the opportunity was taken to prepare a 'Humble Petition' to the two houses of Parliament, from the Grand Jury. The document does not read as a particularly humble one. Although it acknowledges that 'many grievances abounded in the Kingdome, which wee hoped would have bin reformed by this Parliament, gladding our Hearts by the establishing of some excellent Lawes at the beginning', it deplores the dispute between King and Parliament, and moves into a litany of the plunderings and outrages committed in Hereford by the Parliamentary forces under the Earl of Stamford, claiming that some citizens had been hanged or dragged at horses' hooves without charge, 'to the horrible astonishment of His Majesties Subjects of this County'. It protests against the unseemly sermons of Mr John Sedgwick in Hereford Cathedral, and at Stamford's opening of the prisons and release of felons. It also records his oppressive forcing of money from the citizens, his unlawful appropriation of cathedral revenues, and his removal of arms and ammunition. It ends with the plea that the two Houses 'would forthwith submit to such termes of Accommodation, as his Majestie will graciously yeeld unto' and so avoid 'wee say not a civil warre, but that which is like to be the most horrid and desperate Civil warre that can be apprehended to befall any Nation'. Fifteen jurymen signed. Though Abel Carwardine, their foreman (the pro-Parliament Roger Seaborne was not a member of this Grand Jury) was delegated to bear it to London, it is very unlikely that he did. The Lords and Commons would certainly have had him clapped in prison.

Viscount Scudamore was still a member of the commission of array, but Coningsby held the reins of power. He was to write later that Scudamore 'look't with an euill Eye vpon these powers vnited in me' and showed 'the envie that produced Thwarting and Disturbances to the weakening his Majesties Service, and Ruining our Countrey'.[8] Scudamore as High Steward and Coningsby as Governor were at odds. When the King ordered the Herefordshire justices to assist Coningsby in the raising and arming of a regiment, Scudamore objected to the troops being paid out of the county's monthly payment and hinted that the regiment might be taken out of the county (a powerful disincentive to recruitment). Coningsby procured a letter from the royal headquarters promising that Charles would not order his regiment out of the county and ordering that money should be raised in the county to support it. Atherton suggests that Coningsby was exaggerating his claims for money,[9]

Lord Herbert, 2nd Marquess of Worcester, from the frontispiece of his book A Century of the names and Scantlings or such Inventions as at present I can call to mind, *published in 1663*

which would not be unusual for the time. 'A professional officer was virtually self-employed; he bought and could resell his commission, and earned his income by contracting for supplies, collecting pay and allowances for ghost troops and cheating his men on their rations.'[10] Scudamore ensured that all the monthly collections raised in the county for the regular payment of the forces should be passed to Lord Herbert, who had been appointed by Hertford as commander in south Wales and the southern Marches and Coningsby was compelled to use his own funds, or borrow, to equip his regiment. Loyal Joyce Jeffreys sent him £50 on 27 December, and a fat bullock worth £6,[11] and he managed to parade 685 men, plus officers, before the commissioners of array and Lord Herbert, at Hereford on 28 January. When Coningsby wanted the clergy's dues for improving the defences of Hereford, Scudamore wanted them to be used to raise a troop of horse under his cousin John Scudamore of Ballingham. Instead, by royal command the dues were paid to Colonel Herbert Price of Brecon, commanding under Lord Herbert in the southern Marches.[12] In February 1643 Scudamore went to the King in Oxford and procured an order prohibiting Coningsby from raising further troops. To say that 'Scudamore's actions emasculated Coningsby' may overstate the case,[13] but undoubt-

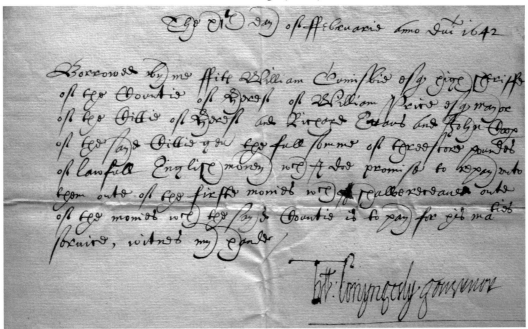

A document signed by Fitzwilliam Coningsby as Governor on 11th February 1642 (in old style dating, when the year commenced on 25 March, so dated 11th February 1643 in our eyes), acknowledging receipt of £60 lent by William Price. Richard Evans and John Cooper, to be repaid from the first monies collected from the county 'for his majesty's service' (HCRO CF50/263)

edly the Viscount's personal connections in court circles enabled him to be obstructive, and he was angrily confronted by the combative Richard Wigmore of Shobdon, lieutenant-colonel of Coningsby's regiment.[14] Scudamore's activities seem to have been entirely negative and unlike the Earl of Worcester, and Coningsby, he disbursed very little of his personal wealth and resources for the King's cause. It could be that his campaign against Coningsby was intended to cover up his own self-serving intention to inconvenience himself as little as possible in this most undesirable war. Meanwhile, a hint that the commissioners were beginning to scrape the barrel comes from a letter of 21 February 1643 to the Mayor of Hereford from Coningsby, Croft and Rudhall, writing as commissioners of array 'under ye greate seale of England', requesting him to liberate one Thomas Watkins, of Bridge Sollers, in prison for debt, 'to do such service as he should be enjoyned for his Ma'tie'.[15]

In February 1643 Gloucester's Parliamentary garrison under Colonel Massey was under threat on the north and east from a Royalist force commanded by Prince Rupert. Lord Herbert, in his new role as military supremo, prepared to mount a supporting attack from the west. Sir Richard Lawdey, promoted to Major-General, was in command of the infantry, around 1,500 men, and Herbert's younger brother Lord John Somerset (their father had been raised to the rank of Marquess on 2 November 1642) led 500 cavalry. Fitzwilliam Coningsby's 685 men had been raised for the defence of Hereford, and he had brought in arms and ammunition, plates to make corselets, and two tons of 'bullet', together with material to assemble brass field guns,[16] but almost all this *matériel* was requisitioned by Herbert,

Sir William Waller (National Portrait Gallery)

along with 400 men under Richard Wigmore, to strengthen his own forces. Coningsby was most unhappy about this but was doubtless assured they would soon be back triumphant. The force set off from Monmouth in mid-February across the Forest of Dean. Parliament had many supporters among the Forest's miners and artisans, and at Coleford they joined with a detachment of troops under Colonel Berrow to hold back the Royalists. In a fierce struggle, Lawdey was killed but the Roundhead force was routed.[17] The Royalists then moved on to entrench themselves at Highnam, two miles west of Gloucester. Robert Kyrle, who had been Sergeant-Major of Stamford's regiment of horse, changed sides during this campaign and became a Royalist. In a long letter justifying his action, he put forward the sermons of John Sedgwick as one of his reasons, for 'traducing the King, and cursing him, while he seemed to pray for him' – in Kyrle's case they were clearly counter-productive. Fighting on the Parliamentary side at Edgehill, he had already felt 'that strange mistery, that fighting for the safety of the King, was shooting at him'.[18]

Having got to Gloucester, the besiegers seemed at a loss about how to proceed. Colonel Massey's chaplain, John Corbet, wrote contemptuously of them, '… they lay five weeks in a stinking nest. They were basely bafled, never attempted our out-guard, never undertook the least party that issued forth'.[19] Massey put up a vigorous defence, leading at least one attack out of the city on 23 March. But by then he knew what his Royalist assailants did not: a relieving army, commanded by Sir William Waller, was close to arriving. On the 24th, with skirmishing still going on around Highnam House, the besiegers became belatedly aware that Waller's army had passed south of Gloucester, crossed the Severn, and come up on their western side. Caught between Waller's force and the city's defenders, the Royalists promptly asked for a truce to negotiate surrender terms. Although some of their officers wanted to make an attack during the night, the men were unwilling[20] and the Royalist army surrendered on the 25th, 150 officers and 1,444 men taken prisoner, and five guns captured. Clarendon's history terms it a 'mushrump army, which grew up and perished so soon'.[21] Herbert himself was not present, being with the King in Oxford.[22] On 27 March, Joyce Jeffreys recorded that 'This Monday morning the men of Little Mansel and all the company of Herefordshire went to Ross to meet the other army'.[23] Herbert's men had been given the choice of joining the Parliamentary forces or of release if they swore never again to take up arms against the Parliament. Almost all would have chosen the second option. Gloucester remained a stronghold of Parliament.

Lord Herbert was highly intelligent, a man of science and invention (some historians of technology credit him with the invention of a steam engine later in his career), but as a military commander he had no talent at all. After the failure at Gloucester, he took no further part in active campaigning, though he retained his military commission for some time and remained wholly committed to the King's cause, in which, by his reckoning, his father and he spent the colossal sum of £918,000.[24] Coningsby was left in a difficult position. In the wake of a surrender, foot soldiers often took the chance to desert, or to join the other side, and he would certainly not have got all his men back, and none of his supplies. With a much-reduced force, his power was greatly weakened. His most loyal supporter, Richard Wigmore, was one of numerous Herefordshire gentry taken prisoner at Highnam, and later transferred to Bristol. John Corbet noted that among those captured were some of the 'nine worthies, who in the first opening of the great breach affronted the Parliament with a scandalous remonstrance'.[25] Coningsby described his force now as 'rather like a Constables watch than a Garrison'.[26] Feeling that he lacked the military support to maintain his position, he despatched a letter to Lord Falkland, Secretary of State, requesting permission to resign as Governor,[27] but no answer came back.

There is some uncertainty about the Governorship after November 1642. From early in 1643, the Governor of Hereford is named in some accounts as Colonel Herbert Price of Brecon.[28] Webb suggests that Price had been appointed Deputy Governor by Coningsby, but Coningsby refers to his deputy as Colonel Talbot.[29] Price was certainly among the officers in Hereford at the time. Coningsby's own account of events shows he certainly considered himself to be the city's Governor, and all surviving evidence suggests the same. Instructions sent from the King's HQ in January about investing Brampton Bryan are addressed to Coningsby.

After the affair at Highnam, a distinguished figure reappeared in Hereford. Lord Scudamore had been in London. Atherton suggests that he was back at Holme Lacy before Christmas 1642, but there is no definite evidence of the Viscount's whereabouts or movements at this time. Webb merely says, '... certain it is that in any case this nobleman returned into Herefordshire'.[31] To Scudamore, who would have needed a pass from the Parliamentary authorities to travel across the country, it would have been a suitable time to visit his estates. Despite the military activity, renewed negotiations for a truce or peace were going on in Oxford, and there were hopes that peace might be restored. Hereford, like the rest of the country, could try to go about its normal business. William Price appears to have recovered from his breakdown and is recorded as paying his accounts to merchants in London.[32]

Following on an Ordinance of 1 April for sequestration of the estates of notorious delinquents,[33] Parliament ordered the sequestration of the estates of the Bishop of Hereford. In addition Sir Robert Harley, Sir Richard Hopton, Walter Kyrle, Edward Broughton and Henry Vaughan were named as commissioners for collection of the weekly assessment of £437 10s on Herefordshire, in the county; and Harley, Kyrle, and Vaughan, with Richard Hobson and John Flackett in the city.[34] As long as the Royalists held the city of Hereford, this authority can only have been exercised on a very limited scale, if at all. Some functionaries – Mayor Price of Hereford is the prime local example – seem to have collected taxes on behalf of both Royalist and Parliamentarian commanders. Among his accounts, his costs in 1642-43 for entertaining the Earl of Stamford, the Marquess of Hertford, and Lord Herbert are all recorded on the same sheet, totalling £26 1s 9d.[35] The changing commands at Hereford would have levied rates and taxes through men they could trust and rely on, but lower down the line of action, the high constables and petty constables could not be bypassed, and they were imposed upon by both sides.

For Waller, the walkover at Highnam was something to build on, and at the beginning of April he left Gloucester with an army of 2,000 men, four cannon and 500 cavalry. His aim was to carry the war into Monmouthshire while Herbert's command was still in disarray. On the 2nd they paused at Ross-on-Wye, then continued westwards to Monmouth, the Royalist garrisons of Ross, Goodrich, Monmouth and Chepstow evacuating and retreating before them, Waller's presence also encouraging local bands of Parliamentary sympathisers to muster and join him. But Herbert was regrouping his forces, and it soon became apparent to Waller that, with a small army, he was unlikely to accomplish anything useful in the region. Shadowed by watchers, he decided to withdraw. Already, however, the Royalists had moved into action. By 7 April, Prince Maurice, the younger of the King's two Anglo-German nephews who had come to join his cause, was on the way with a force to intercept Waller. Maurice's army marched from Tewkesbury through Ledbury and Much Marcle to Ross, and the Prince spread his force to the north of the Forest of Dean, on a line between the Wye and the Severn. (One of the officers in this army was Lord Grandison, but he had no links with Stretton Grandison in Herefordshire.[36])

Prince Maurice sent out a capable officer, Sir Richard Cave, with 80 horse and 100 dragoons, to discourage local Parliamentary bands and to send back intelligence reports on Waller's movements. But Waller crossed the Severn at Aust, well south of Maurice's position. Making for the security of Gloucester, his force passed by Little Dean, where Maurice was not expecting them, and there was some fighting, though the main groups did not engage. Waller got back to Gloucester with little to show for his outing, but almost immediately set out again, with Massey, for Tewkesbury, recapturing the town on 12 April. The Prince did not remain in the Forest of Dean, but withdrew up the Severn, back towards Tewkesbury.

At the northern end of Herefordshire, Sir Robert Harley was back in London together with Edward, and Lady Brilliana was again on her own. Fearing for her security, she appealed to Viscount Scudamore, expressing surprise that members of the Herefordshire gentry should break the obligations of courtesy and friendship: 'When I look upon myself I see nothing but love and respect arising out of my heart to them'.[37] But Scudamore had his own problems. His wife was at Llanthony Secunda and in January 1643 he wrote to Sir Robert Harley, also to James Kyrle and Henry Vaughan, complaining that Lady Scudamore was made 'a prisoner and hostage for the security of Sir Robert Harley's lady'.[38] Scudamore was concerned about depredations made on Llanthony, and threatened the Herefordshire Parliamentarians with retaliation by cutting down their trees. Harley made a placatory reply to this, as did Kyrle, who also pointed out that his own estate at Walford was being raided by the Royalists. Relations between men on opposing sides were breaking down under the strain of war, with the collection of taxes and enforced 'contributions', and simple plundering. Harley at this time was intensely busy in Parliament, as one of the sponsors of a bill for the abolition of episcopacy which was to be included in the latest peace proposals submitted to the King, on 1st February.

As one of the active leaders of the war party in Parliament, Sir Robert was particularly obnoxious to the King, and it was perhaps because of this rather than for any strategic reason, that in January 1643 Fitzwilliam Coningsby received the order from Oxford to make an assault on Brampton Bryan. Preparations for this collapsed with the defeat at Highnam, and Coningsby did not get beyond sending a token force, under Captain Henry Baskerville, on 4 March, demanding that Lady Brilliana should deliver up the castle and its contents to His Majesty's use.[39] Placing her case on the laws and liberties of the land, she refused. Lord Hertford, as commander of the King's forces, replied to her reply, guaranteeing the security of herself, her family and her possessions if she would yield the castle, but she clung on, although 'none that belongs to me dare go to Hereford, nor dare they go far from my house'.[40] In February, Fitzwilliam Coningsby ordered the Harley tenants to pay their rents to him,[41] and Lady Brilliana found it increasingly difficult to obtain payments.

With General Waller's withdrawal, full Royalist control was swiftly restored in the region. Sir Richard Cave busied himself in re-securing the position in Monmouthshire, reoccupying Monmouth on 11 April. Colonel Price's regiment, with two companies at

Abergavenny and one at Hereford, was put at his disposal, as was the 100-strong remnant of Coningsby troops at Hereford. It was at this time, as Webb records, that a troop of new recruits from Hereford, under Captain Wathen of Mere Court, Allensmoor, were on the way to join Cave at Monmouth, when they heard horsemen approaching at Llanlawdy Hill, near St Weonards. Panicking, they prepared to surrender, when the 'enemy' turned out to be a column of charcoal-carriers' horses.[42] This ludicrous incident is also an indication of normal economic activity going on even amid military operations. If this was the general mettle of the Hereford garrison, subsequent events are perhaps less surprising than they would otherwise be. Cave then installed himself and his troop at Hereford and wrote for instructions to Prince Maurice, who was on something of a high since he had inflicted a defeat on Sir William Waller at Ripple Field, by the Severn, three and a half miles north of Tewkesbury, on 13 April. It was a minor battle, with some 80 Roundheads killed[43] but, gained against a general hailed as 'William the Conqueror' by Parliamentary writers, it was good for Royalist morale. Waller retreated to Gloucester, and Maurice moved back on Evesham, leaving Massey still in control of the Severn between Tewkesbury and Gloucester. Maurice's response to Cave was a commission which might be interpreted as giving him overall military command in Herefordshire, Monmouthshire and Glamorgan, on a temporary basis, while forming an Association to combine the military resources of Hereford, Monmouth and south Wales. Herbert, still the King's Lieutenant-General, attended a conference of Commissioners at Abergavenny but was profoundly downbeat about the morale of his Welsh levies and his own ability to keep them under arms.

By mid-April it was clear to everyone that the Oxford negotiations between the King and the delegates sent by Parliament had failed, and that large-scale hostilities would resume.

9

The Second Surrender

On 18 April a muster of Royalist forces was arranged at Hereford, to be reviewed by Lord Herbert and his staff. It was a far less confident assembly than the one held in January, with a depleted garrison and a fever of expectation that Waller was about to turn his attention on Hereford. Herbert brought Welsh troops, but they were in no mood for fighting. Next day most of them deserted.[1] On the 22nd news came that Waller's army was on the move from Gloucester towards Ross and Hereford. Herbert's reaction was to promptly leave the city, though Colonel Price and Sir Walter Pye rode after him to implore him to stay.[2] With no immediate prospect of Maurice's desired Association becoming a reality, Cave also had no reason to remain.

In fact Waller had received an order from the Earl of Essex to leave Gloucester and bring his force to support the main Parliamentary field army in the siege of Reading. Cave was also summoned to Reading, to rejoin Prince Maurice, who was assembling an army to relieve the garrison there. Neither Cave nor Waller obeyed their instructions. Waller's excuse was that he had no funds, but there is little doubt that he had no wish to join up with Essex, and preferred to play his own hand. His lack of money for pay, food and equipment was perfectly genuine, however, and it was probably at Massey's suggestion that he decided to fill his coffers at Hereford's expense. Massey, having been one of Stamford's officers in the brief occupation of late 1642, was familiar with Hereford's resources and its defences, and one historian was to call Waller's attack 'a smash and grab raid'. Cave's order to move came on the same day that Waller's army reached Ross-on-Wye. With a hostile force approaching, the thought of losing this experienced officer and his men caused alarm among those in charge. Lord Herbert had apparently assigned command of the city's defence to Cave, though he had no authority to do this and was aware of Cave's order from the Prince. Cave was, in his own words, 'cast into a great straite'[4] for he had no official status beyond the command of his own troop. Knowing that an attack was imminent, could he honourably withdraw his men? At the urgent pleading of Colonel Price, Sir William Croft, Sir Walter Pye, and Lord Scudamore, he agreed to stay. Coningsby later flatly denied that he had joined in this plea.[5]

Accounts of the subsequent events come from two participants, Cave himself, and Fitzwilliam Coningsby. Both were concerned to justify their own actions. Cave's story hardly mentions Coningsby, and indeed refers to Colonel Herbert Price as the city's Governor, while Coningsby's is a bitter account of being excluded – despite his position as Governor – from participation in the defence. The defending force numbered about 7 or 800, most of whom had never been in action before. One of Coningsby's difficulties was that only around 80 of them were under his direct command.[6] Cave, trying to make the best arrangements he could for the defence of the city, found the inhabitants strangely disinclined to help. Despite the ringing of the Common Bell, a sign of emergency to which all able-bodied men were supposed to respond immediately, very few came forward to join in strengthening the weakest parts of the defences. He wanted breastworks built at each end of the Wye bridge, another to defend the entry to the castle from the mill on the east side, deep trenches cut inside the gates, some old houses on the wall to be pulled down, and Bye Street Gate to be blocked up with earth. Only this last was done. Nor was this the only evidence of the citizens' reluctance to help in mounting a defence. Frantic searching for gunpowder yielded only five barrels. Yet, as Cave later noted, more than 40 barrels of powder were found after Waller had taken the town.[7] Coningsby records that the citizens did not want to take orders from Cave. James Barroll, controller of the magazine, would not furnish powder without an order from Coningsby, but Cave told him: 'I have sufficient power to comand you and Collonell Conyngesby both'.[8]

Waller had around 2,500 men and two light cannons, known as sakers, capable of firing 6lb shots. Early on Monday 24 April they were at Fownhope, only five miles from Hereford. Cave had wanted to hold the Roundhead army off at Mordiford, where the River Lugg joins the Wye, and stationed a force of 50 horsemen under Lt Col Courtney to hold the Lugg bridge there, but Waller ignored the bridge and forded the Lugg, bypassing the outer defence and gaining an easy approach to the city. Courtney and his men retreated into the city at about 9 o'clock at night. Cave now planned a midnight assault on the attackers, mustering his infantry by the cathedral and summoning the cavalry to assemble in Broad Street. But horses were mysteriously lacking. Despite searches, only 20 or so could be found; nothing like enough to mount an attack. Instead he sent out two reconnaissance parties on horseback, who reported that enemy musketeers were already in position behind hedges close to the walls.

At first light on the 25th Cave looked out from the castle to see the whole attacking army within a mile of the city. The defending infantry had dispersed to their lodgings, against Cave's orders to stay in their positions, and it took time to reassemble and station them. Coningsby and his Sergeant-Major, Muntrich, made numerous suggestions for defence, all of which were ignored by Cave. With Herbert Aubrey of Clehonger, Coningsby assembled a party of 40 volunteer townsmen in the churchyard, but they received no orders.[9] Some Parliamentary musketeers were seen crossing the Wye in boats, and Cave organised a sally from the bridge, chasing the musketeers back; but their approach was a feint. While small groups of attackers also appeared at other gates and fired shots, the real thrust was mounted at Widemarsh Gate, where the cannons were used to shoot right through. An officer's head was blown off by a cannon-ball and after that no-one dared stand in the street. Coningsby got the ex-Mayor, David Bowen, to drag timber with his horses to reinforce the gate, but claims Cave told Bowen not to meddle.[10] Waller sent a trumpet forward to demand surrender, but Cave returned a defiant reply: 'He who held the town, held it by commission from the King; if Sir William Waller could produce a better commission from the King, it should be delivered to him; otherwise he who had it by authority from the King, would

Widemarsh Gate with a bastion on the city walls beyond

preserve it for the King.'[11] Cave was accompanied by James Booth, Coningsby's Provost Marshal, and Booth reported to Coningsby that Cave 'gave the trumpeter a farr different answer from what hath beene attested'.[12]

At such a stage, a resolute response from the defenders would be normal, though it might not reflect their real attitude or intention. The reality of events certainly belied Cave's defiance. With dissension among the commanders, the stock of powder seemingly almost used up, most people exhausted after a sleepless night, and evidently very little spirit of resistance, the leading men held a council. The choice they faced, according to Cave, was to break out and try to chase the attackers away, or to open negotiations. With Coningsby absent or dissenting, a parley was decided on. The defenders proposed to deliver up the town if they were not relieved within four days, on condition they should be allowed to march away with their weapons and flying colours, and that there should be no violence to the persons and goods of townsmen and churchmen. Waller replied with a demand for immediate surrender, with the only concession being quarter to officers and soldiers. After some posturing and high talk of dying where they stood, the defenders sent to inquire whether these were the best conditions available. While the parleys went on at Widemarsh Gate, the Royalist troops, Cave's included, were leaving on the other side, by the river gate and bridge. Coningsby claims that Cave ordered this personally, without any discussion with the others.[13]

A sharp little vignette is given by Coningsby, of a meeting – he calls it a council of war – held on Tuesday 25 April, in the dean's house. Bishop Coke, accompanied by Drs Kerry,

Benson and Rogers were present. 'The Lord Bishop said wee heare of a Parley, it concerneth us also to know on what tearmes, looking hard at the Lord Scudamore and my selfe. The said Lord Scudamore spake to the Lord Bishop, My Lord, I pray you speake to Sir Richard Cave, he is the Comander in Chief.'[14]

Cessation of defence was indicated when Captain Rowland Howorth waved his hat, and the captain of the watch waved Lord Scudamore's handkerchief, from the castle mound. On seeing this one of Waller's men turned his back on them and clapped his hand to his backside, in a gesture expressive of contempt.[15] A document of surrender was then completed and signed by Waller and Price (the latter ensuring that his colleagues also signed it). Its terms were moderate, giving quarter and 'civil usage' to officers and gentlemen; quarter to ordinary soldiers; guaranteeing freedom from plunder to the citizens, and 'their persons left at liberty for any thing past'; and freedom from violence and plunder to the bishop, dean and chapter.[16] That afternoon the gates were opened to the Parliamentarians. In less than two days, with the loss of only one man, and a few others injured, Waller captured not only the city but the leading Royalists of the county. The Royalist gentlemen were imprisoned in their lodgings, but Cave, accommodated in the home of an alderman, was helped by the son of the house to escape over the wall and through the moat, 'which was not over my bootes', and get away. Colonel Price also escaped.[17]

It was an inglorious episode. What was the reason for the inhabitants' apparent lethargy or reluctance to defend the city? Perhaps it was simple pragmatism. The more readily a town was handed over, the less likely the victors were to run wild. A surrender would incur fines and other payments, but if the town were taken by storm, it could expect rampaging soldiery, looting, and destruction of lives and property. Nor did the civil and military leaders show much backbone. Colonel Price appears to have been of no help at all; Courtney failed to halt the enemy or spot their detour. The Mayor, the same William Price as had dealt with Stamford, again appeared not unsympathetic to the Roundheads and received a certificate of thanks from General Waller for his help. Fitzwilliam Coningsby is not mentioned at any point in Cave's account as being among the leaders. Atherton considers that Scudamore had managed to exclude him,[18] but since his wish to relinquish the governorship was unlikely to have been a secret, Coningsby may have helped to exclude himself. He was also isolated by refusing to accept the defeatist view of the others. His claim to have opposed the surrender[19] is supported by the fact that, twelve hours or so after the conclusion of the surrender, Cave saw members of Coningsby's company at Eign Gate, who 'endeavoured to hinder and disturb it, yet soe unreasonably and so

Eign Gate in 1784

contrary to the judgment of the rest of the city, that the governor [i.e. Price] and mayor went to the gate, and, reproveing them, made them desist from soe doing'.[20]

Cave was concerned to show that he had merely behaved as an honourable officer responding to the request of the leading men in the city, and had not usurped proper authority. It would not have aided his case to show that the royally appointed Sheriff and Governor was not one of those who appealed to him to stay. Coningsby, writing his account some time after Cave had been exonerated, was concerned to vindicate his own behaviour against those who would 'leave the brand of cowardhood and villainie upon my house and posterity'.[21] It was not just a matter of reputation. Position and advancement depended absolutely on the King's good opinion. Coningsby had staked his fortune on Charles, and to be dropped would be to lose everything.

Whether Scudamore indeed was pursuing a personal campaign against Coningsby, or he and the senior military officers decided that the experienced Cave was better able to organise the defences than the amateur Coningsby, is a matter for personal choice. What emerges clearly from the event is that successful resistance to a siege needed a strong and determined commander whose personality and abilities carried along his subordinates and the citizens. This is what Massey was at Gloucester, and what Coningsby might have been at Hereford, but he failed to assert himself against the others. Instead, Hereford had Cave, whose aim quickly became to go through the accepted gestures required for an honourable surrender, and then get back to his royal patron. Once again Lord Herbert's hopelessness as a commander is revealed. He decamped from Hereford leaving a deeply unclear command structure. Coningsby, having received his appointment as Governor via Herbert, felt he had in the end to defer to someone who claimed to exercise an overriding commission from the same source: 'I might be Governor, by Commission, yet not Comander in Chief, being bound to obey the directions of my Superior Officer', and chose finally to 'swimm with that tide'.[22]

Officers turning up at general headquarters to report their own defeat are rarely given a warm welcome, and when Sir Richard Cave appeared at Oxford with the news of Hereford's loss, he was promptly put under arrest. It was a considerable shock to the King's advisers. For a second time Hereford had tamely yielded to a Parliamentary force. How could a city supposedly loyal, with a garrison, walls and a castle, be so easily captured? Incompetence, cowardice, above all, bribery, were immediately assumed. A court martial was convened, with Prince Rupert as President, and Cave settled down to preparing his defence. Colonel Herbert Price, perhaps fortunate not to be similarly accused,[23] testified that Cave had received the summons from Waller and had dictated the reply. Cave's account of events was accepted without dispute and he was given honourable acquittal. Coningsby, a prisoner of war, was not in a position to give evidence, but later he would hint at dirty work. Captain Gray of Stamford's Regiment told Richard Wigmore (at the time a prisoner in Gloucester) that the Parliamentarians 'were sure of the city before they went', but even Coningsby accepted that this could be mere boasting.[24] He and the other Royalist leaders remained prisoners of the Parliamentarians. Lord Scudamore, with his son James, was required by Waller to go up to London and submit himself to the will of Parliament. The others, including Fitzwilliam and Humphrey Coningsby, Sir Walter Pye and Sir William Croft, with Drs Godwin, Rogers, and Evans of the cathedral chapter and some of the senior officers, were taken under guard to Bristol and confined there.

The loss of Hereford was sharply felt by the Royalists. Satirists and propagandists of the Parliamentarian side, with metropolitan ignorance or insouciance, portrayed Hereford as a Welsh town[25] and jeered in Wenglish at the failure of Prince Maurice to stop Waller in the Forest of Dean, and at the loss of Hereford, ' ... and for te losse of her creat Cosin and Commander, M. Fitzwilliam Conningsby ...'. The fighting spirit of the Hereford men was derided, 'her Welch plood so hot of nature' that the Welshman could destroy his foes 'with te breath of her back parts as soone as pi fighting'.[26]

On his arrival in London, Viscount Scudamore wrote on 14 May to Sir Robert Pye, Sir Walter's Parliamentarian kinsman, hoping for assistance. Scudamore had hoped to avoid having to go to London:

> by the sixt article of the treaty, I conceaved both my person and goods to bee free for any thing past, as being a citizen, and having had the happiness long since to serve under that quality, as an unworthy member of the honourable house of commons. And, therefore, I desired that I might enjoy the justice and benefitt of that article, and if there were no other reason than my being in Hereford when the town was rendered up, I presumed it was in his [Waller's] power to excuse mee from the journey up to London. Hee made answere, that hee had already written up how hee had found mee in Hereford, and that I would shortly bee in London, and that hee had taken my word for it; and that besides hee had represented how much I had suffered, and how little I had acted ...[27]

It was of course in Scudamore's interest to stress how little he had 'acted' on the King's behalf. But he gives no explanation for his lack of support. He also found that his house in Petty France and its contents,

> are nearly sequestered by a general ordinance of Parliament' and hopes this may be lifted, and further, 'that when a thorough search shall have been made of mee, it will bee found, that neither bitternes of mind against persons, nor greedy desire of any worldly thing, have moved mee to or fro in the carriage of my self amid these dismall distractions and divine judgements upon my deare mother England ... I have desired and laboured to keep a good conscience, according to the best of my understanding; and though it should proove to bee an erring conscience, yet it had been sinne in me to goe against it, being mine ...

This dignified plea was followed by a second letter expressing the hope that he might buy his freedom by payment of a fine, since

> I perswade myself every unpartiall eye, comparing both together, will thinke my sufferings already have been so much above the proportion of my desert, that there will remaine very little in reason to be added for this action of Hereford, wherein I was but a volunteer, and had no command, and beeing heer casually and a sworn citizen and steward of the town, I knew not in honour how to run away from it, just when a force appeared before it.[28]

But the Parliamentary leaders showed little sympathy, and the goods in his house were seized and sold as the property of a delinquent. Scudamore's hope to buy his freedom was dashed when Sir Robert Harley, one of the members appointed to deal with the matter, and his colleagues, failed to get the House of Commons to agree to the amount, and Scudamore was to spend almost three years imprisoned in London.

General Waller's men occupied Hereford without plundering or rapine, though it was reported that the citizens had paid £3,000 to avoid looting. Joyce Jeffreys recorded that she paid fourpence to 'Richard Winnye Smith for mending locks and keys at Heriford, which the plunderers broke', but her houses were outside the city, at Widemarsh Gate[29].

Parliamentary troops very soon also appeared in Leominster: 'Sir William Waller, after taking of Hereford, went to Leominster, a very malignant town, but a place of great consequence, and very rich; and having taken that town, and spent some time disarming the malignants, and placed a proper garrison there, he departed'.[30] It is not likely that the troopers, on free quarter, did much to win the hearts and minds of the townspeople, and during the occupancy of this garrison most of the stained glass in Leominster Priory Church was destroyed.[31]

Waller, though humane and courteous (his letter to his erstwhile military colleague, the Royalist general Sir Ralph Hopton, deploring 'a war without an enemie' is well-known[32]), was brisk and methodical in collecting levies and fines. Without delay he issued warrants for the collection of moneys due under the Parliament's various acts and ordinances but which the county and city had never collected. Once again the burden of civil war weighed on those named on the rent rolls: taxes and contributions paid to one side had to be paid all over again to the other side. A meeting of Commissioners set a hefty levy for Herefordshire of £7,146, and Isaac Seward wrote to Sir Robert Harley hoping that an abatement might be possible.[33] For those seen as 'delinquent', further fines were inflicted: a twentieth part of their effects had to be handed over. The high constables in each hundred were ordered to supervise collections and bring the money to John Cooke, gentleman in Hereford,[34] appointed as Waller's receiver. Five trunks full of gold and silver plate were shipped off to London, and John Webb commented that Sir Robert Harley, as Master of the Mint (he was reappointed to his old post in 1643), might have been pleased that in having it turned into coin 'he was converting the extorted aid of the malignants of his own county, who had shut up his lady and children so long in his Castle'.[35] But Hereford Cathedral was again spared the indignities and depredations suffered at Worcester, Lichfield, Chichester and some other cathedrals.

To a local Parliamentarian looking back, the six weeks after Waller's occupation were like 'a jubilee of rest' except for two days, 19 and 20 May; the records of events on these days are confused. With the garrison troops temporarily gone from the city, 'we had a mutiny raised by collegiates [vicars] and some townsmen' apparently in collusion with Captain Henry Baskerville who had entered the city with a troop of Royalist soldiers. There was fighting in the streets, 'the guards were doubled by townsmen armed and Baskervile's party set upon in the streets, many beaten down, wounded, some after died of their wounds, both by the way and in the town, partly some for want of well dressing'. But the writer suspected Baskerville's motive, as 'it was to be believed he came on purpose to yield up his troop' and two months later he did defect to Parliament.[36]

While Lady Harley now enjoyed her freedom, Lady Scudamore at Holme Lacy had to protect the house and estate as best she could against the attentions of Roundhead soldiers and Parliamentary commissioners. As well as Holme Lacy there was Llanthony Secunda, right by Gloucester and all too accessible. The Viscount claimed that he had lost the furniture of both mansions, that buildings had been wasted and trees felled. His wife complained to General Waller, who replied on 4 June to say that he had made inquiries, found that some trees had been felled and had ordered that no more should be touched; and had also ordered that the sequestration on the Holme Lacy rents should not be executed, 'so that, Madam, they are still at your command'.[37] He went on to add that, 'If there be anything else wherein I may advance your ladyshipp's service, I humbly beg the favour to be commanded, that I may have opportunity to give some demonstration with what passion I am, Madam, Your devoted humble servant'. Even in an age of florid compliment, it was a remarkable letter and gesture to the wife of one who was on the enemy side, even if he had not been actively engaged against the Parliament. Waller, incidentally, was a kinsman of Sir Robert Harley,[38] and Edward Harley and his brother Robert would both serve under his command.

Once he had completed his collections, Waller did not remain in Hereford. At one point it seemed he would head north towards Shrewsbury, and an order to the county clergy requiring them to record their loyalty to Parliament and their support for the Parliamentary army, dated 6 May 1643, refers to him as 'General of the army drawn to Salop'. Ludlow and Shrewsbury were both in the King's hands, and Waller did not head north. Without attempting to install a garrison in Hereford, he marched his men back to Gloucester, leaving the city on 20 May. At the end of the month he made an attempt to capture Worcester, but its Governor Colonel Sandys pointedly told him 'he was not now at Hereford',[39] and he withdrew when Royalist reinforcements were said to be on the way. Waller marched off to the south-west. He would not return to Herefordshire.

10

Vavasour Takes Command

Parliament's failure to consolidate its position at Hereford seems surprising, but Waller had no orders regarding the city and no troops to spare for a garrison in what remained a largely hostile area. He had made an effort to secure the county by requiring its men of substance to subscribe to an oath: 'I do swear in the presence of Almighty God that I will defend with my life and estate the King's Majesty's person and both Houses of Parliament now sitting at Westminster, and to the utmost of my power maintain and assist the army raised by the authority of both Houses',[1] but it is unlikely that any committed Royalist took it, or would have considered it binding if taken under compulsion. Hereford could

resume its former ways and business and King's men moved speedily back into control. But with the county Sheriff among the prisoners of the Parliamentarians, provision had to be made for replacements, and King Charles appointed Henry Lingen as High Sheriff of Herefordshire. Lingen had been Sheriff in 1638-39 and was a firm adherent of the royal cause. He had been captured on the surrender of Hereford, but had paid Waller a ransom of £500 for himself and his troop.[2] He had 'a fair house' at Sutton Frene,[3] and was a brother-in-law of Sir Walter Pye. A new Governor was also appointed, Sir William Vavasour, an experienced soldier with the rank of Colonel. Not a 'Native Gentleman', his family roots were in Yorkshire and Wales. Vavasour had been taken prisoner at Edgehill but had later escaped (according to his own side) or broken parole (according to the Parliament's propagandists). His courage was not in doubt, and events would show him as a man of decent instincts but poor judgment, accompanied, as is often the

Sir Henry Lingen

case, by complacent obstinacy. New members were also appointed to the Commission of the Peace: Fulke Walwyn of Hellens; Robert Whitney (eldest son of the former Sheriff); James Rodd, a former Mayor; and his nephew Richard Rodd, a high constable of the Wigmore hundred; and John Skipp of Ledbury, all safe men for the Royalist side.[4]

The Hereford Royalists captured by Waller had an anxious time of it as prisoners transferred to Bristol. Two Royalist burghers of that city, Robert Yeoman and George Bourchier, had been condemned to hang for their part in a plot (which failed) to open the city to Prince Rupert on 7 March. The Governor of Bristol, Nathaniel Fiennes, received a message from the King's General, the Earl of Forth, that if these two men were executed, tit-for-tat executions could be expected among Parliamentarians from Cirencester held prisoner. Basing his case on the fact that Yeoman and Bourchier were not open enemies but 'secret spies', Fiennes informed Forth on 18 May that if the Cirencester men were executed, then Pye, Croft and Coningsby, together with other Royalists held in his custody 'must expect no Favour or Mercy'.[5] Tense days followed. Yeoman and Bourchier were hanged, but the King refused to allow retaliation against his own prisoners, and the Herefordians, though held in close confinement, were spared. Before the end of June they were freed, whether by exchange or ransom is unclear. Fitzwilliam Coningsby appears to have gone to join the King's entourage, while Brilliana Harley noted that Sir Walter Pye, Wallop Brabazon, William Smallman, Richard Wigmore and Henry Lingen were back in Herefordshire in a letter of 30 June.[6] She expected 'new onsets' as a result.

Lingen and Vavasour were certainly expected to show more zeal and energy than their predecessors, and they actively set about rebuilding a Royalist force. Lingen had a royal warrant to raise a regiment of 1,000 men. The need appeared urgent, with Colonel Massey, securely holding Gloucester for the Parliament, as a permanent threat on the horizon. But in the summer of 1643 they were favoured with a period of comparative tranquillity, while military action moved further away. Sir William Vavasour organised the townsmen for defence, with the leading men in each ward named as captains. With Lord Herbert as an honorific Lieutenant-General, Vavasour was appointed Colonel-General for Herefordshire, Monmouthshire, Brecon and Radnor. In Herefordshire as in other counties the former commissioners of array were reorganised as a committee 'for the guarding the county'. Providing men, and the money to pay for them, remained the committee's task. By July, Hereford was on a full military footing under the Royalists, and Vavasour had assembled and equipped 1,200 foot and over 200 horse. The military tax for Herefordshire was assessed at £1,200 a month, of which some was to support Vavasour's field army and some to pay for local garrisons like the one at Goodrich Castle. But payment was slow and in Vavasour's first month he received little more than £100.[7] Loans had to be demanded from some Hereford citizens, as well as further subsidies from Herbert. At this time, a reminder of the way in which war involved family networks across the land came when one of the Tomkins family of Monnington, Nathaniel Tomkins, Clerk to the Queen's Counsel in London, was hanged in London on 5 July. He was involved in a Royalist plot started by the poet-politician Edmund Waller (a relation of the Parliamentarian Sir William), which hoped to end the war by mobilising pro-Royalist sentiments in the City of London. The plot was a complete failure, but the summer was a season of success and promise for the cause of Charles I, reaching a high point when Prince Rupert eventually captured Bristol on 24 July.

Dr Jacqueline Eales suggests that 'The restraint shown by the local Royalist gentry in postponing any direct attack on Brampton for so long stemmed in part from their personal regard for Lady Brilliana, although military considerations also played their part.'[8] This may be the case, though also Brampton simply did not represent a threat. But in July, Vavasour decided to have a go at extirpating this aggravating outpost of Parliamentary support in Herefordshire. The existence of a Roundhead stronghold only a few miles away seems to have been seen by Vavasour as a reflection on his own capacity, especially as it was not strongly garrisoned. He could not feel he had the respect and fear of the community if Lady Harley was there, metaphorically thumbing her nose at him. On 26 July 1643 he said as much in a letter to Prince Rupert: 'I found that I had benn lost in the opinione of thease Countyes, neither should I gett half the contributione promisd mee, unles I made an attempt on Bromton Castle.'[9] Brilliana Harley had lived under the threat of attack for a year, with only brief periods of respite when the Parliamentary forces occupied Hereford, and even these posed a problem, as she noted that any resentment caused by the Roundheads' conduct was inevitably focused on her as soon as they were gone.[10] But when Vavasour himself went to parley with her before the siege commenced, she refused his request for a surrender.

Vavasour laid siege to the castle on 26 July. A blind man, John Pountney, was killed in the village when he replied to a challenge by saying he was 'for King and Parliament'.[11] In a further show of force, Lord Molyneux, a Lancashire peer who had been gathering recruits for the royal army, appeared in Brampton Bryan on the 27th. Observing that he had 'noe arms or very few', Lady Harley promptly sent a message to Massey in Gloucester asking for two troops of horse to chase him away.[12] But Molyneux moved on before anything could happen. Waging a war of nerves as well as of weapons, Vavasour wrote to Lady Harley from Wigmore Grange on 28 July:

> I shall deal fairly with you, madam. I am your servant, and to one so noble and so virtuous am desirous to keep off all insolences that the liberty of the soldiers, provoked to it by your obstinacies, may throw you upon; yet if you remain still wilful, what you may suffer is brought upon you by yourself, I having by this timely notice discharged those respects due to your sex and honour.[13]

Vavasour's presence, and that of most of his men, was soon required outside his own area of command. Encouraged by the recapture of Bristol, the King had resolved on a new and major effort to take Gloucester, to safeguard his rear before advancing on London. Many commentators then and since have expressed surprise that he should not have marched directly on the capital, while the war seemed to be going very much his way. But some 5,000 of his force were Welshmen, who were extremely reluctant go beyond the Severn, and some of his officers believed that Massey was willing to surrender,[14] which, if true, would have made the siege a brief formality. Vavasour was summoned to the greater siege, and was given command of the Welsh levies also, Herbert having withdrawn, 'aware of his unpopularity as a Roman Catholic'.[15] To help compensate for the loss of garrison troops, some hasty defensive work was put in hand at Hereford, with 334 man-days at 8d a day put in by 74 men.[16] From around 6 August Henry Lingen was left with 700 men to maintain the siege at Brampton Bryan, while Vavasour's own force, 300 horse under Sir Walter Pye and 1,000 foot, was placed on the north side of Gloucester, at Maisemore and The Vineyard. Among those who joined in the march on Gloucester were James Barroll, now a ward captain heading 50 men including John Rogers as his lieutenant, Philip Aston the town crier, and John Seaborne.[17]

For six weeks a large royal army, with King Charles at its head, encircled Gloucester, while Edward Massey maintained a stubborn defence. In London, the Parliamentary leaders considered urgently what action to take, and eventually, with six London trained-band regiments and authority to impress another 2,000 conscripts, the Earl of Essex set off with a relief army which reached the neighbourhood of Gloucester on 6 September. The King immediately raised the siege, but placed his force to block Essex's way back to London. For almost two weeks the two armies manoeuvred, Essex trying to make his way home, the Royalists trying to force a battle. On the 19th they finally succeeded in this intention. The encounter, the first Battle of Newbury, was indecisive, but ended with a Royalist withdrawal overnight. Casualties were heavy, and Vavasour's regiments of Hereford and Welsh infantry suffered with the rest.

The gatehouse of Brampton Bryan Castle showing the depth of its defences

The events at Gloucester and Newbury overshadowed those at Brampton Bryan, except for the individuals engaged in the siege. Henry Lingen kept up the pressure, but Lady Brilliana no more thought of surrender than did Colonel Massey. Brampton Bryan Castle was a quadrangular structure set on a low motte and surrounded by a moat. The southern curtain wall had a gatehouse with two massively-built round towers and a drawbridge, and there was an outer gatehouse with a portcullis. It was a distinctly old-fashioned building in 1643, but for that very reason a tough proposition for besiegers. Lingen had 'five great guns', some of which were mounted on the church tower, very close by,[18] but one expert notes that, 'Only the cannon royal, firing a 66lb shot, was in any way effective against medieval stonework, and this weighed three tons and needed a team of seventy draught horses'.[19] After three weeks the besiegers had put up breastworks in the gardens, in order to protect their own positions. They were also building siege engines, or 'hoggs', apparently as protective cover for digging tunnels beneath the house, but the defenders managed to set these on fire.[20] The strong outer gatehouse helped to guard the inner courtyard, while two drakes, or light cannon, mounted on the walls, helped make things difficult for the besiegers, and the castle had long been stocked up with muskets, gunpowder, match and bullets. Within its walls were 50 musketeers and 20 or so other men capable of bearing arms, as well as women and children. Brilliana's three youngest children, Thomas, Dorothy and Margaret, were with her, as well as some family friends including Samuel More, steward of the estate, whose father was MP for Bishop's Castle, and the physician Nathaniel Wright. Priamus Davies, perhaps the same who resisted the Royalist summons at the start of the war, was a Parliamentary army captain who organised the defence and appears on occasion to have slipped out and in again with secret messages, though other letters were allowed out by safe conduct.

Lady Brilliana Harley
(by kind permission of Edward Harley Esq.)

Throughout the siege, Lady Harley kept up a stream of letters, to Vavasour, to local Royalist gentlemen, even to the King. Charles sent Sir John Scudamore of Ballingham to offer her a full pardon on surrender. Scudamore was admitted to the castle on 24 August by a ladder and rope to speak to its chief defender.[21] The Secretary of State, Lord Falkland, also offered her full pardon and safe conduct for all the inmates to leave. While this was going on, for two weeks there was a cessation of hostilities, but Lady Harley was playing for time, hoping that Parliament's commander in Cheshire, General Brereton, would send a force to relieve her.[22] Her delaying tactics proved to be effective, but due to an altogether different reason. With the arrival of Essex's army at Gloucester, Lingen was ordered to abandon the siege of Brampton Bryan. On 9 September, after six weeks, he fell back on Hereford in case of a Parliamentary attack there, his position helped by a load of munitions sent from the King. But there was no attack on Hereford. By early October Vavasour had returned to his command in the southern Marches, with a depleted force, and still having to focus his attention on Gloucester.

Vavasour was given the appointment of Colonel-General of Gloucestershire, with authority also over Herefordshire, still under the titular command of Lord Herbert, but his headquarters were in Hereford. He set about re-establishing the county's commissioners of array, and called in all due and overdue payments. Methodical lists of payers in each city ward were drawn up.[23] His commissioners were Lingen, Croft, Pye, Rudhall and Tomkins, and they in turn leaned heavily on the high constables and their collectors. One who had been a commissioner at the start, Wallop Brabazon of Eaton Gamage, lost heart for the struggle and removed with his family to Worcester.

Sir Robert Harley now finally advised his wife to leave Brampton, and she began to make arrangements to do so while providing for the castle's security, encouraging her son Edward to come and hold it, 'helping to keep what I hope shall be his'.[24] She had no intention of letting the Royalists have it. As soon as Lingen had marched off she had set about reducing his earthworks, destroying his 'hoggs', and restocking the castle with arms and ammunition. At first she hoped for assistance from the locals and tenants, and when they 'barbarously refused', she used her forces to compel them, 'whereby our necessities were in a short time supplied', as Priamus Davies noted.[25] The unfortunate tenants and countryfolk were caught between a rock and a hard place. Any help given to Lady Harley, they knew, would be recorded and punished by the Cavaliers in command at Hereford. And a wide area round the village and castle had been left devastated by the siege. 'This noble lady, who commanded in chief, I may truly say with such a masculine bravery, both for religion, resolution, wisdom, and warlike policy, that her equal I never yet saw' also went on the offensive, sending a troop of some 40 horse to Knighton in Radnorshire, about four miles away, where a party of Lingen's troops were quartered. The surprise attack resulted in the capture of prisoners, arms and horses, with no loss to the raiders.[26] On 9 October she again felt threatened: '… there are some souldiers come to Lemster and three troopes of hors to Heariford with Sr William Vauasor, and they say they meane to visit Brompton againe'.[27] But on 31 October 1643 Brilliana Harley died, still in possession of her home at Brampton Bryan. Her final illness, described as 'an apoplexy, with a defluxion of the lungs',[28] came on suddenly, after what she thought was merely a bad cold, and her death was unexpected. Samuel More recorded that 'this Sabbath day the sweet lady's soul went to keep Sabbath in Heaven, where she can never be besieged'.[28] As the church was badly damaged, her body was wrapped in lead and 'interred within the castle' for the time being. (Although the Royalists promised not to dishonour it after the castle's eventual surrender, 'we are informed that it was taken up under pretence to search for jewels, but the jewels being gone, the cabinet was raked up again in close cinders'.[29]) Dr Nathaniel Wright was made guardian of the estate and the young Harley children by Sir Robert, and appointed Governor of the castle by Parliament.[30] Assisted by Samuel

More, he moved quickly to follow Lady Brilliana's example, raising a troop of horse and commandeering enough basic food supplies to last a year, in the correct anticipation that the siege would sooner or later be resumed.

That autumn, Parliament for the first time in England's history proclaimed an excise duty (though the King had levied 'impositions' on specific items). Proposed in March by John Pym as a tax on 'superfluous commodities', it had been rejected, but the driving need for a steady supply of funds saw it accepted in September and October 1643 on a range of goods, including tobacco, wine, ale, cider and perry (the two latter among the prime products of Herefordshire and the surrounding counties) but also on imported groceries, drugs, mercery, saltery, glassware, and soap, draperies and paper whether home-produced or imported. A hogshead of cider or perry was chargeable at two shillings from the maker, and at a further shilling when bought retail, while the tax on a tun of wine was £5. An excise office was to be set up in each town.[31] The King at first denounced the excise, but when he called his own Parliament in Oxford at the start of 1644, it followed the Long Parliament's example. Dr Sherburn, the strongly Royalist Rector of Pembridge, would later be accused of 'trying to settle the excise at Hereford for the King, but was opposed by the women there'.[32] Both sides claimed it was an emergency measure for the duration of the war, but the excise became a fixture of the fiscal system. In general, the Parliament's greater efficiency in finding ways to raise and collect cash was one of the main reasons underlying its ultimate victory.

Vavasour, keen to exercise his commission in Gloucester, led a force of around 700 horse and foot from Hereford to take possession of Tewkesbury, an unwalled town which had seen far more than its fair share of passing armies of both sides. Massey sent a defending party up the Severn by boat, but Vavasour's main problem was his own men. Mostly Welsh, pressed into service, seeing no sign of payment, and unhappy about being outside their own territory, they deserted *en masse*. Left with only his officers, Vavasour returned to Hereford. But Gloucester was still under blockade. Among other Royalist troops deployed in the hope of blocking the supply-ways were 600 horse around Pershore and Edgbury under Sir Walter Pye, Fitzwilliam Coningsby, Herbert Price and a Mr Finch. Lord Herbert's forces were increased in early November 1643 by the arrival of a regiment of foot, 100 horse and eight field-guns, returned from Ireland. Warfare, more widespread and savage than in England, had been going on there between rebel Catholics and pro-English loyalists (some for the King, some for Parliament) until the controversial 'Cessation' of hostilities engineered by Charles in October 1643. The King's intention was to bolster his English forces with men from Ireland, whether Catholics or not. The Irish reinforcements based themselves at Newent under Colonel Nicholas Mynne. Mynne, an able officer, did not have a high opinion of Vavasour, and seems to have offered scant co-operation. He was quoted as saying he could take Gloucester with 200 men. Complaints were made by Vavasour to Prince Rupert of Mynne's disobedience 'of three several orders' in April 1644.[33]

Gloucester was again in a dangerous situation, cut off and running short of supplies. In command of the Parliamentary cavalry there was Major Robert Backhouse (sometimes recorded as Bacchus). An approach was made to him on 19 November 1643 by an old friend, a Catholic gentleman of Worcestershire, Edward Stanford, now a lieutenant-colonel in the royal army, offering £5,000 if he would open up the city to the Royalists. Vavasour was in on this proposal, and may have been its author. But intrigues of this kind were not his *forte*. Backhouse reported the overture to Massey, and they evolved a plan to string the Royalists along. At several secret meetings, Backhouse and Vavasour discussed ways and means of letting in the Royalists, as well as the terms and conditions of the deal. Soon the high command were informed and lent their support. Lord Digby wrote from Oxford to confirm the bribe, and Prince Rupert came down to Newent to receive details and encourage the scheme personally. Vavasour's confidence carried everyone along, at first. To encourage Vavasour, the Parliamentary forces made no resistance to a second attempt of his to occupy Tewkesbury in early January 1644. While the negotiations were spun out by Backhouse, there was a virtual cessation of hostilities, which made life much easier for Massey and his men. Finally, at a meeting at Corse Lawn on 8 January it was agreed that Backhouse would open the west gate of Gloucester to the Royalists on 15 February. Sir William was so confident of his scheme that he agreed to make various concessions to show his good will, including the disbanding of the garrison at Berkeley Castle and the removal of most of the Tewkesbury garrison. The Governor of Berkeley refused to move, and some of those in the know had begun to think Vavasour was being hoodwinked, but he himself never seems to have doubted. Sir Walter Pye suspected him of treachery to the cause and went to Oxford to lodge an accusation. On 14 February Vavasour duly marched his troops to Gloucester. Massey now told his officers about the plot, and had three guns placed in the west gate, also four 'stout men' in a boat under the wooden bridge over the Severn at Over, ready to pull it down as soon as they heard the cannon fire. Vavasour and his men would have been trapped between the river and the city, but seeing unexpected activity around the gate, they became suspicious and withdrew. This foiled the culmination of Backhouse's and Massey's plot, but even then Vavasour seems to have still believed in their good faith.[34]

11

Sieges and Skirmishes

By January 1644 the country had been at war with itself for a year and a half, and there was no prospect of a settlement in sight. Through the coming year Royalist Hereford and Parliamentarian Gloucester would confront each other and contest for the ground in between, in a series of small-scale but deadly battles.

To show the nation who should summon a Parliament, and to justify his claim to be a monarch who desired to co-operate with its members, King Charles called a Parliament at Oxford, which met on 25 January 1644. Members of both Houses who had been expelled from Westminster, and all others well-affected to the King, were summoned. The initiative was denounced at Westminster as a 'junto' and the only members to assemble were committed Royalists, including the Hereford city and county members Humphrey Coningsby, James Scudamore, Richard Seaborne, and Thomas Tomkins. Lord Ranelagh and Walter Kyrle appear among the names of those listed as in service, or absent by leave or illness. Sir Sampson Eure of Leominster was elected Speaker of this Oxford Parliament.[1]

Also in January 1644 a new element entered the war when a large Scottish army crossed the Border, in fulfilment of the Solemn League and Covenant which had been ratified between the Scottish and English Parliaments in November 1643. More than a military treaty, it was intended to be signed by all well-affected men, and Sir Robert Harley had been one of the first English signatories, on 25 September 1643.[2] The Scots were still far in the north and anyone in Hereford would have laughed at the idea that this force would eventually lay siege to their city.

Occasional signs of the tensions and discords within Hereford itself surface in surviving documents or records. In January 1644, Richard Philpotts faced charges in the Mayor's court of Quarter Sessions following an incident when, 'foaming at the mouth', he had insulted John Clarke, one of the city magistrates. Philpotts (who would be Mayor under the Parliamentary regime in 1647) defended himself with vigour, accusing Clarke of leading the citizens of Hereford 'in blindness'.[3] The Royalist Clarke family had often supplied town clerks to the city.

At this time the three main Parliamentary armies were being increased to 34,000 men, and the Royalists had to strive to match this. Prince Rupert had been named in January as 'Captain-General under His Majesty of all the forces now raised or being raised within Salop and the neighbouring counties and all North Wales', and from 5 February was appointed as President of North Wales. Herefordshire was part of his command area, but his personal campaigning was mostly in Cheshire and the Midlands. As part of the drive for a build-up of Royalist forces, the Coningsbys were recruiting in Herefordshire during February. But the only effective way to gather troops in sufficiently large numbers was by pressing them from an increasingly reluctant population, and the Associated Counties were required in April to find 2,500 men, of whom 600 were to come from Herefordshire.[4] Each district was also re-assessed for its cash contribution to the maintenance of the army. An indication of the efficiency with which this was managed comes in a letter from Henry Lingen to the petty constables of Sellack. On quarterly rent days they had to ensure that tenants of sequestrated properties paid their rent to the King's Commissioners, 'at Mr Norman's house in Hereford'.[5]

Brampton Bryan's defenders had a period of relative peace while Vavasour's attention was focused on Gloucester and the Severn valley, and they took the opportunity to strengthen and install a garrison in a smaller castle at Hopton, across the Shropshire border, among hills three miles to the north. Built around 1300,[6] it was owned though not occupied by Robert Wallop, a staunch Parliamentarian who had inherited Hopton through his mother Elizabeth Corbet, and so was a cousin of Sir Robert Harley. His home was in Hampshire.[7] But Ludlow, only five miles to the east, had acquired a new Royalist Governor late in 1643, Sir Michael Woodhouse. His military experience had been largely gained in Ireland, and his garrison troops were largely Irish or veterans of the Irish war. While the 'Irish' troops included Protestant Englishmen, many others were loyalist Catholics, and Parliamentary propaganda branded them all indiscriminately as barbarians. At the order of Prince Rupert, Woodhouse went into action against the Parliamentary outposts so impudently close to Ludlow Castle.

Samuel More, with Major Phillips from the Brampton Bryan garrison, was occupying Hopton Castle with 31 men. A solid stone building, of three storeys, with square corner-turrets, it was set Norman-style on a low mound above a moat, with an outer wall. On 25 February Woodhouse's men tried to storm the place, but could not break through. On 2 March they returned. Woodhouse offered security to the occupiers if the castle were surrendered to Prince Rupert. More returned the conventional reply, that he held it for King and Parliament, with the owner's consent, and could not surrender it without Parliament's authority. The resultant attack, including an attempt to dig a mine beneath the graffe or moat, was beaten off, and Woodhouse reported to Rupert that he had lost one captain and two soldiers, with 16 men injured; and did not believe that he could take the place without cannon.[8] A few days later he reappeared with around 500 men and at least one field gun. More refused two further summonses to yield. The second of these warned him that there would be no quarter if he refused again. Later, More claimed to have misunderstood the significance of this threat, which is unlikely, since the language and protocols of siege warfare were well-known. Indeed, he followed the same code of behaviour when at Hopton he refused to accept a message from Woodhouse that 'came without drum or trumpet'.[9] Around 13 March, hearing diggers at work beneath the castle, and expecting to be blown up imminently, he finally offered surrender, if he and his men were allowed to march away with their arms and ammunition. This was refused and More then asked only for quarter, receiving the answer that 'they should be referred to Colonel Woodhouse's mercy'.[10] Woodhouse himself was on the scene. On surrendering, More and Phillips were taken

Hopton Castle

prisoner but their surviving men were bound together and 'stripped naked as ever they were born, it being about the beginning of March very cold and many of them sore wounded'. After about an hour the order was given that they should be left to the mercy of the common soldiers, 'who presently fell on them, wounding them grievously, and drove them into a cellar unfinished, wherein was stinking water, the house being on fire over them, when they were every man … presently massacred'.[11] The parish record has this terse entry for 13 March 1644: *Occisi fuere 29 in castro Hoptoniensis* (29 were slaughtered in Hopton Castle).[12] Although the strict rules of war permitted the killing of troops who had refused to surrender after a 'No quarter' warning, the slaughter of the Hopton Castle men was regarded as an atrocity by the Parliamentary side. The Royalists did not try to justify it.

The notion of personal and military honour loomed large in the 17th century. An officer bore his honour as if it were as real as his cloak. One who surrendered too readily lost his honour; as did one who acted with excessive brutality. What constituted 'honourable' and 'reasonable' conduct was much discussed; it was a touchy matter and the cause of many duels. Racial-religious hostility between English and Irish distorted these conventions during the Civil War. Parliamentary propagandists found it easy to magnify the threat of wild Catholic Irishmen (and their women camp-followers) rampaging across the English countryside. Captured Irish soldiers were liable to be executed on the spot, and late in 1644 Parliament formalised the practice in a grim ordinance forbidding the granting of quarter to Irish soldiers captured in England. Woodhouse's men were Irish, but the responsibility for permitting the massacre was his. It is possible, though, that he was following orders from Prince Rupert, whose military education, in the latter stages of the Thirty Years' War, had been in a more ruthless mode than England was accustomed to. It may be noted that the two officers were spared, and treated with comparative civility (though one writer states that Phillips was taken to Broncroft Castle, a few miles away, and stabbed to death).[13] Gentlemen were not to be left to the bloodlust of victorious troopers. After this event, 'Hopton Quarter' was said to have been a retort from Parliamentary troops to Royalists who asked for quarter before surrendering.[14] But events such as Hopton were rare enough for them to stand out as extremes. Against the scale of horrors inflicted on far greater numbers, both soldiers and civilians, in the war still afflicting much of Germany until 1648, the English Civil War is regarded by comparative historians as a 'mild' conflict.[15]

With the Hereford garrison still heavily involved in operations east and south of the city, where Massey and Mynne were struggling for control of territory on the Hereford-Gloucestershire border, Woodhouse kept up the pressure from Ludlow on Brampton Bryan. At the beginning of April 1644, he began siege works: '... the first day they made 87 shots against us with a twenty and twenty four pound ball; these made our walls begin to reel, which we lined within with earth'.[16] To clear the approach, Woodhouse destroyed the church beside the castle, with any other buildings left standing from the previous siege. But the attackers found it difficult to make progress against determined defence. On the 6th Woodhouse reported to Prince Rupert that the defenders had made a sally, killing some of his pioneers. Six days later they foiled a midnight attempt to fire the place: 'I attempted to fyer the breach it being filled with timber, and did it, but the roges put it oute againe with much adoe'. The besiegers were also digging beneath the moat.[17] Rupert sent reinforcements, and Wright finally began to discuss surrender terms. After Hopton, he was understandably apprehensive about Woodhouse's intentions. It was believed that Woodhouse had reneged on a promise of clemency at Hopton, and only when the Royalists prevailed on Samuel More to write a letter from prison confirming that Woodhouse had not broken his word did Wright agree terms of honourable surrender with Woodhouse, Vavasour and Croft, on 17 April. After these had been concluded, orders came from Rupert on how the garrison should be dealt with once the castle had been taken. His command, the defenders later learned, was 'to put us all to the sword, especially Doctor Wright our Lieutenant-Colonel'.[18] Woodhouse convened a council of war to discuss what should be done, and at Vavasour's insistence, the Prince's orders were set aside. Around 70 people were in the castle, including the younger Harley children and three Puritan ministers. The prisoners were taken to Ludlow first, where the townsfolk 'baited us like bears, and demanded where our God was',[19] then on to Shrewsbury, and some to Chester. The three children were well treated, under the protection of Sir John Scudamore of Ballingham. Colonel Massey wrote from Gloucester to Thomas: 'If Sir John Scudamore will be so courteous as to give you a fitting conveyance I shall not only rest his thankful servant but will also send you a safe conduct and passport … If Sir John in his person shall show you so much respect, his person with me shall find the entertainment of a friend.'[20] On 18 June they were released at Rupert's order and sent under safe conduct to join their father in London, spending a few days on the way at Holme Lacy, 'where we were used exceedingly kindly by my lady Scudamore'.[21]

Successive sieges had turned the area round Brampton Bryan into a wasteland. The castle was looted, and destroyed at Prince Rupert's order in order to prevent its re-occupancy. Sir Robert's losses were estimated at £12,990.[22] At the end of hostilities he revisited his old home, and his son Edward recorded that he took off his hat to say: 'God hath visited great desolation upon this place since I saw it. I desire to say that the Lord hath given and the Lord hath taken away and blessed be the name of the Lord. I trust in his good time He will rays it up agayn.'[23] The church and the village houses were rebuilt, but the castle remained a ruin, though replaced by a new Harley mansion right alongside it.

Vavasour's appearance at the siege of Brampton Bryan was his last involvement with Herefordshire. On 12 April he had been named as commander-in-chief of the royal forces in Gloucestershire, but failed to prevent a supply convoy getting through to Gloucester city.[24] As a result, Massey was enabled to go on the offensive. In May Major Backhouse published a pamphlet, *A True Relation of a Wicked Plot*, revealing the details of the failed stratagem to take Gloucester, and providing a painful embarrassment for Vavasour.

On 8 May King Charles wrote to Rupert recommending that 'Hereford should be fortified and placed under a Governor'[25] and on 12 June commissions were drawn up for Nicholas

Mynne as Governor of Hereford and Sir Gilbert Gerrard as Governor of Worcester. Mynne was named Governor and Commander-in-Chief of Gloucester, Hereford and Monmouth, with full power to impress men and to dispose of the levy to pay his forces. He was to rule by martial law and all other functionaries, including the High Sheriff, Commissioners for Contributions, and Justices, were to obey him.[26] It was thus by the King's order that Hereford was first placed under martial law, with all civil officials commanded to assist and obey the military Governor. In fact Mynne's appointment was already effective, as a letter written on 10 June by Lady Scudamore of Ballingham to Thomas Harley refers to him as Governor.[27] In the same month Lord Herbert resigned his military command. Vavasour's effective dismissal was probably at Herbert's request; he felt, or wanted to believe, that Vavasour had lost him the chance of winning Gloucester.[28]

While besieging Brampton Bryan, Woodhouse had intercepted at least one message from Dr Wright to Colonel Massey at Gloucester, appealing for help, and though Massey sent only a barrel of powder, with a few men and their arms,[29] the siege of Harley's castle had an effect on military activity on the other side of the county. On 13 April, borrowing the cavalry who had escorted his supply convoy, Massey launched an attack on Mynne's base at Newent, but was beaten off. Mynne was already in touch with Herefordshire Royalists, and had requested provisions, saddles and bridles from John Skipp at Ledbury on 10 April.[30] Anticipating further attacks, Mynne had the churchyard at Ross fortified by earthworks.

But Massey chose to strike out northwards, and by 20 April he came up past Taynton and Dymock to Ledbury, with a force of 400 foot and Colonel Purefoy's regiment of horse. The Hellens historian, Munthe, relates that a rude palisade was quickly put up round the churchyard at Much Marcle, and a small cannon was hauled up on to the church tower in order to hold off the Roundheads.[31] But they passed by, leaving Hellens House undisturbed. At Ledbury, Massey's troops were put on free quarter and he sought to use the constables to exact a levy from the surrounding parishes. The petty constables of Evesbatch received orders to pay it to Edward Broughton 'at his lodging in Ledbury at Master Winyates or elsewhere, within 4 and 20 hours, hereof you are not to fail … as you tender your persons and estates'.[32] By this time Brampton Bryan was past needing Massey's help, but he made a show of force outside Hereford with 150 musketeers and the cavalry, setting fire to a house near the walls, and meeting no resistance. At Stoke Edith, a Parliamentary soldier shot dead the octogenarian vicar, John Pralph, incumbent of the place since 1602. Challenged as to his allegiance, he had replied, 'For God and the King'. Like the killing of the blind man at Brampton Bryan, this was an isolated action, but it allowed Royalist propagandists to seize on it as an example of the other side's barbarism. Parliament's scribblers duly returned such truculent replies as: '… he was above threescore years in his Idolatry and Superstition; and was it not time, think you, to sequester him out of the world …'.[33]

Massey had intended to set up fortifications around Ledbury and make it a base for operations[34] but, informed that Prince Rupert had left Shrewsbury on the 22nd intending to join up with Mynne, he abandoned the plan, fearing to be cut off from his base, and made a rapid withdrawal to Gloucester. In the event, Rupert was called to Oxford by the King and the attack did not happen. Mynne, however, clearly anticipated further attacks on Hereford and set about improving the city's defences. But he may not have had much help

Wilton Castle as it would have looked c.1785 (Hereford Library)

from the citizens. Joyce Jeffreys, as wholehearted a Royalist as anyone, recorded that in May she had paid a shilling to 'an honest carpinder for preserving my tymber from the Governors knowledge, which sought for tymber to make works to defend heriford'. But she still had to contribute 2d for 'work done in making bullwarks'.[35] For the time being, however, military action was confined to the south of the county. Mynne's forces were divided between Hereford and Monmouth, and Massey struck between them, at Ross, in mid-May. There was a sharp action at Wilton bridge, of which the last arch on the Wilton side had been demolished by William Rudhall in 1643[36] and replaced by a drawbridge. Breaking past a detachment sent from the garrison of Goodrich Castle, the Parliamentarians stormed and occupied Wilton Castle, home of the Royalist Bridges family. Massey held Ross for about a week, gathering supplies and exacting payments as he had done at Ledbury. If he had intended to move on to Hereford, this did not happen. Obeying orders sent from London by the Committee for Both Kingdoms, on 22 May he abruptly moved his force first to the south-west, capturing Malmesbury, and then returning northwards, taking Tewkesbury on 5 June, the same day Colonel Mynne was to have set off from Hereford to prevent him. Massey was very much in the ascendant, but through June, Hereford had a period of peace, albeit with a precarious feeling about it, while armies were on the march elsewhere. The Royalists had a narrow victory at Cropredy Down in Oxfordshire on the 29th, but Prince Rupert suffered massive defeat at Marston Moor, near York, on 2 July. As in other Royalist places, the bells of Hereford were rung to celebrate a victory, and then the premature report was followed by the news of disaster.

12

Hereford vs Gloucester

Nicholas Mynne has left a reputation as a fair as well as a firm Governor. Clement Barksdale, in an elegiac verse, wrote of '… how well The soldier and the city lov'd him', and he permitted, under supervision, trade between Hereford merchants and London suppliers or customers. Ex-Mayor Price was still very much in business, paying some £300 to two visiting Londoners, Richard Newman and Philip Gouldsmith.[1] Mynne and Massey continued to contest for the ground between Hereford and Gloucester. With harvest-time approaching, both had an eye on winter stores, and Mynne was determined to deprive his opponent by burning the cornfields of Gloucestershire.[2] In mid-July Prince Rupert passed through Herefordshire with remnants of his cavalry that had been severely depleted in the battle of Marston Moor, heading for Bristol, and Mynne led a raid almost to the walls of Gloucester. He made a second foray at the end of the month, with 850 foot and 160 horse, and on 2 August was at Hartpury, expecting to be reinforced by 600 foot and 200 horse from Worcester. For a man who had said he could take Gloucester with 200 soldiers, this would have made an army large enough to attack the city. Massey assembled his own forces as rapidly as possible, hindered by a violent dispute between two of his majors, each commanding a company of some 140 men,[3] which ended in one killing the other. Command and soldiers' loyalty were a very personal affair, and disturbance and dissension swept through the Gloucester troops. An officer less resolute than Massey might have failed to hold the men together, but in a despatch to the Committee for both Kingdoms, he reported that 'I persuaded most of the soldiers to march with me'.[4] They almost met the Royalists at Highleadon, but Mynne marched his force north to Redmarley, while Massey ended up at Eldersfield, two miles to the east. At sunrise next morning, he heard Mynne's drums, and advanced. The Worcester contingent had not yet arrived.

In the cheery tone that reports a victory, Massey described the Royalist force as 'drawn out and ordered in battalions, and their hedges lined with musketeers for our entertainment'. He advanced his men in two bodies in order of battle. Edward Harley, by now a colonel of horse, led with three troops, supported by Major Backhouse, who had deceived Vavasour, with three more troops. On the flank of the horse were a body of infantry. The rear was brought up by another troop of horse and infantry. The reserves were stationed in the village of Redmarley.

Driving straight in on the right flank and front, the Parliamentary attack forced the Royalists out of the enclosures and from the hedges. Its violence put the horse to flight, and shattered the whole body of infantry. Mynne fell fighting, with 130 of his men. At the moment of defeat, Colonel Passey, the commander of the Worcester troop, rode up looking for Mynne. He was wounded and taken prisoner, but his men continued to advance until they saw on their right the bulk of Mynne's horse fleeing in disorder, when they halted. Uncertain of what to do, they gave Massey time to call his men together and draw them up in line again. To the Roundheads' relief, the Worcester men then moved off towards Ledbury, and Massey was able to turn back to Gloucester with his prisoners and whatever loot his men had got off the battleground. The survivors of Mynne's force fled to Ledbury. Had the Worcester men arrived a little earlier, Massey himself admitted he might have lost the encounter. Edward Harley had a bullet wound in the arm, but Massey's men had sustained relatively few casualties. In his dispatch Massey noted

> … the troop of Col. [Edward] Harley especially distinguished itself. All our troops, both officers and soldiers, as also our foot, played their parts with much resolution and gallantry, so that we slew many of the enemy, about 100, and took Lieut.-Col. Passey, being wounded, a prisoner, Major John Buller, 7 captains, 3 lieutenants, 5 ensigns, and 12 sergeants, and about 300 soldiers prisoners. Some troops of horse advanced in the pursuit almost to Ledbury, five miles from the first place of our fight. Amongst the dead was Major-Genl. Mynn's body, which with all the rest [of the slain] on our return we found stripped naked.[5]

Mynne's body was taken to Gloucester by the victors, and buried there with military honours.

Probably few Herefordshire men were in Mynne's force, which was formed mainly from his own Anglo-Irish regiment, but the defeat left Hereford without a Governor and with a seriously depleted garrison. Matters had to be taken in hand urgently. Vavasour (still well-regarded by Prince Rupert) was named to replace Mynne as Governor of Hereford,[6] but does not appear to have taken up the role. His appointment was resisted by Croft, Lingen and Rudhall, ostensibly on the ground that his commission had not been properly drawn up, and was probably also opposed by Lord Herbert (on 6 April Vavasour had written to Rupert asking him 'to protect him from an affront which is much laboured here [Oxford] by Lord Herbert' – perhaps relating to the Gloucester trickery).[7] Anxiety and dissatisfaction were strong in the city and the county with the feeling that they were inadequately protected from Massey's raids, and it was reported to Rupert that many of the constables, tax assessors and collectors were Parliament supporters.[8] Clearly matters needed to be taken in hand. A Colonel Barnard or Barnold, first heard of as a major of foot in Colonel Stanhope's regiment,[9] was made Governor, apparently on a temporary basis, until 10 September, when Major Barnabas Scudamore, youngest of the Viscount's six siblings, was appointed. His commission, from Prince Rupert, had been solicited by two prominent citizens, William Cater, the Mayor, and Philip Trehearne, who had been Mayor the previous year.[10] Scudamore, aged 35 in 1644, had joined the King even before Nottingham, having been wounded in a brief action at Coventry on 20 August 1642. A seasoned campaigner, he was one of the officers of the Monmouth garrison and had gained a reputation for ability and courage. He was not wealthy, possessing only a farm at Rowlstone in Little Birch parish and entitlement to the tithe of Bridstow rectory, close to Ross. His eldest brother provided him with £50 a year. Typically, as a younger son of a gentry family, he was expected to make his own career.

On 14 September, Scudamore had 466 men at arms billeted in the city,[11] not enough to make any impact even if they were trained and fully armed. Massey at Gloucester was far better equipped, and his garrison was raiding deep into the southern parts of Herefordshire. A Parliamentary committee for the sequestration of Herefordshire's Royalist estates was sitting in Gloucester in the summer of 1644 and at least one 'delinquent', Thomas Cardiffe, of The Helm, Ewyas Harold, compounded at this time.[12] Royalist garrisons still held Abergavenny, Newport and Monmouth, but Scudamore had hardly taken up his new post when his former colleague at Monmouth, Robert Kyrle, commander of the horse there, defected from the Royalist cause back to the side of Parliament and planned secretly with Massey for the capture of the town. Remembering his own deception of Vavasour, Massey was suspicious, and 'there wanted not those that kept a watch over Kyrle's deportment',[13] but Kyrle's father, always a loyal Parliamentarian, living in Gloucester rather than at Walford, was also involved with the plan. The plot worked. Kyrle, pretending to be returning to Monmouth with 100 prisoners, had in actuality 100 well-armed Parliamentary soldiers, and around 26 September, Monmouth's Royalist garrison was overpowered. Less than two months later, the Royalists reclaimed it, on 19 November, while most of the garrison were absent at the siege of Chepstow Castle. An outer defence of Monmouth, Pembridge Castle, an old fortified house in the Herefordshire parish of Welsh Newton, owned by the Catholic Kemble family but with a Parliamentary garrison, was also regained by the Royalists after a two-week siege.[15]

At this time coins were being minted in Hereford, probably to pay the garrison troops, possibly using minting presses that could be transported from one place to another, under the control of the King's mint-master Sir Thomas Cary. The necessary silver was supplied locally. Documents recorded in the 19th century show the receipt of plate for coinage from certain persons including Walter Kyrle, and others noted simply as Weaver and Harford. Kyrle and Dr Harford were Parliamentarians and presumably their contributions were not voluntary. Edmund Weaver would be elected an MP for Hereford in November 1646,

Pembridge Castle at Welsh Newton

which suggests that he too was not a committed Royalist. The amounts of money coined were modest and Hereford coins are very rare.[15]

Late in the year, Dr Herbert Croft, already a chaplain to the King, was appointed Dean of Hereford. Despite his clerical position – or using it as a cover – the King made use of him 'for conveying secret commands to loyalist generals, often at great personal risk', though nothing specific is recorded of these actions.[16]

In the winter of 1644-45 things were relatively calm in Herefordshire, apart from one short-lived Parliamentary attempt to occupy and fortify a house near Goodrich, quickly put down by Henry Lingen, Governor of the castle there.[17] The county was entirely under Royalist control, and energetic steps were taken to underpin the Royalists' position. A garrison was installed or reinstated at Canon Frome,[18] and apart from Goodrich Castle, troops were stationed at Wilton Castle (reoccupied by the Royalists), The Mynde, Kilpeck Castle, Pembridge Castle, Croft Castle and perhaps other locations, as the existence of a garrison is sometimes only apparent in the records if it is attacked. Lingen, as High Sheriff, was assiduous in collecting imposts and dues with the assistance of the commissioners of array and the constables, and in his military role he appears to have made lightning raids into Gloucestershire whenever the opportunity offered, acting in concert with the Royalist troops at Worcester.[19] Coningsby, Croft, Pye, and Rudhall were all still active, and Parliamentary supporters kept a low profile. Shortly after the garrisoning of Canon Frome, Sir Richard Hopton was arrested, probably for resisting the occupancy of his house and despite his claim to have an order from Prince Maurice guaranteeing the safety of his property. Hopton was taken first to Hereford, then to Oxford. With one son in the King's army and two in the Parliament's, he was a suspect figure, imprisoned and released again eight times by the Royalists between 1642 and 1646.[20]

Yet another semi-reshuffle of military responsibilities saw Prince Maurice named on 6 November 1644 as Major-General of Worcester, Salop, Herefordshire and Monmouthshire, under his brother's supreme command, though Rupert with courtly punctilio placed himself under the nominal authority of the teenage Prince of Wales. In January 1645 Archbishop Laud, half-forgotten to many, was executed on the charge of treason. Negotiations between both sides, the so-called 'Treaty of Uxbridge', were going on, but were abandoned by the end of February. After two and a half years of inconclusive warfare, and no agreement about peace, both the King's council and the Parliamentary leaders had to assess their strength and resources, and consider how to make 1645 the year of victory. At Westminster, the decision was taken to form a new field army.

While there can be little doubt that the troops based in Hereford were well stocked, they were frequently ordered out to support Royalist detachments which were harassing, or being harassed by, Massey in the efforts made by each side to claim supplies from the farms of Gloucestershire and Monmouthshire. The Forest of Dean, with its wood and coal, was also fought over. Skirmishings took place around Ledbury, and Massey brought a force as far as Bosbury where he captured a captain and his troop.[21] But Scudamore's men gained a success at Eastnor. Richard Hopton, youngest son of Sir Richard, had been commissioned by Massey on the quite unfulfillable promise of raising 400 horse and arming them at his own expense. With about 60 horse and 40 foot, he had established himself in early

Shrewsbury Castle (Shropshire Archives)

February at the house of Castleditch, Eastnor (site of the present castle), a place Massey considered impossible to defend. Despite Massey's order or request to leave the place, he remained, and was duly captured by a party from Hereford and brought to captivity in the city. He escaped at the end of March 'by leaping over a wall'.[22] Hopton's escapade is typical of many officers on both sides, who, considering themselves as independent commanders and often with an exaggerated notion of their military abilities, felt free to ignore the orders laid down by the seniors. The Royalist side suffered more than Parliament's from this kind of initiative, which was supposed to show Cavalier dash and spirit.

Firmly under Royalist control, Hereford saw nothing of Prince Maurice, whose head-quarters were in Worcester. But dramatic changes were happening in the region to the north. Montgomery had been in Parliamentary hands since 18 September 1644. The former monastery of Cwm Hîr, in its remote Radnor valley, was stormed just before Christmas by a strong Parliamentary force. Its Governor's name is given by Webb as Colonel Barnold, and he is assumed to be the same man who was briefly Governor of Hereford.[23] Barnold was compelled to surrender but was allowed to make an honourable departure with his surviving men. But it was the capture of Shrewsbury by Colonel Thomas Mytton on 22 February that resounded down the Marches. Shropshire had been a Royalist county, and now the Roundheads were in almost complete control, except for the area round Ludlow; and energetically setting about the business of sequestration, trials, and tax collection.

The disastrous loss of Shrewsbury brought Prince Rupert into the southern Marches, seeking to muster an army to recoup the losses. From Ludlow Castle he sent warrants into Herefordshire commanding all persons aged from 16 to 60 to appear at a rendezvous with arms and other necessaries fit for a march. This was supposedly to 'convoy his Majesty who is coming that way', but was more likely a means of recruitment.[24] Evidently many were drafted or forced into the ranks, since Rupert soon afterwards marched into Cheshire with an army estimated at some 10,000 men.[25] If no actual fighting happened in Herefordshire at this time, it was anything but tranquil. With Rupert demanding men and money, and such resolute men as Coningsby, Croft and Barnabas Scudamore in charge, no excuses would be accepted for failure to pay the levies and contributions needed both for mainte-nance of the county garrisons and for remitting to the King's ever-emptying treasury. And if foot-soldiers were needed, they knew where to find them.

13

The Herefordshire Clubmen

On 16 October 1644 Barnabas Scudamore and Henry Lingen, as Governor and Sheriff, had written to Prince Rupert praying that he would consider the distressed state of the county, and not quarter troops permanently on it. Scudamore also requested 1,000 muskets.[1] At that time Sir Marmaduke Langdale's Royalist Northern Horse, or the remnants of it after Marston Moor, were spread across Herefordshire's northern parishes, taking free quarter and demanding food, fodder, and accommodation.[2] But Scudamore, responsible for the county garrisons as well as that of Hereford, and for troops stationed in such places as Leominster, saw himself as the needful beneficiary of the county's resources, and had no scruples about collecting them. The men under his command were equally liable to help themselves and to demand money with menaces, and the fact that many of them were Irish increased the locals' hostility. On 2 December 1644 Scudamore was appointed Sheriff by the King, in addition to his post as Governor, and so became in effect the dictator of Herefordshire, controlling both military and civil power under the overall authority of Prince Rupert. He was someone to whom the French phrase *à la guerre comme à la guerre* applies – to him, war made its own conditions, which were not those of peace-time. Scudamore was not alone in this: among the pressures which drove the war on was the rise of a professional military caste who saw warfare as their business and who, influenced by European examples but also by a native logic, did not accept that civilians could expect immunity, as if the war did not touch them.

In Royalist areas like Herefordshire and Worcestershire, the dominance of the military governors and the conduct of local garrison commanders unhinged the arrangement of local government as described in Chapter 2. Even before Scudamore's appointment, the author of 'Certain Observations' noted how Mynne's troops 'raked contribution in corn, in bacon, and butter, and cheese faster than ever'[3] – the writer was a Parliamentarian, but it soon became clear that Royalists felt just as victimised. Neither Prince Rupert nor Prince Maurice took any steps to curb the way in which the garrisons and detached army groups battened off the countryside, terrifying the inhabitants and attacking, sometimes killing, those who protested or resisted. Local gentry, once the arbiters of local custom and justice, were marginalised, Royalist or not. For many, this was just what they had feared from the breakdown of consensus which had led to the war, though in a way they had not anticipated. The traditional forms of county administration were being pushed aside by the unchecked power of the military. An effort to stem the slide was begun when at a Special Sessions in December 1644 the Worcester Justices came up with the idea of an 'Association' with the neighbouring counties of Herefordshire, Shropshire, Staffordshire and Monmouthshire. An emulation of the Parliament's successful county associations in some areas, it had the overt aim of 'mutual protection' and the unstated one of clawing back the county gentry's management of affairs. A petition was sent to King Charles, who replied favourably. On 9 January 1645 a meeting of representatives from Worcestershire, Herefordshire and Shropshire met at Ludlow and resolved that, subject to the King's approval, they would 'arm themselves in such a powerful way that the counties should be secured by their own powers, and be in readiness when His Majesty's occasions brought him into any of the counties to have such an army as would be able to encounter the strongest and most able bodies of his enemies'. But also, 'our ancient laws' were to be 'observed in force and reputation, for the Soldier assuming a liberty to rapine and insolence, hath discharged the subject and thrown him into a confused despair'.[4] Free quarter was to be forbidden, along with forced loans and contributions. The King again replied favourably, and gave them authority to raise 600 troops, but the terms of his message did nothing to empower them against the depredations of the garrisons. They had asked for the Prince of Wales to be titular head of their Association, but instead they had the presence of Prince Maurice, who held a meeting for 'Commissioners from the Associated Counties of Worcester, Hereford, Salop and Stafford' in January.[5] Maurice's opinion of the Association was soon passed on to his brother: 'I … desire you to be very careful in the business of the Association, which, I fear, tends much to the destruction of military power and discipline. For there are some cunning men amongst them …'.[6] The Prince did nothing to stop the troops from continuing to commandeer supplies. The Royalists' lack of funds, worsening as more counties came under Parliamentary control, and their relatively loosely-structured command system, combined to make it impossible for all the King's good intentions (he perhaps realised the damage being done to his cause) to prevent the raids.

How far the squires and landowners were influenced by the complaints of their tenants and employees, as well as by the loss of their own authority, influence, and movable goods, is impossible to tell. But it is very likely that they received a torrent of appeals from those who saw them not only as masters and superiors, but also as protectors. To the yeomen, the farmers, the country artisans and the labourers (the group most likely to be impressed for armed service) it was becoming clear that the former order of things had changed. The old masters were not in charge, and the military relied on force and terror to hold control and get supplies of food and money. Insecure, threatened, with old bonds and loyalties proving worthless, the country people were becoming increasingly desperate.

To them, the Association formed in Ludlow offered no security and its license to impress 600 men meant another forcible intrusion in their lives. By late February 1645, anger was driving them into action. Preserved in the letter books of Sir William Brereton, Parliamentary commander in Cheshire, is a document drawn up and subscribed by 'some of the sufficient and best able men' of several parishes in the Broxash hundred of Herefordshire. Dated 6 March 1645, almost simultaneous with one from Woodbury, only a few miles away in Worcestershire, it is a statement of protest and defiance from people who had no part in managing the war effort and only a limited local role, in a few cases, in managing the county's affairs. Yet they were the most potentially dangerous element in society, because they alone could rouse the mass of the population into action. It could be compared to the NCOs of an army refusing to acknowledge the authority of the officers. Suddenly that small caste or clique, so used to deference and obedience, might seem highly vulnerable.

The document is addressed to the inhabitants of Bodenham, requesting their support by signing their names against the list included in the document. The authors clearly felt that they had had enough of the state of affairs which had been prevailing. One reason advanced for banding is defence against 'papists'. They stood for the defence of 'the true Protestant religion, his Majestys person … and our owne estates and privileges'. They also object to being 'led away by papists … out of our own country'.[7] They note that the last commission allowed for 'the forcible impressing of us 600 men at a time, as often as they shall please; the reference to the newly-formed Gentry Association's draft of 600 men makes clear that further 'recruitment' from whatever source was opposed.[8] They proclaim resistance to new taxes: 'other oppressions by way of excise', and to the soldiers' habit of 'fetching in provisions into their garrisons'. Their intention is 'to defend ourselves from all insolencies and violences whatsoever offered us or our estates at home',[9] and they make appeal to the Book of Orders issued by the King's Oxford Parliament to regulate the behaviour of troops. Twenty-six signatures are appended to the manifesto, with Thomas Careless at the head.[10] A high constable of Broxash hundred, rated in the 1641 subsidy rolls as an inhabitant of Withington and Preston Wynne, he was clearly a man of some substance. Two others of the 26, Henry Haywood from Pencombe and John Edwards from Bodenham, were also to be active later, respectively as collector of sequestrations and assessment commissioner for the Parliamentary administration of the county. Another signatory was John Parsons, clergyman, incumbent of Withington. John Morrill points out that Parliament's banning of the Prayer Book (it was replaced by a 'Directory of Public Worship') impelled numerous clergy to take a stand with clubmen,[11] but the ban was not yet enforced in Herefordshire. Parsons may have been defending the produce of his glebe. Among the wealthiest (according to 1663 assessments) was Richard Carwardine, who owned lands in Broxash and the hundred of Radlow. He and two others are also described in the same sources as gentlemen, though 'many farmers in other parts of England were richer than most Herefordshire gentry'.[12] Carwardine would later buy up some of the Hereford dean and chapter properties.[13] Next richest was perhaps William Wootton of Marden, whose properties in 1663 were assessed at £42 a year (though his prosperity may have increased after 1645). But though some of the names indicate links with gentry families, these were not men of great substance. One scholar suggests that 'it may be significant that Broxash contained a higher proportion of small landholders than the other Herefordshire hundreds'.[14]

'Clubmen' simply meant men wielding cudgels and staves, and so without firearms or other purpose-made weapons. Their timing was significant: it was just after winter, with stores and provisions at their lowest, and the prospect of sowing crops for the soldiers to plunder surely played a part. Very soon the protest changed from a paper proclamation to an uprising. In mid-March Scudamore sent to the parishes of Much and Little Cowarne, in Broxash hundred, for supplies of fodder and contributions to his garrison, but the parishioners turned out and chased them away: 'The countrie people of a place called Cowarne did ringe their larum bell beate affrighted Scudamore's troope out of their towneship.'[15] Some troops took refuge at the home of a local gentleman, Mr Berrington, a Catholic, before returning to Hereford to report to the Governor. His response was uncompromising. The country people were branded as Roundheads and traitors. A letter from Scudamore to Berrington, intercepted by the clubmen, announced that he 'was making a rod to whip the men of Cowarne'.[16] A punitive expedition of 30 musketeers and six horse teams were sent from Hereford to seize hay and provisions from Thomas Careless's property. Careless had gone into hiding, but the church bells again rang out as 'some persons or other range the larum bells in some 3 parishes together'[17] and locals assembled in enough numbers to drive the musketeers and hay wagons back to the city: 'the countrie came on apace and rescued some of the teames at a great bridge called Luggbridge'. This was the Lugg bridge to the east of Hereford, where the Little Lugg stream joins the main river. News of the affray came quickly into the city, drums were beaten and troops, ward companies and volunteers rushed out. A party of horsemen took the rustics from behind and scattered them, jumping and scrambling across the Little Lugg and dispersing into the landscape. They were pursued '3 or 4 myle into divers parishes'. Crying for quarter, they were answered, 'We'll give no quarter. You're roundhead dogs and traitors'. Around 16 were killed on the spot or died later of wounds.[18]

This violent and bloody affair did not end the matter. Next day, 19 March, a crowd reckoned at 6,000[19] appeared outside Hereford, demanding restitution and relief and calling for the garrison soldiers to be sent to the King's service elsewhere. Colonel Massey estimated a much higher number, between 15 and 16,000, with 6 or 7,000 possessing 'musquitts and other fire armes' but this is most improbable. All roads were blockaded, and travellers questioned. The mood was fierce, and the Broxash episode has been called 'the most aggressive of the Marcher risings'.[20] Some accounts say that Henry Lingen's house at Sutton Frene was destroyed at this time, but Webb rejects this, and Symonds' record of the King's travels, made later that year, refers to Lingen's 'fair house in Sutton'.[21]

Scudamore issued a prompt Declaration which offered the clubmen no concessions other than a promise to 'vse my best endeavours for easeinge of their iust grievances p'sented in an orderly way' and to 'forgett all that is past on their submission', so long as they paid their contributions and continued to provide free quarter to the King's soldiers. Only the leaders would be punished and he called on the people to hand over Thomas Careless, Thomas Wootton, the two eldest sons of Alexander Walwyn of Cowarne, and one Richard Lawrence, of the same place, 'to receive Condigne punishment according to the knowen lawes of the land'.[22] The clubmen responded with a statement of their demands, which included the removal of the garrison of Canon Frome and a reduction of the number of soldiers in Hereford, to be replaced by local men; as well as protection against further depredations from troops, and provision made for the dependants of the people killed on the 18th. They denied any suggestion of treachery and rebellion, having assembled for the defence of their persons and property according to the known laws. This insistence on 'known laws' reflects an intense dislike and fear of the martial law at the commander's disposal.

The clubmen mostly dispersed, but with their grudges and fears unsoothed. Colonel Edward Massey, with informants both inside Hereford and in the county, lost no time in coming from Gloucester to Ledbury with 500 men and 150 horse, to try to take advantage of the situation. But the great body of the clubmen had no desire to ally themselves with the Parliamentary side. They had come out in their own defence, and despite Massey's persuasive talk they had no intention of exchanging one military occupation for another. Massey really had no more sympathy with their demands than Scudamore; reporting via Sir Samuel Luke to the Committee for Both Kingdoms in London, and forwarding copies of the two declarations, he called their action 'a perfect act of Rebellion to bee justified by noe Law or Statute and their confusion will be certaine'.[23] Massey believed that if he could be sent reinforcements, he could get the clubmen to declare for Parliament and enlist their aid in an attack on Hereford. This rather sanguine notion was perhaps encouraged by the fact that Careless was a Parliamentary sympathiser (in July 1645 Edward Harley and James Kyrle gave him authority to raise 100 foot 'for the service of the King and Parliament and the defence of the county of Hereford'[24]), and he served later in the decade as treasurer to the Herefordshire sequestration committee. But General Brereton in Shropshire also believed that if the Parliament could muster a significant force in the Marches, 'a strong party, who are now overawed, would declare themselves to the Parliament'.[25] Scudamore, who knew Herefordshire much better, probably never expected the clubmen to ally themselves with Parliament, which would explain his tough response to them. The Hereford clubmen, unlike those in some other counties, made no political claims at all. The entire tenor of their case was against the presence and oppression of the troops and for a return to 'known laws', and they were not likely to feel that the Parliament would bring that about. Dore quotes from an anonymous 'Royalist's Diary' four political claims allegedly put forward by the Herefordshire clubmen, arguing for the King's deposition because he had come in a warlike manner to the House of Commons, had arranged for his daughter's marriage without consultation, had raised his own Parliament in Oxford, and had concluded a peace with the Irish without consulting Parliament;[26] but there is no direct record of such sentiments coming from Herefordshire at this time, and the reputed claims are likely to be part of a propaganda campaign or simply the fruit of their writer's imagination.

Nevertheless, among the local Royalist leaders, reaction to this

General Sir William Brereton

sudden popular mobilisation was panicky. Sir Walter Pye, always quick off the mark, set off to Prince Rupert, reaching him at Newport, Shropshire on 22 March with the news that in pro-royal Herefordshire, something of a popular revolt was going on. Scudamore, undoubtedly aware of the Ledbury meeting, had to negotiate, though he settled with the clubmen 'on terms which he probably made in bad faith and which, in any case, offered them much less than they had demanded'.[27] Around 2,000 clubmen, unsatisfied or perhaps rallying round their threatened ringleaders, remained in the vicinity of Ledbury. Massey had returned to Gloucester, though he kept in close touch with events. King Charles himself weighed in with a letter to the Governor of Hereford, approving his action and instructing him, if the clubmen should ally with Massey, to proceed against them as rebels, 'according to your Power and Strength you have', with support to come from Prince Rupert at Newport.[28]

Pye's story was dramatic enough to bring Rupert straight down with a substantial force of royal troops, 'at least 5,000',[29] and the intention 'to refresh after the Dutch [i.e. German] fashion'. Far from making concessions, they 'brought all their power on Bromyard and Ledbury side, fell on, plundered every parish and house, poor as well as others, leaving neither clothes nor provision; killed all the young lambs in the country, though not above a week old'.[30] On 29 March, 1,000 foot and a party of horse went to deal with the clubmen still assembled at Ledbury, most of whom scattered and fled, but 200 or so put up a vain fight against trained and well-armed troopers. Some were killed, prisoners were taken to Hereford and three men were executed. One of these, Henry Smith (not listed in the first outbreak), was reported to have been 'a troubler of many that had been under-sheriffs and feodaries, escheators and jailers, for corruption and extortion'.[31] Ambrose Elton, a declared Parliamentarian, was briefly imprisoned by Rupert's order.[32] The Prince, no apostle of compromise, had an oath drawn up which every man in the city and county was supposed to swear, or face imprisonment for refusal. It pledged to oppose Parliament and to renounce clubman leagues,[33] in a complete and absolute assertion of loyalty to the King. Its eight clauses included rejection of the pretension of the two Houses of Parliament to make laws or ordinances without royal approval, and a promise to assist the King's cause with 'the hazzard of my life and fortune', all to be vowed 'without equivocation, or mentall reservation'.

Rupert made Hereford his headquarters until the beginning of April,[34] and took the opportunity to reorganise the county's muster areas.[35] A senior Royalist officer, Lord Astley, was raising troops in the north of the county, where there had been little or no clubman activity, and on 22 April took 'a large number of pressed men'[36] to assist in the Royalist effort to relieve Chester.

Clubman assemblies were not restricted to Herefordshire and Worcestershire. In Somerset, Dorset and Wiltshire many thousands turned out. Scholars who have examined the clubmen's protests have made the point that risings came from areas whose underlying sympathies were Royalist as well as from Parliamentarian areas. David Underdown's 'social geography' approach sees the downland clubmen of Somerset as largely Royalist in their basic sympathies,[37] and this – despite the evidence of some Parliamentarians among the moving spirits – is evidently also true of the Broxash men, so long as 'Royalist' is understood as 'traditionalist' and not implying an attitude of active commitment. In an article that touches only peripherally on the Herefordshire clubmen, Simon Osborne suggests that the risings were made possible by weakened Royalist military power. But this was certainly not the case in Herefordshire.[38] The clubmen of the southern counties have been more

Prince Rupert (National Portrait Gallery)

closely scrutinised than those of Herefordshire, partly perhaps because the Broxash manifesto is of more limited scope than some of the others; but also in Somerset and Wiltshire they seemed a genuine third force, and had General Fairfax to negotiate with, whereas in Broxash hundred they had Prince Rupert, whose 'Dutch' method of dealing with them was brutally effective.

So the Hereford clubmen's protest came to an end, though one or two isolated incidents occurred in April and later, and the protestors were forced back into anonymity and resentful compliance with the demands of the military governors. If they had had more of a political programme, they might have had more impact, but that would have required a strong leadership, able to convert anger and frustration into determined purpose; and there was no such leadership on offer. In the end they gained little or nothing at all from their uprising. Events generated outside Herefordshire were to have more effect on the county, and even if Scudamore had intended to keep his promises, he soon had other preoccupations.

14

Prince Rupert Takes a Hand

Prince Rupert was frequently in and around Hereford in the wake of the clubmen's rising, drawn by the need to contain Massey who was pressing the Royalists hard in the Forest of Dean, but also building up his forces. A sub-headquarters was established at Ross-on-Wye, from where two Royalist commanders, the veteran Sir Marmaduke Langdale and Bernard Astley,[1] mounted forays into the Forest and, of course, supplied themselves from the local countryside. Meanwhile a Parliamentary newsbook reported that the Prince had collected a considerable force in Herefordshire, quartered – surely not by chance – around Brampton Bryan and at Bodenham, Rosemaund and Moreton Jeffrey in the Broxash hundred. At Mordiford, it reported,

> a party of Rupert's foot came into severall houses, and plundred all the money, and all that was good, that they could lay their hands on, and made them to fetch in roested Mutton, Veale, Lambe, poultry, and I know not what, and when they had done, they having eate and drunk while their bellies would hold, tooke the rest and threw it up and downe the house, and let out a great deale of drinke out of their barrels, and did such barbarous practices as is most wonderfull … if any oppose them it is no more but knocking them on the head, or pistolling those who speake against them.[2]

The Prince hoped to regain Shrewsbury and also to break the long-standing Parliamentary siege of Chester. When the Royalist army began to move north, Massey immediately sent a detachment of his own troops to Ledbury. Rupert's movements at this time are hard to pin down; the *Journal of Prince Rupert's Marches*[3] records that, on 19 April, learning of events in Worcestershire and Herefordshire, Rupert marched to Bewdley and then on to Bromyard, where, 'hearing of a Rendezvous in a village, he marcht out of the waye surpriz'd and freed the people', and carried on to Hereford and thence to Monmouth and Bristol, which seems impossible, since on Monday 21st it has him back in Hereford. There Astley brought him the news that Massey was at Ledbury. Rupert marched his men through the night of the 22nd, capturing Massey's scouts as they advanced, so that the Roundheads were unaware of his approach until he was almost upon them.

Ledbury was formed of two streets, where the roads from Gloucester to Hereford and from Malvern to Ross intersect, with side alleys and lanes. The Roundheads had to improvise their defences, and a writer in the Royalist *Mercurius Aulicus* records that they barricaded the streets with carts.[4] It was a brief though sharp encounter. Within half an hour the barriers had been broken through by Astley's and Colonel Washington's foot-soldiers, and

*The Market Hall in Ledbury,
behind which a lane leads to the
church (Herefordshire Library)*

once the way was clear, Lord Loughborough led a cavalry charge that swept up to the cross-roads. The Parliamentarians were forced out of the town and into the wooded slopes on its eastern edge. Around 120 of Massey's men were killed, some of them fighting in the street, some while fleeing towards Tewkesbury, and around 400 prisoners were claimed. According to the Royalists, their own losses numbered only five men, one of whom was John Lingen, brother of Henry. Massey, making the best of things in a report to the Speaker on 1 May, describes the fight as a holding action to enable his troops to make a safe retreat towards Gloucester. He claims that his side had killed 'near 40' and 'we had very few killed, not above 6 or 7'. Edward Harley had a head wound, and Major Backhouse, wounded more severely in the head, was taken as a prisoner to Hereford, where he died. It was beyond question a Royalist victory, and Rupert used Ledbury Place, still standing at the crossroads, as a temporary headquarters. But Massey, though beaten, was not broken, and Rupert did not remain in Herefordshire, marching his victorious force on to Worcester and then to Oxford (according to the *Journal of Prince Rupert's Marches*), though Massey reported that he had gone north into Shropshire.[5] Massey's credit with Parliament remained high and the Commons resolved that he should have all Sir John Wintour's Dean Forest ironworks and mills for his own use and benefit, and also six horses, fully equipped, to the value of £200, and a payment of £1,000 a year.[6] Wintour had abandoned the struggle and gone to join Queen Henrietta Maria in France. That summer, Massey was promoted to major general and moved from Gloucester to field command, being replaced as Governor of Gloucester by Colonel Thomas Morgan.

For a time, the pressure of combat, if not of military occupancy, was off Herefordshire. Walter Powell (a Royalist) noted grimly: 'Conisbye's trowps deuouring my hay meadowes'.[7] But Astley's pressed men from Herefordshire were participating in the siege of Hawkesley Hall, near Droitwich, and Scudamore brought troops to join the King for a planned effort to break the siege of Chester. Brereton abandoned the siege, the King moved east into

Derbyshire, and Scudamore returned with his men to Hereford.[8] Probably as a result of Prince Rupert's visits – the Prince was in Hereford again on 29 April[9] – Scudamore organised further work on the city's defences during May. To clear a space round the walls and gates, houses and shacks abutting the walls were pulled down, and houses along Widemarsh Street, outside the gate, were ordered to be demolished. Three of these belonged to Joyce Jeffreys, who had been renting them out. Now she had to take away everything salvageable – shelves, doors and panes of glass – leaving only shells to be pulled down.[10]

At Ludlow, Colonel Woodhouse was concerned about encroachments into southern Shropshire from the Parliamentary base at Shrewsbury. Stokesay Castle had been wrested from its Royalist owners, the Cravens, as had Broncroft Castle in Corvedale. Garrisoned by Roundhead troops, they represented a serious threat to his supplies and security. He mustered a substantial expedition in early June, little short of 2,000 men, from his own troops backed up by detachments from Hereford, Worcester and as far away as Monmouth, to reclaim the lost ground. Among the commanders were Barnabas Scudamore and Sir William Croft, with Sir Thomas Lunsford heading the Monmouth contingent. A Shrewsbury officer's report states that the Parliamentarians felt too weak to confront the Royalists. Withdrawing from Broncroft, their force, around 600 strong, assembled at Wistanstow, a mile or so north of Stokesay Castle, awaiting reinforcements, when the Royalists appeared on 8 June. Resolving to fight, the Parliamentarians 'beat up all their ambuscades in the hedges for a mile together, untill they came to the main body, which after an houres fight, we routed and dispersed'.[11] According to the Royalist Sir Edward Walker, 'This Defeat was ascribed to the ill Conduct and strife of those Collonells about Superiority and Command …'.[12] Woodhouse lost his horse, and Thomas Lochard of The Byletts was killed, but the Royalists' chief loss was Sir William Croft, killed either in the battle or in the pursuit which followed. Clement Barksdale, one-time master of the Hereford Cathedral School, later wrote elegiac lines:

> Perish may the place, perish the day
> When sober Croft came to so mad a fray.
> Name me not subtle Birch or Morgan. There
> When Croft was slain, they conquer'd Herefordshire[13]

The defeat at Stokesay was a severe dent to Royalist prestige in the region, but was not a strategic victory or disaster for either side, though to Sir Edward Walker the effects of the defeat were noticeable when a week or so later 'we retreated into these Parts'.[14] The Parliamentarians did not attempt to advance further, and the surviving Royalists returned to their bases, leaving almost 100 dead and 360 prisoners, as well as all their baggage. Less than a week later, on the 14th, a far larger and, for the King, vastly more disastrous battle was fought at Naseby, in Leicestershire. Parliament's victory there did not end the war but from then on, Charles was on the run. He still held a few cards, however. Bristol was his; and he still had loyal supporters. In Scotland, the Marquis of Montrose was winning notable victories on his behalf. It was not time to give in, though the need to build up a new field army which could match Parliament's shatteringly effective 'new model' was a daunting challenge, and he retreated into friendly territory.

Riding south-westwards via Bewdley, the King dined at Bromyard on 19 June and arrived in Hereford later that day. Prince Rupert was with him and left on 26 June to take command at Bristol. General Gerrard arrived with 2,000 men,[15] who were sent on to Bristol. Hereford's welcome to the fugitive monarch was warm enough for Charles to write to Lord Herbert (whom he had recently created Earl of Glamorgan) striking a note of slightly forced optimism: 'As myself is nowais dishartned by our late misfortune so nether this Country, for I could not haue expected more from them, than they have now freely undertaken, though I had come hither absolute Victorius …'.[16] But, as so often in the course of the war, Charles found that displays of enthusiasm and popular support in the streets did not result in either volunteers or material contributions. Lodging in the Bishop's Palace, the King wrote from 'Our court at Hereford' to the Prince of Wales (then at Barnstaple) on 20 June, reaffirming the powers entrusted to the Prince and allowing him 'to make your personal residence in what place soever you shall judge most expedient. And so we bid you heartily farewell.'[17] Whatever opinion may be held of Charles I's intelligence, percipience and judgement, he was the only person among the main protagonists who had no choice but to be there and to do what he considered his destined duty. He could not throw up his hands and go home. His grandmother, as an unsatisfactory monarch of Scotland, had been forced to abdicate in favour of her baby son. But abdication was not an option in Charles's mind, and the Prince of Wales was not an infant who might be brought up in a right-thinking manner, but a lusty adolescent who had been taught to believe in the divine right to rule. The King's time in Hereford was largely taken up by debates and councils, all focused on how to retrieve his fortunes. Notes survive from a council of war, held on 23 June, with the King, Prince Rupert, Lord Digby, the Lord Chancellor, the Duke of Richmond, General Gerrard, and Lord Astley. They resolved to immediately 'send to break down the bridge at Ross', but the prime subject was the recruitment and deployment of fresh troops. They hoped to raise 6,300 men and 160 horse from Herefordshire and south Wales, including 2,000 men and 50 horse from 'Sheriff Scudamore'.[18] But most of the impressed men promptly deserted. Charles complained to Barnabas Scudamore about the quality of the Herefordshire levies and wrote peevishly on the same topic after he had left Hereford: '… very many of those raysed in several Hundreds of that County and delivered for our Life guards are already ran away'.[19] Scudamore had to make efforts both to track down the runaways and to get the constables to provide able-bodied replacements.[20] But the best and most willing men must have long been used up. The King was also desperately short of funds. However, 'before 30 June he succeeded in obtaining a considerable sum of money', some £5,000, which must have been raised in Hereford.[21] Not all Royalists had given up hope. Dr Swift, of Goodrich, was reputed to have sent to the King a waistcoat with 300 guineas sewn into its lining: 'No gift the King received was more seasonable or acceptable'. Swift was said to have mortgaged his property to raise the money.[22] On 1 July Charles left Hereford for Abergavenny and Raglan, escorted to the county boundary by Scudamore, Lingen and others. Stopping to dine at a yeoman's house near Grosmont, he knighted Henry Lingen, and borrowed some money from the householder, one Pritchard, which was never to be repaid.[23]

15

The Scottish Siege of Hereford

Barnabas Scudamore had little time to recover from the defeat at Stokesay and the royal visitation before being confronted with a new and daunting challenge. The Scottish army, Parliament's ally, a full-scale field army with a large cavalry force, hitherto occupied in the north of England, was moving south. At first it was not clear whether Worcester or Hereford was its target:

> Now the question was, Whether the Scots should set down before Worcester or Hereford. At the first they would more easily and better be provided of all Necessaries, both for the Siege, and Entertainment of the Soldiers; the King had not another Pass upon the Severn, and it brought much Trade to London: But on the other side, Hereford was nearer the King's Quarters, where they could more hinder his Recruits, and break his Forces, and thereby Worcester too would in a manner be Block'd up, the Parliaments Troops having three sides of it already; therefore it was concluded they should attempt the latter.[1]

The approach of the Scots, after Naseby and Stokesay, pushed the Herefordshire Royalists into demolishing The Mynde and the castle at Kilpeck, in case these too should become fortresses of Parliament. Stapleton Castle, on the Radnorshire border, was also slighted, by Woodhouse's Ludlow men.[2] But they did not abandon or slight Canon Frome. Sir Richard Hopton's house was a battlemented building with a fosse round it and a drawbridge. Since early in 1645 its Royalist garrison had been commanded by Colonel John Barnold, formerly at Cwm Hîr. The Scottish advance guard, some 4,500 strong, under the Earl of Callendar and General David Leslie, was pursuing a Royalist force which was retreating before them (it ultimately took refuge in Monmouth) and had no particular intention of taking Canon Frome. As they came up, Callendar summoned the garrison to surrender. Barnold returned a defiant reply, and Callendar resolved to attack the house. Earthworks had been thrown up around it, and it was reported that the ditches were nine feet deep and nine feet across, mostly filled with water.[3] The attackers had not been able to find ladders long enough to scale the defences, but, relying on weight of numbers, they scrambled up and over and forced the Royalists back to the house. Inside, the defenders 'fought desperately'[4] but were overwhelmed. Seventy of the garrison's 120 men were killed, including Barnold, who was 'deadly wounded' in the battle. The Scots' losses were 16 dead and 24 wounded. Although some accounts state that the surviving defenders were put to the sword, all the deaths appear to have been in the actual fighting. Thirty men were taken prisoner. The Parliament's committees for Gloucestershire and Worcestershire considered destroying the house, but finally resolved to take it over as a strong point. Its first Parliamentary Governor was named as Colonel Edward Harley, but he being on service with the army, a deputy, Major Henry Archbold, a Scot who had been active in Monmouthshire, was placed in charge.[6]

Presumably because of their pursuit of the Royalist party referred to above, who may have been the remnants of the garrison of Carlisle, the Scottish army did not march directly from Ledbury, where it encamped on 23 July, to Hereford, but continued south as far as Mitcheldean and Newent before swinging back northwards. The cavalry arrived first. Barnabas Scudamore had sent out a party of 20 horsemen who encountered the Scots' advance guard and retreated before them after a short skirmish. By 10 o'clock on the morning of 30 July, the main body of Scottish horse was drawn up outside the city, incautiously within cannon-shot and, wrote Scudamore, 'were welcomed with our metall'.[7] But Scudamore did not mention that he had tried, and failed, to rouse the county to arms by summoning the *posse comitatus* 'to come both with horse and Armes at ye generall meeting on Thursday next in Wigmarsh-Street by Tenn of the Clock in ye morning being the last day of this instant July'.[8] Anyone failing to appear would be considered 'a newtrall and disloyall subject'. The squires and gentlemen of Herefordshire stayed at home. Scudamore had ordered the town clocks stopped, to prevent 'their telling tales, to the advantage of the Enemy', and so his own times and even dates are suspect. By the next day the full army had arrived and the city was surrounded. The besiegers were attended by 'many hundred of women':[9] wives, concubines, camp cooks and servants, who had accompanied them from Scotland. The Earl of Leven, as commander, sent his summons to the Governor:

> SIR, Our appearance before you in this Posture is for no other End, but for the settling of Truth with Peace in England, without the least desire to shed the Blood of any Subject in it: Our by-past Actions may be a sufficient Evidence thereof. This is to Summon and require you to deliver up the City unto me, to be kept for the use of his Majesty and the Parliament of England, whereunto if you shall be so wise and happy as to condescend, you may have Conditions Honourable and Safe; but if otherwise worse Counsel shall so far prevail with you, as to contemn this Offer, I am persuaded all the World, and you also will acquit us of the manifold Inconveniences which will undoubtedly ensue upon your Refusal. Consider sadly of your own Condition, and of those now under your Charge, whose Blood will be laid upon your Account, and return Answer unto me within three Hours after the Receipt hereof. Given at the Leaguer before Hereford this last Day of July about Ten of the Clock in the Forenoon.[10]

Scudamore replied with the conventional form of defiance: 'I was set in here by the King's Command, and shall not quit it but by Special Order from His Majesty or the Prince.' Four commissioners from Gloucester had been appointed by Parliament to attend on Leven's army, and they, John Corbet, William Purefoy, Edwin Baynton and Humphrey Salway, also wrote a letter, addressed to the Mayor and Townsmen, advising speedy submission, since 'by a wilful delay or refusal you bring utter ruin and destruction not only upon yourselves, but all that are with you'. Their trumpeter was refused admission and 'threw his message over the works'. No reply came back.[11] And with that, the siege of Hereford began.

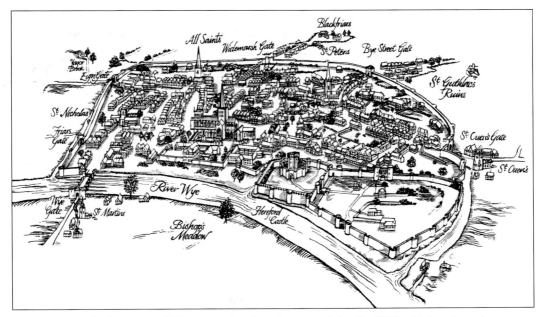

Hereford as it would have appeared at the time of the Civil War (Brian Byron)

At first (if the Governor's account is reliable) more action was initiated by the defenders than by the besiegers. But the Scots were occupied in setting up camp and throwing up their 'leaguer', a massive earthen rampart, with a ditch, some 20 feet high from base to top, along the southern bank of the Wye and at a number of other locations east and west of the walls. Dinedor and Aconbury hills were occupied and new earthworks raised over their ancient British defence-lines. Several sorties were made from the city across the Wye Bridge, one of them chasing Scottish troops all the way back to their main lines. Another destroyed the steeple of St Martin's church, which could have been a vantage point for attackers.

The spirit of the town was evidently very high, and credit for this must belong chiefly to Barnabas Scudamore who was in charge of military resistance. The threat was serious, with an army of some 10,000 outside the walls.[12] But there were hopeful signs, too. King Charles, now at Cardiff, was making efforts to cope with the difficulties of his situation, and organise his resources of men and materials so as to get a new army together and unite it with the surviving elements of his former armies. Scudamore's defence works of May proved valuable. The Scottish army was not equipped for siege warfare, and despite the modest victory at Canon Frome, its morale was not high. News of Montrose's devastatingly successful campaign against their own Covenanter Government in Scotland could not be kept from it. The Commons had passed an ordinance that the counties of Worcestershire, Herefordshire, Staffordshire and Shropshire should be taxed 'to the Payment of the Scotts Army', but promises of food and money supplies were not fulfilled[13] and the army 'never saw a farthing' of the £200 a day supposed to be levied for its upkeep.[14] This is borne out by the experience of William Pullen and Richard Woodlake, constables of Bosbury, who used their own cash to buy up cattle, bedding and provisions against warrants issued by Scots officers, but also appear to have requisitioned goods from some inhabitants who later sued

Central Hereford somewhat as it would have appeared at the time of the Civil War. Top: Butcher's Row and High Town by an unknown artist (Hereford Museum & Art Gallery) Bottom: High Town by Cornelius Varley (Hereford Library)

them in Chancery for 'what the petitioners tooke upp of them by virtue of the said warrants'. The constables had to appeal to the Committee for Indemnity, after the war, to get their money back and avoid the debt.[15] Miles Hill, variously described as a lawyer and as a mercer of Leominster, bailiff of that town in 1637,[16] who also owned property in Weobley, was appointed as commissary to help organise supplies. Writing later, he called the levy 'far above the ability of that poore County'.[17] A letter from John Corbet to Speaker Lenthall of the Commons noted that Hereford's walls were much stronger and the moat deeper than they had supposed, and '… our Souldiers meet with all discouragement that can be imagined to bee in any Army … the greatest part of the food of our Infantry is Apples, Peases and greene wheate'.[18]

Leaving Cardiff, the King 'passed as a fugitive by the Scottish camp' at Hereford on 7 July according to one account,[19] though he had an escort of 300 horse and rode via Radnor to Ludlow, keeping well to the west of Hereford,[20] then made his way north-eastwards towards Doncaster. Almost immediately, Lieutenant General David Leslie, in command of the cavalry, left the besieging force, taking eight regiments of horse, one of dragoons and 500 mounted musketeers,[21] in pursuit of the King, 'to attend his Motions'. Leslie was acting under orders, but he never returned to join Leven, instead returning to Scotland, on his own initiative (and his men's insistence), to meet and defeat Montrose at Philiphaugh on 13 September, thereby dealing a final deadly blow to Charles's chances of keeping up the struggle. Leven's army, deprived of cavalry, found it hard both to make scouting sweeps and to send out foraging parties. While the bakehouse chimneys of Hereford smoked tantalisingly, they lived for ten days without bread, on 'beans, green corn and fruit'.[22] It is surprising, not that the Scots went looking for what they could find, but that they were not more rapacious and violent. As it is, 'no instance of cruelty or personal violence is recorded against them',[23] though in some cases isolated Scots soldiers were attacked and killed[24] by local people. Nevertheless, their demands and snatchings were deeply resented by a population that objected to them in every way. Particularly short of horses with their cavalry gone, the Scots seized every horse they could find, and a rough hide-and-seek was played out in many a farmyard.

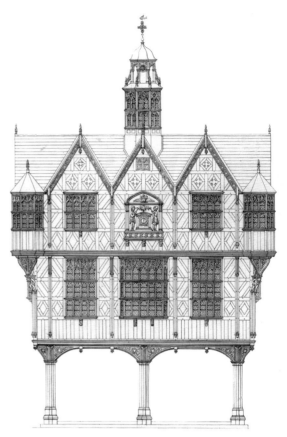

Hereford's guildhall
as it would have looked in 1645

Leven had ample troops for his purpose but his main tactical problem was a lack of heavy artillery and siege equipment. From Gloucester he received three 18-pounder field guns, and 150 cannon-balls, and had to have a further supply of balls cast by 'the Iron Mills' which took a long time.[25] Hereford's moat, described in 1643 as 'in most places of greater breadth than any ordinary Graffe, full of liquid Mudd, and a continuall running water'[26] never seems to have offered much of an obstacle to those who sought to cross it, but the Scots drained it. Fifty miners were brought in by the besiegers to undermine the walls, but inside the city too were 'skilfull Miners'.[27] On 11 August, it was found that the Scots were digging under 'Frein Gate' (probably Friars' Gate) and a counter-mine was dug. When the same thing was tried on the eastern side of the city, a sortie broke it open and burned its wooden supports. Another mine being dug from St Owen's church was also foiled by the digging of a counter-mine to smoke the attackers out: 'what our fire could not perfect, though it burnt farre, and suffocated some of their Miners, our water did, breaking in upon them and drowning that which the fire had not consumed'.[28] This mine was discovered in 1858.[29] Leven recorded that, 'when the Mines were brought to perfection, they were drowned by reason of eight days continual Rain, the Town being low in Situation'[30] while Scudamore's account does not mention rain at all, but claims that the besiegers' mines were either fired or flooded by the defenders. The Scots concentrated their attention on the eastern walls and a local tradition recorded the existence of 'a wide entrance leading to a subterranean passage called Scots' Hole',[31] though when Alfred Watkins investigated it he concluded that this, and other hints of tunnelling under Eign Hill, were caused naturally.[32] Above ground, cannon-fire from both sides caused destruction and loss of life. The churches outside the walls, St Martin's and St Owen's, were reduced to ruin. During the 19th century, cannon balls weighing from 1lb to 15lb were found in the city.[33] Archaeological work in 2010 found numerous burials in the cathedral precinct from this time with head wounds, due perhaps to flying fragments as cannon balls struck brick- and stonework. An early form of shrapnel bomb was found,[34] packed with round shot which would spray in all directions when the ball crashed against a solid object. In a siege, civilians were on the front line.

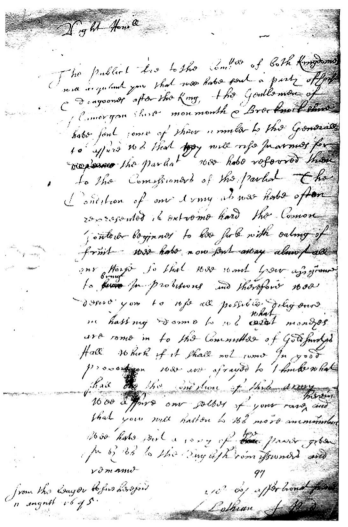

A letter written by Lord Leven 'from the leaguer before Hereford' on 11 August (© Frank Bennett)

In an effort by the attackers to keep up the propaganda battle as well as the actual siege, a further letter was sent in to the Mayor, aldermen, and citizens, on 14 August. It was a direct appeal from some of Hereford's Parliamentarians, with Edward Harley and Thomas Seaborne of 'The Lloyds', Francis Pember, John Herring of Holmer, John Styall and Eusbare Hardwick as the signatories.[35] In anticipation of victory, a Committee for Herefordshire had been set up at Gloucester, its members including Edward Harley, James Kyrle, Henry Jones (a lawyer of the Inner Temple, son of John Jones of Putley), with John Herring, Miles Hill of Weobley, and Thomas Seaborne to be treasurers.[36] Writing as friends and fellow-citizens, 'who have, and must live amongst you', they emphasise the heavy burden which the besieging army placed

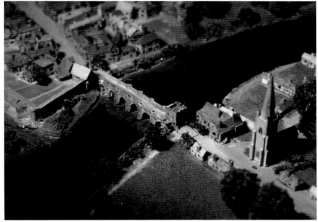

Top: The Wye Bridge and St Martin's church as they are believed to have appeared at the time of the Civil War (from a model in the Old House Museum, Hereford City Museums & Art Gallery)
Lower: The Wye Bridge showing the arch that the defenders destroyed as rebuilt

on the countryside, and insist that surrender is the only remedy: 'in so doing, you shall preserve your Lives and Goods from the rage of the devouring Sword, your Country from approaching Famine …'. Two days before, however, Leven had warned the House of Lords that he had many soldiers sick through eating unripe fruit, that he lacked horses to gather provisions, and that if money was not sent, 'we are affrayd to thinke what shall be the condition of this army'.[37] Rejection of the letter provoked a heightening of the attack. Although the Scots' cannons damaged the walls, the defenders proved able to quickly repair them. The Scots now concentrated their efforts on the Wye Bridge Gate, the weakest of the city gates, and succeeded in smashing it, but the defenders blocked it again with woolsacks and timber. Finally, they demolished the last arch of the bridge, building up 'a very strong worke' behind it.[38] But the besiegers then built a wooden bridge across the river, which remained in place for some time after the siege, until the stone bridge was repaired.[39]

These five weeks of siege were probably the most alarming time any inhabitants of Hereford have ever lived through, in their own city. Indeed, the experience can be compared to the 'Blitz' on London and other cities in 1941, though without the devastating power of high explosives. Survival was far from certain. Cannon balls could strike anywhere. Constant bombardment could be demoralising, and capture of the city would certainly result in wholesale looting and destruction. Apart from the very real likelihood of a catastrophic fire, or the walls being stormed, Scudamore had to guard against the possibility of betrayal from within. A woman, apparently a widow with a young son, was hanged for passing information about a planned sally from the city to the besiegers.[40] Life for known or suspected Parliamentary supporters must have been anything but easy. Their allies were attacking the city; yet if the siege succeeded, they would join the rulers, and perhaps help to temper the rage of the victors.

Some people might well have argued that surrender was the safest option. But the evidence suggests strongly that the whole city came together in resistance, townspeople joining with the garrison troops in repairing damage, hustling up new defences, and issuing in sallies from the gates when there was a chance of attacking isolated groups of besiegers, or siege works. Women and children helped to fill up the gaps and repair damage, and the Governor reported that 'even the Women (such was their gallantry) ventured where the musquet bullets did so'.[41]

Another effort to end the siege was made around 14 August, when three of the county gentlemen, Herbert Westfaling, Roger Hereford, and James Newton, all Parliamentarians, but not prominent activists, and perhaps chosen for that reason, put forward a proposal for handing over the city. Scudamore, however, considered it 'frivolous and impertinent' (i.e. irrelevant) and its authors, who had been admitted into the city under safe conduct, were dismissed 'not without some disrelish and disrespect'. Their safe-conduct had been requested by Dr Rowland Scudamore, vicar of Fownhope, a son of William Scudamore of Ballingham. When he again approached the walls, apparently desiring to speak with a 'lady named Skinner' from the city, he was shot dead, both sides denying responsibility for the deed.[42]

Scudamore describes a 'notable Sally' made on 17 August, at St Owen's church, to destroy siege-works being prepared. Not only men but 'little boyes' were involved, the boys carrying firebrands and faggots in order to set fire to the wooden structures and competing to see who could be first. Boys were employed again in the same area to set fire to the scaling platforms being assembled. This was a highly dangerous game and musketeers were placed on the wall to cover their retreat once the fires were lit. The defenders thought up and carried out constant ways of disturbing and disconcerting their besiegers. Fire-balls were aimed from the city at their camp-lines. Lights on the steeple at night suggested an imminent sortie. Old horses, even dogs and cats it would seem, were turned out of the city with blazing strips of match tied to them in order to distract the enemy. One morning, Scudamore organised a fox-hunt around the walls.[43] All these actions were meant to show the besiegers that the city was in good heart. Nothing in any record suggests that Hereford in those weeks was running short of food, and it seems that Scudamore had made good provision in this respect as well. Food prices are not recorded, but in Worcester and Shrewsbury, in similar circumstances a few months later, they rose steeply. When Scottish bombardment put the powder mill out of action, the master carpenter John Abel supervised the construction of a new one,[44] and did the same when the corn mill was destroyed. Since Hereford's long-established mills, Castle Mill and Dog Mill, were both outside the walls, on the stream east of the castle, they cannot have been usable by the defenders. Details of mills set up within the walls do not survive; presumably they were worked by horse-power. Scudamore was also proud of his sharpshooters. Two senior officers of the Scots were killed: a lieutenant-colonel of engineers by a cannon-ball, and a senior staff officer, Major-General Lawrence Crawford, by a musket-ball.[45] One writer suggests that lead from the chapter house roof may have been used to make bullets, and another that cathedral brasses were melted down for the same purpose,[46] though there is no direct evidence of this, and Scudamore makes no mention of it, or of any shortage of ammunition.

The most critical time came in the last days of August. On the 29th, Leven had made a final offer to allow honourable surrender (Scudamore notes that he was 'a mercifull Generall'), but it was rejected like the previous ones. Now from the look-out points of the city, intense activity could be seen, with scaling platforms, ladders and hurdles being got ready for an attack, and a heavy cannonade was mounted against Bye Street Gate and 'the halfe moon next St Owen's Gate'[47] in preparation for a full-scale storming of the city. Hasty efforts were made to reinforce the defences at these points. But the threatened assault did not materialise. Leven had already issued orders to his regiments to make ready for storming the walls on the morning of the 2nd, when messages arrived from Evesham and Gloucester with information that the King's Horse, around 3,000 strong, with Charles himself, were heading towards Worcester from Broadway and Moreton in Marsh. At the same time, a letter arrived for Leven from David Leslie, 'shewing he was gone to Scotland with the whole Party of Horse and Dragoons under his Command'.[48] No general in the 17th century would have risked a full battle without adequate cavalry support if he could possibly avoid it; and Leven was a prudent commander. Deciding that it would not be possible to capture the city before the arrival of the Royalist forces, he decided to put the safety of his army before the hazard of being caught between two fires. The assent of his committee-men was given reluctantly, and Purefoy claimed that, '... we urged them to storm before the King could arrive there ... The General said it was too dangerous to be attempted'.[49] Braced to repel a major onslaught, the defenders saw the Scottish regiments moving away. Promptly Scudamore sent parties of horse to harry the rearguard, and others down the river in boats, but Leven claimed to have driven them off without loss.[50]

Hereford's travail was at an end, and the threat of plunder, fire, slaughter and rape had vanished like a Scotch mist. Celebration and self-congratulation were in order. Songs were made, and a derisive ballad recalled that Scots were often seen as chapmen or pedlars:

> Did you not see the Scotchman's wallet
> Lately hanging on Beare's Court;
> The Countrye's treasure pleased their pallet,
> Their complayning was their sport?
> Did you not see old Leshlye stout
> With all his Scottish ragged rout?
> Then drinke your drinke and fill your vaine,
> The Scotch shall nere come here againe.[51]

The raising of the siege of Hereford was a boost for the Royalist cause, now in desperate straits – indeed, it was the last episode that could be considered a real victory – but it did not change the overall situation. After the Scots had gone, the Parliamentarian Sir Robert Honeywood wrote to his colleague Sir Henry Vane, commenting adversely on the 'slow proceedings before Hereford'.[52] While the Scottish army was in England as an ally of Parliament, there was undoubtedly a reluctance on the part of its senior officers to confront the King directly, not only through respect for his person, or perhaps fear that he would be killed and they would be held responsible, but also because some of them were keen to discuss a deal with him. An intriguing sidelight on this is found in information given by William Barry, a Royalist, of Tregiett in Llanrothal parish, to Major Edward Smith in Chepstow on 16 May 1646. Barry stated that in August 1645, when the Scottish army was at Mitcheldean, 'about 1,000 horse came on the Saturday before the siege of Hereford to his house & carried him away prisoner'. He was brought before the Earl of Callendar, at Ross, then taken to Lord General Leven at Dean, where he was questioned concerning the King's strength. He then 'unwillingly' undertook to carry a message from another staff officer, Lord Montgomery, to Sir William Fleming (Callendar's nephew) at the King's court at Raglan. When he had done this, and been questioned about it by Charles himself, Fleming went with him to Caerleon, where they met Montgomery, Lord Sinclair and Lord Leveston (*sic*, probably Lothian). After an all-night discussion, the Scots lords departed to join the siege of Hereford, but further meetings were had at Monmouth, Didley in St Devereux, and Henllan.[53] The prospect of an accommodation with Charles had been under discussion among some of the Scottish lords for some time, though Leven had forbidden Callendar to make contact with Fleming.[54] Already, deep in the Herefordshire woodlands, machinations were beginning for the 'Engagement' between the King and the Scots, which would be disastrous to both.

Miles Hill, not a very effective commissary to the Scottish army, published a self-exculpatory pamphlet in London in 1650,[55] explaining that 'I myself was a great Proselite of them till I had experienced their oppressions, self-seekings and cruelty at the siege' – by 1650 of course the Scots had become the enemies of England's Parliament. Hill claimed that 'an orderly course was taken for their subsistance' but it is evident from Leven's and Corbet's reports that they were seriously short of provisions. Using figures he had gathered in September 1646, Hill set out the extent of the Scots' plunderings, having obtained figures from 106 parishes; another 70 did not report, 'by reason of some disaffected to the business, being Scotified persons', though it is difficult to imagine that there were many such in Herefordshire. His pamphlet tells of houses rifled, horses and cattle taken, along with clothes, rings, books, money, and 'other rich commodities'. Linen and plate were taken from churches. Hill's record shows Mordiford as having lost £490-worth of goods, Holmer 531 7s 4d, Hampton Bishop £511 18s 4d, Withington £485 13s 8d, and Huntington £140 9s 3d, but the raiders went as far as Ross-on-Wye (£1,189 18s). Hill's estimated total was £61,743 5s 2d. The extent of physical damage caused to Hereford by the siege is hard to assess. Some structures in the city appear to have disappeared in the mid-17th century, including the old market hall and St Peter's Cross,[56] but this may well have happened after the siege.

16

The Last Hurrah

King Charles returned to Herefordshire on Wednesday 3 September. He slept that night at Mrs Baynham's house in Bromyard, and entered Hereford next day. In the glow of the city's relief, the King's visit was a far happier occasion than his tetchy stay after Naseby. The breath of his coming had driven off the enemy, and the bells rang out,[1] with ringers at All Saints paid 6s 8d to ring for victory, and people thronged out to meet him. Honours were bestowed. Barnabas Scudamore and his deputy, Nicholas Throckmorton, were knighted. To commemorate its heroic stand the city was awarded an augmented grant of arms: 'About the ancient arms of that City being Gules, three Lyons passant gardant argent, on a border Azure ten Saltires Scottish Crosses argent, supported by two Lyons rampant gardant argent, each collared Azure, and on each Collar three Buckles Or, in reference to the rebellious Scottish general, Leslie, Earl of Leven, and for the Crest, on a Helm or Torse of the Collars, mantled Gules doubled argent, a Lyon passant gardant argent, holding in the right paw

a sword erected, proper hilted and pommeled Or',[2] and was given a new motto: *Invictae Fidelitatis Praemium,* 'the reward of unconquered loyalty'. The heraldic embellishment was a reminder that the King, among the unique qualities of his position, was the fount of honour: the drab functionaries of Parliament could not make a knight, or authorise a coat of arms (later, Cromwell, when Lord Protector, gave knighthoods and baronetcies and life peerages). The fact that Charles had been trading titles for cash for almost two decades was no doubt forgotten in the emotional warmth of the moment. John Abel was designated 'one of His Majesty's Carpenters' for his services.[3]

It was in Hereford that Charles I received 'the last loyal acclamations he was ever destined to hear'.[4] Special

The city's arms granted by Charles I

111

The building now known as The Throne, then the Unicorn tavern, in Weobley, where Charles stayed

prayers for the city's deliverance were made on the following Sunday. One effect of the Civil War was that far more of the inhabitants of provincial England saw their King close-up than ever before: not a remote, inaccessible and hieratic figure but a real man, not very tall, and despite his regal manner and ability to speak persuasively, lacking the common touch that might have endeared him to the people (Charles I was notoriously unwilling to touch against the 'King's Evil'). How far this affected his cause is impossible to measure, but certainly his two short stays in Hereford, at a time when he desperately needed to recruit more troops, failed to mobilise popular support, though by then many sympathisers may have thought it a lost cause.

Charles's situation was deeply uncertain, and there is a sense of restless ranging about his movements. On the 5th he went to Leominster and Weobley, staying the night there at the 'Unicorn' tavern. He wrote to Barnabas Scudamore on that day giving him full authority to seize upon the persons and estates of those who had joined with or had given assistance to the Scots.[5] Next day he was back in Hereford, at the Bishop's Palace, then left for Raglan, where he received the shocking news that Prince Rupert had surrendered Bristol to General Thomas Fairfax on the 10th. On the 11th 'His business was to committ five cheife Hinderers from relieving Hereford';[6] the trial was held at Abergavenny and the accused were Welsh notables who had resisted Astley's attempts to form a force to relieve Hereford. On the 12th he was back in Hereford, with Prince Maurice; at this time around

Arthur's Stone, above Dorstone

200 enemy horse were said to be in the neighbourhood of Leominster. A dismayed and angry letter to Prince Rupert is dated from Hereford, 14 September. On the 15th he and his escorts set off towards Bromyard, but 'Gerrard's horse had not orders soone enough to appear at the rendeszvous',[7] and without this support, they turned back to Hereford, where the King sat again in the Bishop's Palace, writing letters. Once again they set off, on the 17th, heading west, then turning northwards into the Golden Valley, pausing to dine and meet supporters at the neolithic tomb site of Arthur's Stone, near Dorstone, then reversing direction again, to spend the night at Lady Scudamore's at Holme Lacy – news of this hospitality would not have made the Viscount's situation in London any more comfortable. These abrupt changes of direction were prompted by the presence of Parliamentary forces under Major General Poyntz and Colonel Rossiter who had been following Charles since he left Oxford, and appear to have based themselves at Leominster and Weobley. Next day, intending to continue eastwards, the King's party had only gone five miles to Stoke Edith when they were informed that the Parliamentarians were coming from Leominster with an intercepting force, and they turned back yet again, 'towards Hariford, so to Lempster, then to Webley, thence to Prestene,'[8] successfully dodging the pursuit, on a wearisome march from 6 a.m. to midnight, and from there continued north to reach Chester on the 23rd. The King would not be seen in Hereford again. Almost 20 years later, after the Restoration, his visit was still being invoked by petitioners. Jane Merrick, 'who when the Scots besieged the city was wounded by a cannon shot in the leg as she was doing service for the city in making up a breach in Wigmore Street', claimed that 'his late majesty, of ever blessed memory, promised she should be taken care of'. She got £1.[9]

The writer of 'Certain Observations' turns a jaundiced Puritan eye at Hereford during its last year as a royal stronghold. The Mayor, William Cater, is castigated as corrupt and a keeper of alehouses 'in all his tenements'.[10] The town clerk, James Lawrence, was a disorderly figure: a city captain who sat in council of war instead of remaining independent as clerk of the justices; in fact he was said to have killed another man, Richard Rodd, with his sword and escaped prosecution. Others named as pernicious 'against any godly person' were James Booth the marshal (the Booths of Breinton, just west of the city, were a Catholic family)[11] and William Marten the hangman. Many Catholics came in to the city, and Roman Catholic services were openly held in two places. 'Tippling houses' were many, and brewing flourished. With some 1,500 soldiers and their officers quartered in a small city, a degree of disorderly behaviour could be expected, and among the officers were some at least who justified their opponents' by name of 'roisterers'. The heroism and endurance of July and August, and the triumph and relief felt after the siege, seem to have quickly decayed into a rather seedy complacency. *Mercurius Civicus* also refers to 'roysterers from Hereford' at this time who burned down Eardisley Castle, home of the Royalist Sir Humphrey Baskerville. But this was done as a precaution against enemy occupation, and other houses in the west of the county were also made uninhabitable for the same reason.[12] It seemed a characteristic of Cavalier-held towns that a gamey, somewhat dissolute element would dominate social life.[13] Heavy drinking, card-play, crude humour, sexual licence, violence and duelling marked their behaviour, as the perhaps inevitable antithesis of the more strait-laced sort of Puritanism. Extreme behaviour could be shown by both sides, but Cavalier ease and jollity carried with it Cavalier carelessness, something that infected all ranks, not just the gentry. Although Scudamore, perhaps because of his local connections, had been backed by the council, his relations were deteriorating both with the city authorities and the officers, not all of whom might have acknowledged his command.

For anyone who looked beyond Hereford, the prospect was threatening. On 10 October Parliamentary forces took Chepstow, and on the 24th Monmouth changed hands yet again to come under Roundhead control. The Royalist troops in both places were allowed to leave with their horses and arms, and they fell back on Hereford. The disreputable Sir Thomas Lunsford, among the most notorious of Cavalier 'swordsmen', who had been Governor of Monmouth, had a falling-out with Sir Nicholas Throckmorton, Deputy Governor of Hereford, who accused him of basely yielding his trust. It almost ended in a duel until the exasperated Scudamore had them both locked up for a few days.[14]

If the King's military position had looked bad in the summer, it was even worse as a cold and snowy winter was setting in. Shortage of military supplies at the Oxford headquarters prompted a letter to Barnabas Scudamore instructing him to send as much brimstone and saltpetre as he could spare to Worcester, for passing on to Oxford where it would be made into gunpowder.[15] Under Rowland Laugharne Parliament was making great gains through south Wales, and Herefordshire, Worcestershire and south Shropshire were becoming an isolated patch of Royalist territory. Chester was again under Parliamentary siege, and a relieving force raised from the Hereford and other garrisons, with a few pressed men from Herefordshire and Radnor,[16] was sent north under Sir William Vaughan, the King's General of Horse for Shropshire, Staffordshire, Worcestershire and Herefordshire. Scudamore made a belated effort to recall the Hereford contingent,[17] but they were routed at Denbigh on 1 November. Many of the horsemen fled back to Leominster, but north Herefordshire was no longer sure ground, with Parliamentary troops raiding freely into it from the garrisons of Stokesay, Montgomery and New Radnor. The fugitive cavalry gathered in the area round Dilwyn and Pembridge, where on 23 November there was a fight between a Parliamentary raiding party and two Royalist regiments, or their remnants.[18] From Ludlow, Vaughan, 'the Devil of Shrawardine',[19] struggling to assemble another force, was demanding men from the Hereford garrison. The volatile, jaundiced mood of Hereford's citizens and their defenders cannot have been eased by knowing that only some miraculous turn of events could change the King's fortunes. Men like Sir Thomas Lunsford would not have installed themselves in Hereford if there were a more entertaining place of safety. But there wasn't.

Nevertheless, the Governor of Hereford was determined to strike his own blow for the King, by the recapture of Canon Frome. The decision may also have been prompted by the need to get food and fodder from the district controlled by that garrison. Scudamore had just been reprimanded by the King for allowing his under-sheriff to seize cattle, oxen and sheep from a farmer, Henry Hyet of Burton, despite Hyet having a certificate to show he had compounded with the Royalists.[20] Bolstered by soldiers from Ludlow as well as his own men, Scudamore called on Canon Frome to surrender on 9 October, but withdrew on Major Archbold's refusal. But the mill and the hay reserves were lost to the Royalists, and the Parliamentarians expected or were warned of further action. On 3 November, from the Parliamentary army in Somerset, Edward Harley wrote to Archbold, '… you must soe fortify the place that it may be tenable against a considerable enemy'.[21] John Abel's skill as an engineer in wood has traditionally been ascribed to the siege engine which Scudamore now commissioned, a wheeled tower hauled by oxen, with bullet-proof walls, internal ladders, shooting positions and boarding platforms, high enough to overtop the breastworks round the old house. Though no doubt the builders incorporated many useful touches, it was in effect a medieval engine of war.

A completely clear account of this foray is lacking. They set off on 5 November and trundled the 'sow' to a location close to Canon Frome. Archbold, meantime, had sent a call to Colonel Morgan in Gloucester for assistance, and 500 horse and 200 foot from Gloucester city, with 300 foot from Corse Lawn, were on the move towards Ledbury and Canon Frome.[22] Scudamore in turn called for additional troops from Malvern and took his combined force from Ledbury to meet the Roundheads, leaving two or three troops of horse to guard the 'sow'. But this guarding party was surprised by a Parliamentary scouting group, 'a quartermaster of Canon Frome, with around 12 horse'. According to a Parliamentary source, the Royalists were chased out of Ledbury[23] and fled, abandoning the huge contraption to the enemy. That seems to have ended the attempt, with the various troops dispersing to their bases, but the congregation of colonels in Hereford were maybe not over-sympathetic to the Governor's discomfiture. A Parliamentary news-sheet noted a foray from Monmouth which may have hoped to catch Hereford off-guard at this time: 'Lt-Col. Kirle did very lately march from Monmouth, within two miles of Hereford, took eight prisoners and ten horse, routed a party of 50 or three-score, and lost not one man; had not the Club-men held together, we should have heard of more action out of these parts by this time …'.[24] There is a hint here that perhaps local communities were again banding for their own protection. Certainly in Worcestershire another clubman-type rising was going on at this time.

A further skirmish took place at Ledbury on 12 November, when Richard Hopton with a troop of 15 chased away some 60 Hereford horsemen, and then retrieved 100 cattle which another Royalist party, 30 strong, had seized from their drovers.[25] Herefordshire was being raided from west and south, with Parliamentary forces now also established at Presteigne, but the Royalists struck back with a night attack on Abergavenny, where Morgan had set up a garrison under Hopton. Another displaced Royalist force, 'Lord Gerrard's troop of reformadoes' from south Wales, was quartered at Pembridge, and with another regiment, Colonel Gradye's, 'at three o'clock in the morning were beate up, one or two killed, most lost their horses and armes'.[26] With winter setting in hard and fast, both sides were relentless in demands for contributions. Scouts, spies and informers fed information on the other side's intentions and whereabouts back to the garrison commanders. Life for the inhabitants was hard and dangerous, with armed parties which might belong to either side suddenly appearing, suspicious and trigger-happy, seeking one another out or enforcing demands for supplies. Herefordshire's heaths and downlands had become bandit country. Webb records 'scenes of plunder' at market days in Ross.[27] Canon Frome controlled a wide sweep of countryside as far as Malvern, where a patrolling troop captured a party of Royalist horsemen in early December, and sent them as prisoners to Gloucester. It soon transpired that they had been under armistice from the Houses of Parliament, as officers of Prince Rupert, whose commission had been withdrawn after surrendering Bristol and who was no longer a combatant. At yet another fight in Ledbury around this time a Royalist troop was scattered.[28]

17

'A New Tricke to Take Townes'

While these raids, depredations and skirmishes were harassing the local population, a new plot was being hatched. On 10 November, 1645, Colonel John Birch, a Parliamentary officer who had distinguished himself for cool courage in the second Newbury battle and several other hard fights, apparently dissatisfied with the role of Governor of Bath,[1] applied for a more active post, or for permission to retire from the army. He was aged only 30 – one of many young men whose careers had been accelerated by warfare; Barnabas Scudamore and Henry Lingen were in their early 30s, while Colonel Edward Harley was 21 and his brother Robert was a major at 19. The Committee for Both Kingdoms commissioned Birch on 5 December to take 1,000 foot and a troop of horse from Bath and Bristol and march to Herefordshire, there to join with Colonel Morgan, Governor of Gloucester, short in stature but fiery in temperament, 'to endeavour to distresse the cittie of Hereford, and vse all meanes to take it in'. The committee's attention had been drawn to Hereford by a disgruntled and disaffected Royalist, Sir John Bridges, whose family home was Wilton Castle, just across the River Wye from the town of Ross. Bridges had commanded a regiment on the King's behalf in Ireland, and, back in Herefordshire to raise recruits,[2] had fallen out with its Royalist leaders. Sir John's father, Sir Giles Bridges, was related by marriage to the Scudamores and was godfather to Viscount Scudamore's son James,[3] but this did not prevent a bitter dispute when the Royalists wanted to make Wilton Castle uninhabitable to prevent its possible use as a Parliamentary garrison. Despite Bridges' opposition, the castle was burned down by Lingen's and Scudamore's men. A later writer claimed that it was done 'through spleen and malice',[4] but Wilton, on a strategic river crossing, had already seen military action; and Barnabas Scudamore also refers to Bridges as 'angry with me for not having something that he desired, which yet I could not give him'.[5] Scudamore claimed that Bridges had then removed to Gloucester, from where he came back into Herefordshire occasionally in disguise, 'the better to lay his designe',[6] and had finally gone to London to propose ways in which Hereford might be taken. Bridges was in touch with two officers of the Hereford garrison, Captain Daniel Alderne and Major Epiphan Howorth, who also considered themselves to have been victims of the Governor's high-handedness. Both were members of well-known families in the city and county. Alderne's father, Thomas, had been the reluctant Sheriff in 1640, and Dr Edward Alderne was a prominent Royalist sympathiser. The Howorths were established at Whitehouse, in Vowchurch parish, where the major's grandfather, also named Epiphan, lived. Rowland Howorth, the major's father, married to Jane Smallman of Kinnersley, was recorded as being of 'Wigmarsh More' (Widemarsh Moor). Familiar with the garrison's dispositions and habits, the two officers suggested that it might be much easier to take the town by surprise rather than by a formal siege like Leven's.

Evidently thinking it was worth a try, the Committee for Both Kingdoms empowered Bridges on 11 November 'to treat with such persons as he should think fit for that purpose, and to promise a sum of money, not exceeding three thousand pounds'.[7] The action-hungry Birch was named to lead the operation. Granted a week's pay for his men and promised a month's more if he should be successful, Birch returned to Bath to prepare his regiment for departure. With marching made easier by hard frosts, he reached Gloucester, where he conferred with Colonel Morgan, Sir John Bridges and Mr Hodges, MP for Gloucester. Leaving his men quartered at Gloucester, Birch with Bridges made his way to Ledbury and then to a house nearby called 'Sissels'[8] where he met Howorth and Alderne, who had moved out of Hereford to Nunnington, two miles east of the city.

Birch himself, through the *Military Memoir*, an unusual vicarious autobiography written by his secretary, Roe, in the form of a lengthy memorandum addressed to him, has left an account of the capture of Hereford, and another is given in a pamphlet quickly issued in London in December 1645, *A New Tricke to Take Townes, or the just and perfect relation of the sudden surprisall of Hereford taken December 18. 1645*. This pamphlet[9] claims to have been written by one who was 'an instrument in the design', and as it assigns a principal role to Alderne, was probably written by him or from his information. Scudamore also produced his own report, having read the pamphlet and some of Birch's printed letters. From these various documents, it is possible to put together an accurate account of events. Roe plays down the roles of Morgan and Bridges, but there can be little doubt that though Alderne and Bridges were responsible for the broad idea, Birch devised the strategy and organised its successful execution. Morgan, however, was in overall command of the force, which included a regiment of horse from Worcestershire as well as Birch's regiment and some of his own Gloucester men.[10]

From the turncoat officers' information, Birch knew that though the garrison comprised around 1,500 men, there were often no more than ten soldiers on night guard, and 'the officers in the towne vsually dranke and gamed all night, and lay in bedd the forepart of the next day'.[11] No guards were posted at Lugg Bridge on the eastern approach. Alderne and Howorth had a collaborator still in the city, 'a Reformado officer' (Reformados were officers whose companies had been disbanded or destroyed, and who attached themselves to other commands) who would hinder any attempt to pull up the drawbridge once the attack was under way. Within musket shot of Byster's Gate stood the ruined walls of St Guthlac's Priory, where 500 men might lie close. It is surprising that they had survived the demolitions of May that year, but they were presumably thought to be far enough from the city walls not to be a danger. Two hundred yards further back, on Aylestone Hill, another 1,000 men might be drawn up.

The hard frost was still persisting, freezing up the river and moat, so that the Governor had sent out warrants to the constables requiring men to be sent each morning to break up the ice. Birch's first plan was to take six carts, four apparently loaded with wood and two with straw, but actually each concealing six men who would leap out to attack the guards as soon as the carts were inside the gate. The party from the Priory would race up to support them. But heavy snow began to fall, quickly making the roads impassable for carts, and he came up with a second, more subtle scheme. As soon as the drawbridge was let down in the morning, seven men, one acting the part of a constable, with six carrying spades and pick-axes, were to approach the gate, pretending to be one of the teams coming as ice-breakers. Birch went to the garrison at Canon Frome to select likely men, and chose as their leader one Berrow, perfect for the role, 'whose face and bodie promised, when fitly clad, to bee noe other than a constable; and vpon conference with him found his resolution answere-able and yet his understanding not so pearceing as to afright him with the enterprise'.[12] Returning to Gloucester, Birch assembled his force, and with Colonel Morgan advanced as far as Ledbury, arriving on Monday 15 December. Scudamore was informed of their pres-ence early on the next morning, and arranged for scouts to watch their movements. Birch now embarked on an elaborate deception. Knowing that secrecy was vital, he kept Alderne and Howorth under 'honerable arrest', just in case they might be acting as double agents.[13] No doubt Major Backhouse's trickery at Gloucester had not been forgotten. Bringing his men on a trudge through the snow to within four miles of Hereford on the Tuesday night, in freezing cold (three died from exposure), he informed his officers that his orders had been to march to Chester, to support Sir William Brereton, the Parliamentary general who was besieging that city. However, in these conditions it was impossible to march north, and so he proposed a return to Gloucester and Bath. This was well received by the cold-nipped officers and their men, and the news was soon spread around the locality that the Parliamentarians were about to withdraw: 'the Governor of Hereford not wanting friends in the country presently was advised of the whole business'.[14] But Scudamore neverthe-less sent out scouts to check the accuracy of the rumours, who duly reported that the enemy were making their way back towards Ledbury. In that town Birch made a point of staying in the house of a leading Royalist, perhaps Skipp, and of telling him and others they would be gone the next day. On the Wednesday night, he put his plan into action. Making the drummers beat the alarm, he told his officers he had received news that Scudamore was advancing from Hereford with his troops: should they stay and fight at Ledbury, or advance to take them by surprise? It was immediately agreed that they should advance, 'the snowe and moone both giving light enough'.[15] Expecting to confront the Royalists at any moment, the troops marched towards Hereford, 'speedily, but soe silently that a dog scarce barked all the night, though wee marched through three or 4 villages; but in deed that was not strange, for if a dog had been without doores that night he would have been starved to death'.[16] The Alderne pamphlet says that they marched by way of Canon Frome,[17] while Roe, more convincingly, has Birch make a detour there to get his 'constable' and team on the move, before rejoining his force, by now very near Hereford and wondering just what was going on. Only now did Birch take his officers into his confidence. His main force was placed in a 'large dingle' on the slope of Aylestone Hill, facing south towards the city, and 150 men with firelocks were set in the priory ruins, along with the disguised labourers. Horsemen were stationed to secure the bridges at Lugg Bridge, Lugwardine and Mordiford against Royalist informants who might have followed the march from Ledbury.[18]

Birch, either through instinct or from awareness of how many plots went wrong through loose talk, had kept up an obsessive secrecy which paid off. Though Governor Scudamore anticipated an attack, he expected it to be of the conventional kind, and this prompted his urgent letter of 14 December to a High Constable: 'These are straightly to charge and command you to send to my Garrison at Hereford out of your hundred, a hundred able men with spades, Shovells, Pickaxes and other necessaries fit for Pioneers, for his Majesties Service, whereof you are not to fail, as you will answer the contrary, at your utmost peril.'[19] He also drew in all the horse troops that had been quartered in the country around. This provoked a near-riot by the townsfolk, who had to provide free quarter: 'the townesmen and souldiers going together by the ears'.[20] Scudamore had arranged to bring the obstreperous citizens before a military court first thing on Thursday morning. Meanwhile he took other precautions, ordering the night guard to be doubled on Wednesday, arranging for horse patrols to be made outside the walls at night, and for snow to be shovelled off the walls so that men could 'stand with their Armes upon the first Alarum'. At 1 o'clock in the morning, the Governor, accompanied by Lieutenant Ballard, made the 'grand round' to inspect the guard. What he found was disconcerting. Town-Major Chaplaine had failed to double the guard numbers, Captain Traherne was not at his post, and at the Bye Street Gate, he found 'the Corporal so drunke he could not give me the word'. Scudamore beat the man with his cane, and ordered Ballard to find an officer to take command at the gate and to 'lay the Corporall by the heeles'.[21]. At 5 a.m., leaving Ballard in charge, with instructions to maintain strict watch on the sentries, Scudamore went to snatch a few hours of sleep.

By then, the assault force was assembled on Aylestone Hill, 'hope keeping them warme'.[22] In the late dawn of 18 December, they heard the morning-prayer bell ring out, breaking the frost-bound silence, then the drum-beats of reveille in the city. Someone inadvertently fired his musket, 'which possessed us with a great fear that our projects were frustrated',[23] but it passed unnoticed. At about 8 o'clock, the drawbridge was let down, and fifteen minutes later, on Birch's signal, the surprise party walked up to the gate. While the pretend-constable was showing his warrant to the officer in charge, the musketeers from the priory began to run forward: 'Wherevpon the guard began to crye "Arme." The constable with his bill knocks downe one: the rest with their spades and pickaxes fell vpon others'.[24] Almost immediately the musketeers were pouring through the gateway, and the main force was hurrying down from Aylestone Hill. With most of the garrison in their beds, the struggle was brief: '… after half an howers dispute in the street, and the loss of about tenn of your [Birch's] men, that great and strong garison, which soe long held out a great army, was taken'.[25]

Sir Barnabas Scudamore was awakened by a servant with the news that an enemy force was in the city. 'I leapt up, commanded him to get me a horse, and slipping on my cloathes, I ran … instantly downe with my Sword and Pistoll in my hand, to the foregate towards the street, where the Enemies horse already come fired upon me, and shot my Secretary into the belly.'[26] Retreating into the house, Scudamore came out by a back way towards the Wye,

> in hopes still of my horse. Vpon the left hand, towards the Castle, I was shewed the Enemy gallopping towards me; vpon the right hand, going to the Bishops Pallace, I found a body of their foot coming into the Pallace yard: and seeing myself thus beset,

The Bye Street Gate in the 18th century (Hereford Library)

my boy shewing mee that a couple were gotten to the other side of the River over the Ice, by which I perceived it would beare; I passed over, and got to the gate at Wybridge, where intending to get into the Town at the wicket, I saw most of the guard gone, and a body of their horse coming upon the Bridge; and then, understanding the Enemy to be fully possessed of the Towne, and no possibility of resistance left, I resolved to cast myself at the King my Master's feet.[27]

'A New Tricke to Take Townes' refers to help given by an unnamed Reformado officer in the city, and Roe also notes that Alderne had accomplices among the garrison. Scudamore accused Lieutenant Ballard of drawing off most of the guard from Byster's Gate and of disabling the 'Murthering Peece', a cannon set in the gateway. Captain Chaplaine, the Town Major, and another officer, Lieutenant Cooper, are also accused of colluding with the plotters, Cooper having opened the main gate and lowered the drawbridge to let the raiders in.[28] While there was evidently considerable disaffection among Scudamore's officers, it seems very unlikely, given Birch's consistent secrecy, that they could have known what was intended. There is one odd discrepancy between the accounts. Scudamore insists that the river ice was broken up by garrison troops, not by labourers from outside. He says that Cooper would have known that Berrow's workmen were impostors. But he himself had certainly summoned outside workers, if not for this specific purpose.

Apart from Scudamore himself, about 50 others got away including Sir Henry Lingen who made his way to Goodrich Castle; the rest were taken prisoner, among them Lord and

Lady Brudenell (Catholics who had fled from Wales; he had appeared on a Parliamentary list as 'one incapable of [receiving] mercy'[29]), Sir Henry Spiller, Judge David Jenkins of Glamorgan – another particular enemy of Parliament – along with 16 knights, five lieutenant-colonels, four majors, nine captains, and 39 gentlemen of quality, five Royalist Seabornes among them, including Richard Seaborne; also Thomas Tomkins, one of the Weobley MPs.[30] Some writers, including Webb, list Bishop Coke among the prisoners, but this is unlikely as he is not mentioned later as a prisoner.[31] The Roundhead troops, perhaps hardly less astonished than their prisoners, set about the plundering which was usual in a city that had been taken by storm (though there had of course been no invitation to surrender). Resistance did not cease immediately and the soldiers were said to be enraged by shooting from windows and in the streets,[32] while Birch and Morgan tried without success to restrain their men.[33] Later, 54 inhabitants redeemed looted property by paying £870 16s 8d composition.

Known Royalists and those who had helped in the defence had to pay a ransom to Birch to avoid imprisonment and likely raids on their property. Among them is listed Dr Harford, who had to pay £10, which suggests that, if a Parliamentarian at heart, he had had dealings with the other side.[34] Among those offering resistance and taken prisoner was John Traherne, master shoemaker, of Widemarsh Street, who served as an officer in the city militia. He paid £4 to regain his freedom.[35] His son Thomas was then aged around 9, probably one of Barksdale's pupils at the cathedral's school, one of a generation of children whose early years were passed in that contentious and strife-torn era. Yet it seems to have left no mark upon Thomas, a most unusual child, far more sensitive to the natural and spiritual worlds than to the human goings-on around him. Later, as a poet, he looked back on himself in those years as 'A little Adam in a sphere of joys!'[36] though he seems to have thought little of his education:

> … childhood might itself alone be said
> My Tutor, Teacher, Guide to be,
> Instructed then even by the Deitie.[38]

– and equally little of his fellow-citizens:

> Mens Customs here but vile appear;
> The Oaths of Roaring Boys,
> Their Gold that shines, their sparkling Wines,
> Their Lies,
> Their gawdy Trifles, are mistaken Joys:
> To prize
> Such Toys I loathed. My Thirst did burn
> But where, O whither should my Spirit turn!
> Their Games, their Bowls, their cheating Dice
> Did not compleat but spoil my Paradise,
> On things that gather Rust,
> Or modish cloaths, they fix their Minds …[37]

While adult opinions may colour his recollections, his verses are suggestive of the city's atmosphere in those days. Other writers of the time also commented on the profanity to be heard in the streets of Hereford.[39]

The Committee for Both Kingdoms may not have had much hope of Birch's success, since on 10 December it issued a directive to the Governor of Canon Frome, along with those of Tewkesbury, Gloucester and other towns, in an attempt to stop trade between Hereford, Worcester and London. By ongoing commerce 'both the people are enabled to pay the contributions laid upon them by the enemy … and the garrisons are supplied with what ammunition and other necessaries they require'. Clearly this was a new policy and trading had been allowed previously, since the order refers to 'some connivance hitherto at that trade', and requests the governors to allow carriers to return home with their goods rather than have them confiscated.[40]

Birch installed himself in the Bishop's Palace where King Charles had not so long before held his court. News of the city's capture was relayed quickly up the Marches. At Shrewsbury 'we discharged four great pieces of ordnance in a triumph'.[41] In a significant ascription to a rapidly rising reputation, the Governor of Stokesay Castle gave credit for Birch's stratagem to 'Lt-Gen Cromwell',[42] who had nothing to do with it. The news reached London by the 22nd, and a delighted Parliament appointed Birch as Governor of Hereford, and £6,000 was voted for the payment of his troops. He was requested to increase his regiment to form a garrison of 1,200 men and to exercise martial law. This was by now standard procedure for a garrison town. The intrepid Berrow was rewarded with £100 and was brought to the House of Commons to be thanked by the Speaker. The committee nominated to manage city and county on behalf of the Parliament, impotent since April 1643, now was enlarged and set about enforcing Parliamentary rule and imposing Parliamentary taxes and fines. Soberly glad at what he would have considered a sign of divine grace, Sir Robert Harley prepared a Parliamentary ordinance 'for the Settling and Maintaining of able preaching and godly Orthodox Ministers, in the City and County of Hereford',[43] and the House of Commons recommended Colonel Edward Harley to the Committee for Both Kingdoms 'to have some command or employment worthy of him in the County of Hereford',[44] while Richard Seaborne was disabled as a Member of the House and ordered to be sent up as a prisoner to London, along with the other notables arrested by Birch.

The Committee for Both Kingdoms had assumed that the moneys made available to Bridges were in part for a bribe to Barnabas Scudamore, and wanted to be informed who the recipients were, by a confidential messenger if necessary: '… the money is ready, and we desire your speedy answer'.[45] Alderne and Howorth were rewarded as agreed, but their nomination of Rowland Howorth, Charles Booth, Dr Edward Alderne and Clement Clarke to be relieved from the status of Delinquents, as part of the agreed reward package for their betrayal, brought a testy response from the committee to Morgan and Birch:

> We have received your letter from Droitwitch of the 6th, intimating that the persons and estates of Mr. Rowland Howorth, Dr. Edw. Alderne, Mr. Charles Booth, and Mr. Clement Clarke should be freed from delinquency and sequestration by virtue of an engagement from you to Major Howorth and Capt. Alderne, who were agents

in the reducing of Hereford. We gave power to promise 3,000*l.* to such as should be instrumental in it, which accordingly has been paid, whereof 300*l.* to Alderne and 400*l.* to Howorth. As for taking off delinquencies and sequestrations, we then gave no power to promise it, nor made any engagement of ourselves to endeavour [to obtain] it from the Houses, neither did we in all this time hear a word of it till now, although it be full four months since; and it will seem a very strange thing to the Houses, who alone can grant what is desired, to make a report for this after so long time; and if it were otherwise fit to do, yet we should desire to be better satisfied of the service that Howorth and Alderne did therein, and of the quality and condition of the persons mentioned, before we take it into any further consideration.

Finally approved by the committee, the agreement was not passed by both Houses until March 1647.[46] By that time the name of James Rodd, Sr, had replaced that of Clement Clarke.

In late December 'the Hereford forces' were recorded as having fallen on a Royalist party near Redstone Ferry, on the Severn close to Stourport, and having killed 150, taken prisoners, and scattered the rest,[47] but this is more likely to be an exploit of men returning to Worcestershire than a 30-mile sally by the newly-established garrison. Birch did move quickly to establish control of Leominster, with its 'malignant' reputation, and with Royalist troops known to be roaming in the vicinity. Placing cannon in the churchyard, he threatened to fire on the town if he met any opposition, but his rule was unopposed, and once again Roundhead soldiers were quartered on the townspeople. The change in the local balance of power prompted the Royalists to destroy Croft Castle: 'Ludlow men upon Sabbath day last at night burnt Croft his house'.[48]

Part Three

Years of Uncertainty

18

Rule by Committee

Parliament's previous occupations of Hereford had been short-lived, but circumstances now were very different. There was no royal field army, and Parliamentary troops controlled most of the countryside. Though Worcester, Ludlow and Chester were still held for the King, they were in no state to come to the relief of Hereford. Goodrich Castle was an isolated outpost, though a defiant and active one where Sir Henry Lingen and his friends certainly hoped to draw on the county's latent royalism to throw out the Roundheads. No doubt they were in contact with supporters in the city and elsewhere. But John Birch was not a general on campaign, like Stamford or Waller; he intended to remain in Herefordshire, with his regiment employed in helping to capture the region's remaining Royalist strongholds. With the King's cause in calamitous decline, in January 1646 Hereford figures for the first and only time in the annals of the *Signoria* of Venice, when its ambassador in London, an acute reporter of the war, informed his Council by despatch that: 'Necessity will drive the king to make some compact, because his affairs are at their last gasp. Hereford, which bravely withstood siege by the Scottish army last summer, has now been surprised in a moment by the Parliamentarians ... The loss is great for the king's side, because the place kept the surrounding country in awe, and now it will bend to the yoke of the more powerful.'[1]

Ambrose Elton Jr of Ledbury was appointed Sheriff, aged 24. Sir Robert Harley could also resume a part in the county's affairs, albeit from London. But Edward was in Hereford, keeping him informed, and the Harleys, by virtue of the part they had played in the war, their previous high status in the county, and the occlusion of prominent Royalists, were clearly poised to take the leading role. There was however a new and substantial presence in the person of Colonel Birch, a remarkable man who was to have a long and active life in the county.[2] Born in Ardwick, near Manchester, to a family of minor gentry status, he had little formal education but acquired his father's Presbyterian beliefs. At 18 he moved to Bristol, entered the wine trade, married the widow of a wealthy grocer and established himself as a merchant (enemies and gossips claimed falsely that he had started work as a humble packman). He had lost his business when Prince Rupert captured Bristol in 1643, and joined the Parliamentary cause. Birch might be described as a child of the Civil War: it gave him openings which he seized and developed to become wealthy, a landowner, and a person of consequence in Parliament and government. Of imposing physical size and presence, he was a rousing public speaker and a careful and exact accountant. Despite being a newcomer to the county, and installed by force, he meant to consolidate his personal position in Herefordshire. He brought his younger brother, Samuel, with the rank of major, to assist him.

Colonel Birch as depicted on his monument adjacent to the altar in Weobley church

By ordinance of Parliament, Birch governed Hereford under martial law, as his Royalist predecessors had also done. But it was not a dictatorship, for there was the committee. 'Committee' originally referred to an individual person to whom some charge was assigned, but from the 1620s on it came to designate a group with a specific function. Parliament's method of governance caused an explosion of committees from 1640 onwards (it is almost surprising that the King was not replaced by a committee) and, as in Herefordshire's case, the Long Parliament appointed committees to manage the affairs of individual counties, even before they could exercise actual authority.

At first in Hereford a single committee dealt with all issues of administration and control. It was intensely busy, holding sessions on six days a week throughout 1646, though receiving five shillings a day, plus the opportunities offered to members both of accepting 'compliments' for favours and of buying sequestrated property at specially low rates, its members were well rewarded for their efforts.[3] Among its most active members were Edward Harley, John Flackett Sr and Jr, Thomas Blayney, Edward Broughton, Robert Higgins, Martin Husbands, Henry Jones, Thomas Rawlins, and Nathaniel Wright. The treasurers were John Herring, Thomas Seaborne and Miles Hill. Already a striking difference to the pre-war management of affairs was clear: of these men, only young Harley came from the topmost layer of gentry that had formerly run the county. His colleagues were men of second- or third-rank gentry status, but all had been open Parliamentarians. Others who had been more discreet also now came out, among them the late convert Sir John Bridges and the equivocal Robert Kyrle (it was not until the end of March 1647 that the latter was freed from the threat of sequestration).[4] Isaac Seward reappears, and there were three other Kyrles, Francis, James and Walter; two Scudamores, William and John (of Kentchurch); Thomas Seaborne, the new Mayor, and Richard Philpotts, now an alderman. In 'Collectanea Herefordiensia' 73 supporters of the new regime are listed, some of whom were newcomers to Hereford.[5] It also seems to have been possible for members of adjacent county committees to sit in on an occasional basis. Unsurprisingly, most of Hereford's 'old' Parliamentarians were friends or associates of the Harleys. Together they had borne the brunt of the years of Cavalier control. Now surely they could come into their own, and they made up most of the committee. But it very soon became clear that Sir Robert was not going to have his own way unchallenged. Colonel Birch was Governor of Hereford, administering martial law, and had over 1,000 armed men at his command. He had every intention of taking a leading, perhaps *the* leading, place in the county's affairs. To Sir Robert, however brave Birch might be, and however correct his opinions (identical to the Harleys' on religio-political matters), he was a vulgar upstart who was in Hereford by mere chance, and should move on somewhere else. From the start, Birch and the committee were at variance.

The division among the new rulers can hardly have gone unnoticed by the inhabitants. But for them, it was as seamless an exchange of power as could be possible. In practically no time at all, all civic and county functions were being exercised again, by different men. One garrison had been replaced by another, even larger though (at least at first) better-behaved. At a local level, there were few changes of officials. The hundred of Stretford had the same high constable, Jon Crofte, from 1641 to 1646.[6] In most parts of the county there was a welcome cessation of menacing 'visits' by armed bands looking for provisions or plunder. With the country more or less at peace, commerce was easier, and when the troops had been paid, there was money to be spent. Birch was not an oppressive Governor, and the writer of 'Certain Observations' notes that there was a considerable and open Royalist element in the town calling themselves 'the true blues' who wore a little blue knot on the inside of their hats.[7] A few were arrested and jailed but most hung around in the alehouses, jeering at the new regime and its ordinances. Colonel Birch wrote to Sir Robert Harley on 10 January 1646 that 'I find this town very much disaffected … I think the castle ought to be fortified, which then would be a very strong place. When that were done I should be able to draw out part of the garrison, and march to Ludlow or Worcester, and rescue that part of the country.'[8] His comment underlines the general ascendancy of Parliament: the task now was mopping up pockets of resistance. Still trying to pull together the dispersed remnants of his forces and form a new field army, the King appointed the veteran Lord Astley as General of Hereford, Salop, Worcester and Stafford in January 1646. Astley set about the task, but there was little he could do in the western parts of his fief.

In many respects the new administration simply took over the functions and routines of pre-war times. The Commission of the Peace, the high constables and their assistants, the work of the Sheriff's men, the activities of the city's common council, all continued. Taxes, levies and excise payments had to be collected and accounted for, and law and order kept. Under Parliament the Quarter Sessions and Assizes continued to be held. But there were new tasks for the committee, including provision of supplies for the garrison troops, and it ordered that hay and fodder be brought in from the lands of Sir Henry Lingen, Wallop Brabazon (now an absentee landlord), Mrs Monnington of Sarnesfield, and Mrs More of Burghope, 'all noted delinquents'.[9] The committee also had to ensure that active Royalists were disarmed and could no longer form a military threat. It had to put the Government's policy of sequestration into effect, so that 'delinquents' – persons who had given support to the King's cause – paid for their opposition to Parliament. Another task was to ensure that religious observance was maintained according to Parliament's ordinances.[10] With authority and responsibility to enforce these ordinances, backed up by military force, the Hereford Committee was by far the most powerful civil body ever to exercise power in the county. In the course of 1646 its functions were split between a Sequestration Committee and an Assessment Committee, the latter concerned with basic taxation. The Sequestration

Committee determined who were delinquents and whether their estates should be confiscated or whether they should simply be fined. Owners of sequestrated estates could 'compound' with it, and regain all or some of their property by paying an agreed fine and swearing not to take up arms against the Parliament. This committee controlled the 'Fifth' and 'Twentieth', penal levies inflicted on all non-Parliamentarians, including neutrals and inactive Royalists, and also managed the sequestrated estates, including those of the bishop and the dean and chapter, and the rental income: 'These revenues were largely used for very traditional purposes – to pay the schoolmasters of the City, the artificers and artisans connected with the cathedral and the castle, the regular doles of bread to the poor of the City, the salaries of the corporation's baker and of the preaching ministers, who had been

The interior of the now ruined chapter house, and the remains as depicted by Thomas Hearne in 1784 (Hereford City Museums & Art gallery)

appointed to replace the resident canons and the previous parsons of the City's churches.'[11] It also maintained the cathedral custom of aiding the poor, giving the Mayor £35 in February 1647 for distribution to the needy and deserving.[12]

Birch put work in hand at Hereford Castle, primarily to provide weatherproof accommodation for a garrison which would remove the need for quartering soldiers on the townspeople, and provide a citadel in the event of revolt. For this purpose, lead was taken from the chapter house roof, and stone from the demolished house of the Royalist Aubrey family at Clehonger.[13] Removal of the lead accelerated the ruin of the chapter house, but some may have already gone during the siege, and it had also suffered from cannon-fire[14] and may have been unusable. In any case, it was redundant. To the new regime, the chapter house, a superb late Gothic decagonal building of the 14th and 15th centuries, was merely an example of the unnecessary and unseemly decoration and pomp with which the cathedral clergy had adorned their lives. One of the first actions of the committee had been to sequestrate the property of the dean and chapter, on the basis of an Ordinance of 1643 permitting this if the chapter had helped raise arms against the Parliament. Dean Croft, the canons, and the vicars choral were all compelled to vacate their houses. Birch was already occupying the Bishop's Palace. Although the office of dean, along with other cathedral clergy, and choirs, would not be abolished until 1648, it was impossible for them to discharge their responsibilities. Soon after the surrender, Croft is recorded as having preached a sermon in the cathedral against sacrilege, to which some of Birch's officers took exception. A guard-party of musketeers levelled their weapons at the intrepid orator, and Colonel Birch had to restrain them.[15] Herbert Croft retired to Cotheridge in Worcestershire, the home of the Royalist Sir Rowland Berkeley; he would return to Hereford in 1661 as bishop, after the Restoration.[16] Clement Barksdale, schoolmaster, pluralist clergyman and poet, was ejected from his several Hereford posts. With a satirical touch, he wrote about Birch's turning over the college of the vicars choral for use by paupers and beggars:

Sir, we are not bold to fight with God
But meekly to submit unto his rod;
Yet we may ask, why do you thus give leave
The nasty beggars should our chamber have.[17]

The cathedral archives were picked over by Silas Taylor, a captain in the Parliamentary army, whose tastes, untypically, ran to music and antiquarianism; he was both a composer and performer. Although Rawlinson in 1717 made the accusation that in 1645 Taylor 'did ransack the library … of most, or at least the best manuscripts therein',[18] it seems that: '… remarkably, the Library survived the Civil War without major losses', and Taylor took mostly documents from the archives of the cathedral or the vicars choral.[19] The library was at that time kept in the Lady Chapel, as was the cathedral's 'Mappa Mundi',

Herbert Croft as bishop

already a venerable antiquity. A tradition suggests that it may have been buried beneath the floor of the adjoining Audley chantry chapel during the disturbances.[20] Although one writer says that the cathedral organ was destroyed[21] it may merely have been left in neglect. The cathedral was not silenced, but no more voices rang out in anthems, even those approved by the pre-Laudian Church. The Directory of Public Worship had replaced the Book of Common Prayer in 1645, (though the churchwardens' inventories for All Saints, Hereford, show that copies of the Book of Common Prayer were kept in the church into the 1650s[22]) and the staple item of the service was once again a lengthy sermon, not at all to Herefordian taste. Walker, chronicler of maltreated Royalist clergy, records 50 in Herefordshire who suffered during the Civil War for expressing Royalist views, from 'molestation' to the murder of Mr Pralph at Stoke Edith. Rice Morris, vicar of Ocle Pychard, was 'pulled from his pulpit by soldiers; his wife and children turned out', but few actually lost their livings. The vicar of Norton Canon 'was molested, robbed of his hat on a wet day, borrowed his maid's'. Thomas Swift was ejected from his living at Goodrich and was also deprived (in 1647) of his rectorship of Bridstow.[23] Some left of their own accord: Henry Wright, Vicar of Ashperton and Stretton Grandison, quitted his parish to live in Worcester 'with confederate clergy and malign gentry' and was said to have opened an alehouse.[24]

When in need of ready money, Birch's methods were direct. On 20 February William Price, ex-Mayor, now an alderman, had a letter from 'your very loving friend, John Birch'. As one 'having aided and assisted to the warr against the Parliament', Price was informed that his estate was liable to sequestration, but a payment of £100 within six days would remove the danger: 'considering that your welfare will bee my owne I am loath yor estate should be sequestrated but by the advise of those whoe are authorised for the raysing of money in this County have rather chosen to chardge you with a sum of money farr below what in rigor you are liable to paie.' Poor Price – brandishing his certificates from Lord Stamford and General Waller seems to have been of no avail. Birch had already 'borrowed' £100 from him in January (see below).[25]

Thomas Tomkins, one of the Weobley members elected to the Long Parliament back in 1641 after his brother's death, had made some pro-Parliamentary noises in the summer of 1642[26] but then chose the King's side. He decided to make his peace with Westminster and attended, on his knees, at the bar of the House of Commons on 7 January 1646. This did not save him from imprisonment and a fine of £2,110. In February James Kyrle died. Although he had always been stoutly for the Parliament, Governor Massey at Gloucester had often found him something of a trial as a critic and complainer; he described him as 'old choleric Mr Kyrle' in a letter to Edward Harley.[27] Robert Kyrle, his standing with the Parliament restored since the capture of Monmouth, became the master of Walford.

Receipt for £100 borrowed from ex-Mayor Price by Col Birch, signed by Miles Hill, witnessed by Thomas Symonds (HCRO CF 50/278)

19

Mopping Up

After the snow and the long frost, February 1646 was a month of overflowing rivers and flooded fields, but military operations splashed on through water and mud. During that month, Lord Astley and Sir William Vaughan combined their forces at Ludlow, where Woodhouse was still Governor, and there were sporadic skirmishes among the hills and valleys of Radnor and west Herefordshire. According to some accounts,[1] Royalist forces from Ludlow and Goodrich, with Sir James Croft, joined in an attempt to oust Birch's troops from Leominster, but he was informed of the plan, sallied out with his men and defeated them in a midnight attack at Eyton, three miles west of the town. But this fight is not mentioned in Birch's own vicarious autobiography, which misses no opportunity to note his successes. Those of Birch's troops who had been left in Bath now came to join their comrades, bringing his regiment's field guns. On 13 February Richard Hopton joined the Hereford garrison with a troop of horse. Edward Harley had been appointed General of Horse for Hereford and Radnor in January but Hopton was under Birch's orders. Robert Harley Jr, with the rank of major, was also back in the county.

Birch and the Harleys were well aware that Parliament's control of Hereford was dependent on military power, and that the continuance of Goodrich and Ludlow as Royalist fortresses helped to keep up a sense of instability and menace. They had every reason to co-operate with each other. Birch was Governor but Sir Robert Harley had powerful contacts in London, and was also regarded as a leader by most of the members of the new County Committee. John Birch and Edward Harley had some things in common: both had fought with conspicuous courage, both belonged to the Presbyterian wing of the Church, and neither harboured a spirit of revenge against the erstwhile enemy. But from the first, it was a strained relationship. Professor Aylmer considered that 'it does look as if the quarrel was of the Harleys' not of Col. Birch's making, and as if they were jealous of a military man, an outsider to the county and one of plebeian origin at that, gaining the credit for the final capture of Hereford and then holding the important post of Governor there'.[2] Birch, as noted, was not of plebeian origin, but his bluff and hearty personal style encouraged the myth. He was aware of the Harleys' hostility, writing to Sir Robert on 25 February to express regret: 'It troubles me that there should be any misunderstanding between us. I am confident you have no reason to think ill of me.'[3] The Herefordshire Committee seemed to echo this, writing to Sir Robert on 5 March of the 'good correspondence we have with the Governor, of whose care frugality and wisdom we need not give a better account than his own actions,'[4] though only five members signed it.

Sir Henry Lingen, smarting perhaps at his own hasty exit from Hereford, was determined to make trouble for the new rulers of the city, but his position at Goodrich was isolated. Monmouth was in Parliamentary hands, and Raglan Castle was under siege. Chester had finally fallen to a Parliamentary force on 3 February. But Lingen had the sympathy of the county Royalists, which ensured him supplies and horses. Possession of cavalry was his main asset, apart from the castle walls, enabling parties to come out from Goodrich, claim contributions on behalf of the King, and inflict annoyances on the occupying forces. The existence of an active Royalist stronghold only a few miles away made Birch's task of holding down a town of largely Royalist sympathies more difficult. But there was much for him to do, and two months elapsed before he attacked Goodrich. Lingen's garrison was not just sitting around during this time, and the route from Hereford to Monmouth and Gloucester was safe only for a heavily-armed party. Lingen gathered his supplies from the estates round about, especially that of Pengethley which had been sequestrated by the Royalists in the absence of Sir Edward Powell, and which Lingen (his own land then being under the Parliamentary committee) treated very much as his own.[5] Colonel Birch made a first attempt to take Goodrich Castle on 9 March with the help of a party from the Monmouth garrison commanded by Robert Kyrle. In a night assault, the attackers failed to break into the main keep, but the stable-yard was breached, the stables were opened, and some 80 horses turned loose before the buildings were fired. The guard troop at the Wye ferry below the castle was also overpowered after a fierce two-hour struggle. Lingen's mobility was drastically reduced, but his intelligence system was functioning well. Birch, riding to Monmouth with a small party to confer with Colonel Morgan, was ambushed at Old Gore, east of the Wye and about five miles north-west of Ross. As soon as he realised what was happening, Birch ordered his party to charge forwards and their onrush broke up the ambuscade. Of the 14 men lying in wait, only two escaped death or capture. Addressing Birch, his secretary gives a graphic account of the close-quarters fight: 'The fury of your

Goodrich Castle and the site of the ferry on the Wye which lay below it

Goodrich Castle as it appears today

horse overthrew one, and dismounting one or 2 more, the comander of them turneing about his horse to clap his pistol to you, I was soe neare you that my pistoll touched his side; where I shott him, his scarf was fired with the powder, and downe hee fell.'[6]

The subject of the Parliamentarian commanders' meeting was Astley's mustering of an army of 3,000 or so Royalists at Bridgnorth. Formed mostly of experienced soldiers, it represented a serious threat to the Parliamentary garrisons and there was widespread spying and scouting on both sides. Early in March, a combined operation was planned. Forces from Shropshire, Hereford, Gloucester and Evesham, under the overall command of General Brereton, were to meet and engage the Royalists. No ambiguity was allowed about the command structure, unlike the Cavaliers' at Stokesay. Colonel Morgan of Gloucester was in command of the non-Shropshire contingents, though that impression would not be gained from Roe's 'Military Memoir' of his master.[7] Perhaps in anticipation of action, Hereford's stock of munitions was substantially boosted, taking in 40 barrels of powder, with 'match and bullet proportionable', 200 cases of pistols, carabines, saddles and bridles, and 200 firelocks, and 1,200 suits of clothing for the garrison.[8] In the third week of March Astley's force moved off in the direction of Oxford to provide King Charles once again with a field army, but Birch and Morgan were already in position to intercept him on the edge of the Cotswold scarp, awaiting the arrival of Brereton. Between them they had around 2,700 men, but as they watched Astley's army approach, Brereton was nowhere in sight. Five hundred of the Roundhead horse and some of the foot harassed the Royalist column, to delay them as they climbed up. Late on 20 March Brereton finally appeared, having failed to keep on Astley's track. Very early on the 21st, the last real battle of the war's first phase was fought, near Stow-on-the-Wold. Birch was in the heart of the struggle and his horse was killed, but after two hours' hard fighting, having withstood two desperate thrusts by the Cavaliers, the Roundheads broke Astley's ranks, and the King's veteran general surrendered. Five days later, the victorious Parliamentary army drew up outside Worcester in what was a show of force rather than a serious attack. In the exchange of fire, Birch once again had his horse shot under him.[9] He was probably relieved to get back to Hereford and find that the force he had left there, 700 foot and 50 horse, was still in control of the city. But if messengers had not already told him, he found out that he was luckier than he knew. During his absence, Sir Henry Lingen had made an appearance before one of the city gates, at noonday, with a force of thirty horsemen. Hacking their way past the turnpike (a pole with radiating spikes set in the roadway to form a barrier) they charged through, cutting down four of the guards, and moved on into the city. Lingen hoped to raise the townsmen in revolt against the Roundheads, but few, if any, responded. People stayed indoors, while the garrison swiftly mustered. When they saw there was no chance of support, Lingen and his men left, pursued, perhaps largely for show, by a party of Parliamentary horse under Captain Benjamin Mason.[10]

During February and March, the House of Commons, Presbyterian-dominated, was devising a Presbyterian structure for the Church of England, recording on 14 March that 'the Lords and Commons having removed Prelacy, with the Common Prayer, and its unneces-

A skillet dating from the time of the Civil War found at Goodrich Castle, showing the wording on the handle: 'Loyal to his Magiste' (Hereford Museum and Art Gallery)

sary Ceremonys, and establish'd the Directory, they have begun to lay the foundations of a Presbyterian Government in every Congregation'.[11] Harley's ordinance had provided for six 'able, learned and godly' ministers to be appointed in Herefordshire, and after its approval by Parliament on 28 March, four Puritan ministers appeared in Hereford and took up residence in the dean's and prebendaries' houses, and the voice of Presbyterian orthodoxy spoke, lengthily, from the city's pulpits. With no administration or head, the free grammar school may have been closed for a time until the committee could appoint a suitable master and supply funds. In Ross-on-Wye, the parson, Philip Price, was turned out for refusing to use the Directory of Public Worship, and was replaced by John Tombes, who had once fled from Leominster.[12]

On 10 April Birch received orders from the Committee for Both Kingdoms 'to take all your horse and the foot belonging to Hereford, besides such forces as are coming to your assistance from Salop, Montgomery and Radnor', to march to Ludlow and set about taking it. Two hundred troops were to form the assistance. On the same day, another message informed Birch and the Committee of Hereford: 'The whole county of Hereford being now subject to the Parliament, and there being no enemy in the field, we conceive there is but little use for the garrisons of Canon Frome and Pembridge [Castle]. We refer it to your consideration whether those garrisons may not be slighted; and if you be of that opinion we desire it may be done, and the forces now there be drawn out by Col. Birch, and receive orders from him.'[13]

Birch duly marched on Ludlow, where the castle's massive walls, topping a steep hill, might have daunted the most experienced siege-master. Setting up position, he sent to Gloucester for siege equipment, including a battering ram. An attempt by Royalists from Raglan, Goodrich and Madresfield in Worcestershire to dislodge the Roundheads from Ludlow was fought off with no great difficulty on 29 April, and efforts by Woodhouse's horsemen to break out through the leaguer were equally unsuccessful. At that same time came startling news. On the 27th, King Charles had left Oxford, in disguise, with a minimal escort, and had vanished into the heart of England. For the Cavaliers, it was a portent of disaster, for the Roundheads, it seemed the beginning of the desired end. Very soon, however, Birch was instructed to pull his troops back to Hereford, since 'it has suffered much from the enemy, some men having been killed even at the gates of Hereford'.[14] Sir Robert Harley was pulling strings here; he had informed the Committee for Both Kingdoms of Lingen's bravura entry. A letter to his father from Edward Harley on 8 May bemoans 'the grievous & sad complaints of our country men' and lists various complaints against the Governor. He had failed to remove the threat of Goodrich, despite promises of speedy action. He had imprisoned Dr Bridstock Harford on his own arbitrary authority, although it was the committee's business, 'if any charge of Delinquencies shall be brought in and proved against him it is our business to receive it & to proceed against him accordingly'. Meanwhile, he wrote, the committee has wholly suspended the execution of sequestration orders on delinquents' estates, 'only out of this consideration: that the proceedings might in likelyhood be more dangerous than at another tyme & surely if it be no wisdome to provoke our enemyes very much, it will be as little pollicie to destroy our friends'.[15]

On 5 May, the King gave himself up to the Scottish army which was besieging Newark. While the possible repercussions of this caused intense speculation and argument throughout the country, the siege of Ludlow went on. On the 18th, Woodhouse indicated that he would surrender at the end of the month if nothing happened to change his fortunes. Perhaps he feared 'Hopton Quarter' from the Shropshire contingent under Samuel More as he apparently refused to deliver the town to anyone other than Birch,[16] who returned to Ludlow to agree conditions for an honourable surrender.

From 21 May, Worcester was also under siege, and one of its most determined defenders was Fitzwilliam Coningsby, who could not safely remain in Herefordshire. He was described as 'head of the recusants and reformadoes',[17] shouting down any suggestion for negotiation or surrender. But he had no official position, and no seat at the Governor's council. When Worcester was surrendered on 19 July, he was among those taken prisoner, with Wallop Brabazon, Sir Barnabas Scudamore, his own son Lt-Col Thomas Coningsby, and probably numerous other Herefordshire Royalists. Sir Barnabas had had a hard time of it since his flight from Hereford. Having reached Ludlow safely, he was making for Oxford when he was arrested by the King's order at Worcester, and kept in confinement there. Knowing himself to be widely suspected of accepting a bribe, it was here he wrote his account of what happened on the fateful night of 17-18 December.[18]

In June, Birch renewed his attack on Goodrich. The castle was placed strongly on ground rising steeply from the river, with a deep moat cut from solid rock on the landward side. Its outer walls are seven to twelve feet thick. Apart from the drawbridge, the entrance was guarded by two semi-circular towers and opened into a vaulted passage 50 feet long with successive portcullises and 'murder holes' for pouring molten lead. Eighty barrels of powder were supplied from Parliamentary stores to help in the attack, and Birch arranged for the casting and assembly of a siege mortar, one of the largest of its kind yet made, which he later referred to as 'a mortar piece, which I have cast here'.[19] Probably cast at the Old Forge close to Goodrich Castle, it fired shot of 13.25 inch diameter, weighing 'above 2 cwt'

(112kg). Scrutinising it in 1919, Alfred Watkins noted that the barrel carried the raised letters '16 Co. Jo. B. 46', and also considered that it 'does not show skilled work'.[20] Given the name of 'Roaring Meg', the mortar tossed its massive stone missiles right over the walls. In the same letter, Birch noted the determination of the defenders: 'they are excepted persons, and Papists very desperate'. He had offered honourable surrender on the 13th, informing Lingen that Oxford had agreed to surrender terms, but got a haughty reply, 'as for the delivering up of Oxford, (if it be so) the fortune of another man's command shall not be leading case for my loyalty, and the

Roaring Meg

trust reposed in me, and this I will assure you is the resolution of your loving friend, Hen. Lingen'.[21] Birch had signed his first letter as 'Your real friend', now he replied using Lingen's phrase: 'Sir, I have received your resolution by your drummer, which far better contents those under my command than myself, who really desired your welfare. In honour, Sir, your loving friend, J.B.'[22] Perhaps Birch hoped that an early surrender would diminish Lingen's reputation and so make his own life as Governor easier, but there is no reason to doubt that he had a real desire to avoid bloodshed. Now, for another six weeks the siege continued. The attackers cut a mine through thirty feet of solid rock and the defenders opened a counter-mine to meet it. In the end, relentless cannon- and mortar-fire reduced the walls sufficiently for a storming party to break through,[23] and finally Lingen asked for terms. By the grim protocols of the time, the only terms now on offer were the mercy of the victors. But Birch was not a bloodthirsty commander, and tradition records that he allowed the Cavaliers to march out to their own tune, 'Sir Harry Lingen's Fancy'. When Goodrich was finally surrendered, on 31 July, the roll-call of surviving defenders was like a list of the county's most strongly Royalist (and Catholic) families: Bodenhams, Berringtons, Cornwalls, Lochards, Pyes, Vaughans and Wigmores all had at least one member in the garrison.[24] Only one of their number, Miles Lochard, is known to have been killed in the course of the siege. Lingen was imprisoned in Hereford until October, when he petitioned to compound for his estate and was allowed freedom on parole[25].

Oxford, Charles's 'capital', had indeed surrendered, on 29 June. One of its defenders, issued with a safe-conduct, was Sir Edward Hopton, the Royalist son of Sir Richard Hopton.[26] Among other Royalists in the city were Sir Walter Pye and Sir Sampson Eure. Raglan was still being held for the King by the old Marquess of Worcester, though now under siege by a range of Parliamentary forces, joined by the victors of Worcester and Goodrich, the latter bringing 'Roaring Meg' as a contribution to the assault. Lord General Fairfax was there in person to superintend operations, surrounded by colonels, and on 19 August the Marquess, having agreed surrender terms, left his great castle to end his days in prison. Raglan was plundered and half-demolished, rendered uninhabitable and undefendable.

20

Birch vs Harley

Birch returned to Hereford in the knowledge that all serious opposition in the region was at an end. He had sent in a bill for £162 in March for the works done at Hereford Castle,[1] and on 11 August he became its owner when Edward Page conveyed the title deeds to him. At that time it appears that the castle grounds had been sub-leased to one Richard Ravenhill, and Birch's clerk John Edmunds noted that 'Ravenhill he is a papist and his house in town is seized uppon by the Government … he lives at a place called Holmer within a myle of the City'.[2] From Raglan Birch had written to the Speaker to ask if it was Parliament's wish that Goodrich should be demolished or kept, his own preference being for the former, and also took the opportunity to remind the Speaker of 'my petition to the honourable house'.[3] On 25 August Parliament ordered the demolition of Goodrich Castle, though the work of slighting does not seem to have been done until the Spring of 1647.[4]

As the mention of his 'petition' suggests, if Sir Robert Harley was better connected in London, Birch was working very hard to make himself known by, and useful to, the men in power, with frequent communications relating to his successes and difficulties. His main problem was the continuing presence in Hereford of his regiment, around 2,000 men who after the fall of Goodrich Castle had nothing to do, but needed feeding and accommodation, and refused to be demobilised until they had been paid. As their arrears of pay mounted up, the soldiers were becoming increasingly disgruntled, while the citizens of Hereford were equally irked at having to pay for their presence. In February, Parliamentary ordinances stipulated a tax of £600 a week to maintain the troops stationed in the county, which should have covered the needs, but it may have been impossible to collect so much. In the same month, the garrison had protested about its lack of pay and accused the County Committee of holding back money.[5] One might wonder about the £6,000 voted to Birch by the Commons in the previous December, but, arrears apart, his regiment cost £53 a day to keep,[6] and three months would see most of that sum swallowed up. In any case, to be voted a payment did not mean instant, or even early, receipt. In May, following the suggestion of the Committee for Both Kingdoms, the garrisons at Canon Frome and Pembridge Castle were withdrawn, and the troops added to the number in Hereford or quartered elsewhere in the county. On 11 June 1646 Birch received a payment of £1,000 with interest, 'for the disengaging of an undertaking made unto him by the Committee for Both Kingdoms'.[7] Birch's attempts to enforce contributions, like those earlier in the year from Alderman Price, brought complaints, and the Committee for Both Kingdoms gave him a mild reprimand, pointing out that such actions could cause 'some distempers'.[8]

Edward Harley kept up his desire to turn former enemies into present friends by not pressing them too hard. On 23 July 1646, Fitzwilliam Coningsby's wife Cecilia wrote to him from Hampton Court that 'My misfortunes are so great as to be interested in this busines so farr as to bewail my child's unhappines. Howsoever I should be glad to do you any curtesie within my power, but I have so small power over my tennants I cannot command my dues'.[9] A few days later Bishop Coke wrote to thank him: 'I have heard of your favour in moving to the committee of my state. It is a manifest declaration of the continuance of the favour of that noble family to which I have ever been bounden.'[10] But Harley's emollience was his own policy and not that of the government. On 5 September an ordinance of Parliament decreed that the 'title and dignity' of archbishops and bishops were to be wholly abolished.

From summer into autumn there was mounting agitation within the county to have the number of troops reduced. In August the House of Commons had considered a report on which forces might be 'conveniently spared out of the City of Hereford' but took no action.[11] The County Committee appealed to the Speaker of the House in September for a reduction in the numbers, and the Herefordshire Grand Jury sent a petition, backed by Sheriff Elton and conveyed by Sir Robert, to Parliament in October, requesting that no writ be served for elections in the county until the troops had been disbanded.

Resentment of the Roundhead soldiers helped to keep Royalist feelings inflamed, and a contemporary report noted 'the Potent number of Cavaliers most of them very lately in Arms against the Parliament, and these very popular and of great interest [influence] in City and County', with their 'admired Jollity, and frequent drunken meetings' with threatening behaviour and language. Sir Henry Lingen is particularly mentioned.[12] Some of the Herefordshire Committee-men, though they may not have been active Royalists, were certainly not dedicated to the service of Parliament. Among these were Isaac Bromwich, of Bromsberrow, who had been mostly in Gloucester during the fighting years, and Herbert Perrott or Parrett. Bromwich, a relative of Lord Scudamore, was in touch with the Viscount during October 1646, helping him in the effort to avoid or minimise the penalties he faced. Massey and others had complained of Bromwich's doubtful loyalty in 1644-45.[13] Perrott, of Moreton-on-Lugg, had returned to Hereford from Pembrokeshire in 1645-46. On 5 October, while Birch was absent from the city conducting a registration of delinquent persons of the Wormelow hundred, at the New Inn in Archenfield, Sir Henry Lingen, newly paroled, appeared in Hereford wearing a sword and behaving in a challenging manner to the Parliamentary officers. Lingen ended up in the Falcon tavern drinking with Bromwich and Perrott. It seems likely that they were making trouble rather than trying to start an uprising, but the soldiers were in a constant fret about conspiracies. The Town Major attempted twice to arrest Lingen but was prevented by Bromwich. A 'great broil and tumult' ensued, with fighting inside the inn and many people running in and out, until Lt-Col Raymond, in charge during Birch's absence, restored a degree of order. Birch got back at around 4 in the afternoon and soon afterwards the brawling broke out again. Brought before the Governor, Bromwich refused to answer questions and demanded a hearing from 'the High Court of Parliament, which all the officers readily assented to', and Birch adjourned the court. Bromwich, as he was being led out, challenged the Governor to a duel.[14] Under martial law this was a capital offence, and Bromwich was sent to London under sentence of death. The affair released a wave of anti-Birch feelings. The County Committee backed Bromwich, claiming that Birch had no authority to judge one of its members and ordering his immediate release.[15] Sir Robert Harley presented a petition to Parliament levelling various charges against Birch, among them that he had allowed one of his officers, Major Humphreys, to illegally take oxen and detain £200 belonging to

Edward Harley (by kind permission of Edward Harley Esq.)

William Scudamore of Ballingham. The dispute was referred to a committee of the House, which treated it lethargically.[16] Meanwhile Bromwich was released on parole by order of the Speaker, but no action was taken against Birch.[17]

Another central body, the Committee for Plundered Ministers, ordained on 4 November that the tithes of Leominster, previously payable to Viscount Scudamore and Wallop Brabazon but now sequestrated, should be put to maintain preaching ministers in Leominster, Lean (perhaps Leen, the district west of Leominster) and Docklow.[18] In the autumn of 1646 Sheriff Elton transferred the Quarter Sessions from Hereford to Leominster, apparently to protect the justices from undue influence from Birch and his military force, and refused a request from Birch, supported by Sir Richard Hopton and Sir John Bridges, to restore it to Hereford.[19] With the Bromwich affair and the forthcoming Parliamentary elections raising the temperature, disputes, personal, political or both, were rocking the committee. On 12 November its proceedings were suspended while some members went to Leominster, perhaps in connection with the election. Some of those who remained in Hereford, including Higgins, Husbands and Jones, then reconvened. On the following day the clerk, Nicholas Philpotts, was dismissed from his post. Philpotts, a lawyer, had been charged with delinquency, but was cleared in February 1647. The events underlying this drama are obscure; one writer speculates that Higgins and the others were a pro-Birch group[20] and certainly there is evidence of anti-Birchian activity. Hopton and Bridges, allies of Birch, had their estates sequestrated by order of the Herefordshire Committee in November. Both men had slightly shady records as Parliamentary supporters, but it looks like a tit-for-tat action. The sequestrations were cancelled in March 1647.[21]

Such apparent digs by the committee at Birch's supporters are at variance with its efforts to act fairly, even leniently, to the wider community, adjusting constables' assessments on occasion, and in the summer of 1646 proposing (at least) to refund contributions raised for a cavalry force, since: 'It hath pleased God to settle their county in more peaceable condition than we expected in so short a time'.[22] In general, the 'localism and leniency'[23] of the committee was conspicuous – perhaps too much so to some of the increasingly confident and vocal 'godly' element. With commercial activity now free of the hazards of warfare, John Vaughan rented a furnace in Bishop's Wood, near Ross, for £4 in 1646, in a contract with Walter Kyrle as steward for the manor, property of the Earl of Essex.[24] Fairs resumed, including Hereford's great cattle fair on 19 October.

Walter Kyrle featured in the proceedings of the House of Commons on 15 October 1646. As a member for Leominster, he had been inconspicuous since July 1642 when he 'went into the Country, without Leave, for Recovery of his Health: That, about Michaelmas following, he was coming up, and the Earl of Essex sent Two Mesengers for him; and said, if he would not come, he would send a Troop of Horse for him: He remained at his House, at Rosse in Herefordshire; and was Two several Days imprisoned by the King's Forces'. With Sir Robert Harley's backing, Kyrle was admitted to sit.[25] It seems that Walter Kyrle had managed his affairs rather well, since he had also contrived to be listed as a member of the King's 'junto' Parliament at Oxford in 1643, being noted as one absent with leave, or by sickness.[26] James Kyrle was not so fortunate. A month later, the House of Lords was petitioned by some Monmouthshire gentlemen to find a worthy position for Mr James

Kyrle, 'One of the committee, who first delivered Monmouth into the Parliament's Hands, and hath since shewed himself very active, faithful, and serviceable, in reducing both Monmouth and those Garrisons lately under the Power of the Enemy'; but it was reported, further, 'That the Committee for both Kingdoms were informed, that the said Mr. James Kyrle, about Two Years age, was active for the Enemy; which they thought fit to acquaint this House withall.' James Kyrle was taken off the Herefordshire Committee.

With military conflict at an end, Parliament called elections in November 1646, not on a general basis but to replace those members who had absented themselves since 1642 and were declared unfit to sit. In Herefordshire, James Scudamore, Richard Seaborne, Sir Sampson Eure and the two Weobley members were 'disabled'. Any candidate had to take the Covenant oath and declare loyalty to Parliament, thus excluding Royalists from standing. John Birch sought nomination as a member for Herefordshire in these 'recruiter' elections, but the Harleys used all their contacts to ensure that Edward was chosen. They spent £402 12s 6d on entertaining voters to 577 suppers and 2,898 dinners.[27] Despite the family's Puritan style and standards, the guests at these dinners reflected all shades of opinion including Catholics and Cavaliers; indeed Puritans would have been a small proportion of those entitled to vote. But the Harleys' lack of vengefulness, and moderation in applying the sequestration and fining policy, now stood them in good stead. With Edward elected, father and son were the senior and junior members for the county. Before the end of the year Sir Robert had also replaced Viscount Scudamore as Steward of the city.[28] Birch however managed to procure election as a member for Leominster, replacing Sampson Eure. James Scudamore and Richard Seaborne were replaced as Hereford's MPs by Bennet Hoskins and Edmund Weaver. Hoskins, of Morehampton Park, was a thoroughgoing Puritan reformer; Weaver was the son of the popular one-time MP Richard Weaver, and was married to a sister of Ambrose Elton Jr. Weobley was now represented by Robert Andrews, from Northamptonshire, and William Crowther, perhaps a Ludlow man by origin,[29] who had made money as a London haberdasher, bought the Wormsley Priory estate in Herefordshire, and founded the grammar school in Weobley.

During 1646 the Committee for Taking the Accounts of the Kingdom, responsible for collating the reports of county sequestration committees, set up sub-committees in each county to check on the work of the sequestration committee. In Herefordshire this checker-committee, like the main committees, was formed largely of Presbyterians, probably at the nomination of Sir Robert Harley and his closest associates. But there are some indications that it was becoming difficult to find men who combined the necessary calibre and willingness with the right principles and loyalties. One of the checker-committee was Richard Wootton of Marden, a Royalist whose small estate had been sequestrated to another Wootton, John – possibly his brother (the same family had been involved in the clubmen rising), and another ex-Royalist on the sub-committee was Arthur Cockerham or Cockram of Adforton. These were relatively obscure men who are unlikely to have been chosen if others of more substance (and a better record) had been available,[30] but their emergence into public office may also be an indication that ideas were on the change and that in Herefordshire reformism was gaining ground against traditionalism. Apart from the tiny handful of 'Brownists' complained of by Stanley Gower before the war, the godly community had been overwhelmingly Presbyterian in its views. Now, not only the prewar tradition of an episcopal Church and a gentry-led administration might be questioned, but also the views of the Harleys and Birch, who wanted to replace one monolithic Church structure with another and who remained thoroughly attached to the rights of property-owners. Influences of newsbooks, pamphlets, preachings of the new clergy, the experiences of friends who had travelled beyond the county, might all serve to open people's minds to religious and political ideas which were becoming common currency in some other parts of the country.

Mr George Coke, once Lord Bishop of Hereford, died on 10 December 1646, at Lower Moor, Eardisley, in obscurity and comparative poverty. His personal estate as well his diocesan possessions had been subject to sequestration, as had the property of his sons Richard, John and William, respectively chancellor and prebendaries of Hereford Cathedral. In 1641 Lord Falkland had quipped that 'they who hated the bishops hated them worse than the devil and they who loved them did not love them as well as their dinner'.[31] A victim of circumstances, Coke was buried in Eardisley church, and a memorial was later placed in Hereford Cathedral. Several staunchly Royalist clergymen were still in office, but at the end of 1646 the County Committee engaged in a new round of ejections. Dr Thomas Edwards, vicar of Kington, was ousted 'for malignancy' in December; Dr Rogers of Stoke Edith was sequestrated as 'a fomenter of this unnatural war' in January 1647; Roger Breinton, rector of Staunton-on-Wye and Credenhill, was sequestrated of both livings in February and was said to have died of a broken heart. John Pember, vicar of Bodenham, was ejected in April.[32]

Tension between Birch and the Herefordians did not let up. A letter from the Governor informed the committee that, 'I understand you are of opinion that I am preventing my horse and foot from disbanding, which is not the case', and went on to say, 'I will not permit any under my command to receive any orders except from myself or my deputy, viz. Major Hopton for the horse, and my brother for the foot.'[33] Hostile rumours about the Governor were being passed around. Thomas Seaborne wrote from Lugwardine to Edward Harley at Westminster with the insinuation that Birch at the siege of Worcester had forced his way into a bedroom occupied by two sisters, 'the one a widdowe, the other a maide, and there did attempt the chastitie of them both'.[34] When Major Richard Hopton was due to bring his cavalry troop to Hereford, the committee issued instructions for their quartering. The Governor immediately countermanded them.[35] Birch was not going to have his authority infringed, but when he adopted a more emollient tone and invited the committee to suggest things that might conduce to the welfare of city and county, some of the committee sent a copy of his letter to Sir Robert Harley with the observation that 'If you knew not the gentleman you might take him for one whose thoughts were taken up for the good of this county.'[36]

Miles Hill had been one of the few committee-men to associate himself from the first with Birch rather than with the Harleys. Whether or not it was caused by hostility between the factions, then at a peak, he was soon at odds with the checker committee. Summoned to present his accounts to it in November, he delayed appearing until December, when he 'entered in a promiscuous and confused manner' and with an incomplete set of accounts.[37]

Rivalry and infighting within the committees did nothing for the inhabitants, whose resentment at military occupation, taxation and committee-men's officiousness was in some instances becoming anger. In December 1646 the sub-tenants of episcopal land at Colwall refused to pay rent to John Flackett Sr, who was leasing it from the committee of which he was a member. Flackett seized their cattle. The committee revoked his lease and had the rents paid directly to itself.[38] On 21 December 1646, William Phillips, the Mayor, wrote to Sir Robert Harley, as Steward, asking him to assist in relieving the city of Hereford from the grievous pressure under which it was groaning.[39] Sheriff Elton wanted to be 'delivered from this troublesome office'.[40] Amid these strains and stresses, Birch struggled to keep some goodwill in Herefordshire and cautioned his officers to keep within bounds: 'for the care of the well affected I desire you to quarter upon those who are in arrear of their contributions for the six months; and besides those, quarter as much as may be on delinquents and "neutors"'.[41] In late January 1647, Hill was arrested by the under-sheriff, presumably with Elton's sanction, for an alleged debt of £153. This action against Birch's prime supporter certainly raised the stakes. Birch was attending Parliament in London. Hill was locked up at Bye Street or at the Freemen's Prison for about three weeks, until in mid-February he was forcibly released by Major Samuel Birch with a troop of soldiers. As the city was still under martial law, this was not illegal, but the slap-down to the civilian committee-men reminded them where power ultimately lay. Hill was unchastened, and verbal warfare with the sub-committee resumed. By March he was accusing it of harbouring delinquent Royalists as well as being financially incompetent. He appealed to Parliament, and the sub-committee appealed to its parent body, the Committee for Taking the Accounts. This central committee was managed by Presbyterians, still the dominant group in the House of Commons, and Hill was excluded from a role in Herefordshire's affairs until 1649. In March the Hereford Committee was still informing the county MPs (except Birch) of the grievances arising from quartering.[42] Birch made a proposal that if the soldiers would be paid, they would then pay up for the free quarter and for all horses and goods wrongfully taken, and would march away.[43] Evidently the committee was still failing to collect enough to pay the soldiers, as he offered an alternative: 'That what is unpaid in the county of the nine months' contribution of £600 a week be paid within ten days', along with two months' contribution at the same rate to himself or his nominee.[44]

Birch's offer is surely connected with the Parliamentary order, made on 1 March, that the 'City of Hereford be disgarrisoned, and new works slighted'. Only the castle was to be garrisoned, with 160 men.[45] Disbanding could be a dangerous moment, resolved by Richard Hopton when his regiment of horse, 500 strong, was dissolved at Withington on 19 March. At first the men refused to go, and it required much diplomatic talk and a hogshead of wine, supplied by the commander, before the disbandment was effected, and 'departed every man to his home with abundance of love and civility'.[46] The disbanding of Hopton's troop acknowledged that there was nothing for it to do. But Birch's regiment, equally idle, unpaid, with nowhere to go, refused to leave Hereford. Birch, as a Member of Parliament and well-regarded by its leading men (Harley excepted) was in a position to press for action to resolve the problem of his unpaid regiment. Bodies of unpaid and resentful soldiers were a problem in many places, with the New Model Army the biggest of all.

Early in 1647, Major Robert Harley was elected as Member of Parliament for Radnor Boroughs, a traditional Harley seat, joining his father and brother in the House of Commons. In March events in Herefordshire took a dangerous turn. Violence flared in Ewyas Lacy hundred, where a party of soldiers under Captain Thomas French had been quartered, against the order of the committee. When the locals protested, a fight began in which three civilians and a soldier were killed. The fracas led to a wider 'countryman rising' which went on into May, with a clubman-type force assembled at Longtown, in the Monnow valley, led by a former Parliamentary soldier. Edward Harley investigated the affair, achieved pacification by promising redress on behalf of the committee, and reported back to his father.[47] The presence of his superfluous troops was a major obstacle to Birch's ambition to establish his position in the county, and on 25 March he came to an agreement with the Committee for Ireland that 1,000 foot and two troops of 100 horse would be sent to Ireland, on payment of two months' arrears and one month's pay to come, a total of £6,740, to be advanced by the County Committee and repaid at 8% interest by the national committee at Goldsmiths' Hall. Harley had for some time been urging that the regiment (along with its colonel) be sent to Ireland. Pressed by both Harley and Birch, each for his own reasons, the Committee for Compounding with Delinquents ordered its treasurers to pay £6,740 to the Committee at Hereford.[48] At last, it seemed that the log-jam might be shifted.

The political scene, nationally and locally, was becoming very different now. The Scots army had returned home in January 1647, having handed the King over to the English Parliament. But although hostilities had come virtually to an end, no settlement was in sight. The Presbyterian majority in Parliament was still intent on pushing through its Church reforms. The Army, demanding its arrears of pay, balking at being sent to Ireland, and rife with vocal opposition to any kind of imposed Church structure, was moving on a collision course with the Presbyterian policy. In May, the Commons decided to reduce the Army in England (around 30,000 strong) to 15,000. Of the rest, 11,800 would be sent to assist in the subjection of Ireland, and the remainder disbanded. All would be paid two weeks' wages. The Army reacted with a degree of outrage that should have been predictable. On a local scale, the greater drama was reflected in Herefordshire, though Birch's troops were far less politicised than those closer to London and appear to have had no agenda beyond getting paid. But if the New Model was being fobbed off with two weeks' wages, what could they expect?

21

Trouble with the Army

Birch may have acquired Hereford Castle as an investment, but if there were to be no troops, there could be no rent, and on 12 April 1647 he sold it to the county for £600, 'for the public use and defence of the county',[1] with the other Members of Parliament acting as trustees. Sir Robert advanced the money as a loan, which was never repaid. On 15 June 1647 the House of Commons approved Colonel Birch's accounts, as certified by the Committee of Accounts on 21 May, for the sum of £4,907 7s 4d, 'in full of all Sums and Demands now due to him from the Parliament and Kingdom of England'.[2] They comprised his losses at Bristol, £4,907 7s 4d, and a loan to the Governor of Bristol on 15 December 1642, of £1,050 at the standard 8% interest. On 15 June Colonel Samuel More, survivor of Hopton, was appointed Governor of Hereford Castle, with 160 men. Re-enactment of the Self-Denying Ordnance on 10 June meant that John Birch, as an MP, could not retain a military commission, and the increasingly precarious command of his 1,000-plus men was transferred to his brother.

Edward Harley, colonel of a regiment in the New Model Army, was in the same position and also caught in the growing tension between the Independent-minded troops and many of their officers, and the Presbyterian Parliament. An unsigned letter on 27 March 1647 had warned him that his lieutenant-colonel, George Pride, had got more than 1,100 of the regiment to subscribe to the Army's Petition setting out its grievances. Harley presented this letter to the Commons as evidence of the dangerous spirit among the troops.[3]

As opinions began to polarise on what should be done about the King, the Harleys were to be increasingly out of sympathy with the trend of events. Their hope was to get an agreement which would restore the King to his proper position, along with a Presbyterian Church structure at least for an experimental period, but the likelihood of achieving this, between the King's unwillingness to compromise and the Army's growing radicalism, was increasingly shaky. After a long period of stalemate during June and July, events speeded up dramatically. The Army seized control of Charles's person at Holmby House in Northamptonshire on 4 June 1647. On 5 June, a General Council of the Army was set up. The nature of political discourse was radically changed by these events. On 16 June, eleven members of the House of Commons, all Presbyterians, were charged, in the name of the Army, with treason, plotting to restore the King and restart the war. They included Edward Harley (and two others who had played some part in events in Herefordshire, Edward Massey, now a Major-General, and Sir William Waller). The eleven were suspended from Parliament, and on 20 July obtained leave to go abroad and were allowed to postpone making their defence against the charges for six months. Edward Harley remained in England, staying with his Royalist cousin Edward Smith at Hill House in Essex, and returning to Herefordshire late in the year.

Sir Robert Harley wrote in alarm at these events to his friend the influential preacher Stephen Marshall, hoping to effect a compromise between Parliament and Army: '... as a native of England bewailing the distractions we are under and apprehending the imminent miseries we may justly fear'.[4] But the divisions he deplored only got wider. Meanwhile a further tax was levied on Hereford city and county, of £828 2s 3d per month for a year, for the maintenance of the Army and the carrying-on of the Irish war. No less than 27 commissioners were named as responsible for gathering it, including both Harleys and Sir Robert Pye Sr, the Herefordshire-born Parliamentarian uncle of Sir Walter.[5]

During this time of confusion and flux, John Birch's ability to prise money from the Government was remarkable. Keen to restore normality in Hereford, he managed to procure an order for £3,700 from the House of Commons, to be paid by the Bristol Committee. This was half the estimated cost of transferring his regiment to Ireland. But, en route from Westminster to Bristol, he was stopped at Bagshot by the troops of Colonel Rainsborough, one of the keenest of the Army's radicals, and taken to General Fairfax's headquarters at St Albans. Fairfax sent him back to Westminster, but Birch, never easily diverted from his chosen course, succeeded in returning to Hereford in mid-July, where he tried to persuade his unwilling men to accept the move to Ireland. But the restive troops had been infected by the mood of their fellows elsewhere: it was noted that 'Colonel Birch's agitators do tread the steps of the Northern [army]',[6] and their impatience boiled over into mutiny. Birch and his brother were made prisoners, and the troops seized control of the castle treasury, where Birch had £2,000 stashed away, along with a stock of boots and clothing. Birch soon talked himself free, but his brother was held hostage. On 15 July, Birch wrote to the House of Commons, somewhat understating the case, informing it of 'Distempers and Differences among the forces' in Hereford, and Parliament asked General Fairfax to arrange for the speedy sending of the Hereford regiment to Ireland.[7] But this never happened. Eventually Major Birch was released, but the soldiers kept the money,[8] and there were no prosecutions for mutiny.

Crises at national and local level meant that '... by 1647, any personal or political rivalry between Colonel Birch and the Harleys was overtaken by, or subsumed under the more general tension between the civil and military authorities'.[9] Ordinary business went on; even without Edward Harley the Herefordshire Committee-men mostly shared his views and his approach. They kept an eye on the constables, and a preserved letter from Thomas Rawlins to William Scudamore of Ballingham notes that one constable in his area had been discharged and another, James Roberts, who had misbehaved in the past (he had been appointed by Sir Henry Lingen) was again behaving unfairly in arranging the quartering of soldiers.[10] News from the capital was keenly awaited in Hereford, with its own problem of mutinous troops. When the City of London opened its gates to the Army on 4 August, and Parliament's Presbyterians were clearly sidelined, accusations flew from Hereford to London. Sir Robert Harley was accused of having abandoned the 'godly party'[11] and of offences including soliciting the votes of papists in the county elections, of packing the County Committee 'with his own creatures', and embezzling public funds. Although anonymous, the accusations clearly came from sources familiar with Herefordshire's affairs. On 8 September Sir Robert was summoned to attend the Commons in three weeks' time to answer 'matters objected against him'. He survived without having to stand trial but did not attend Parliament in the autumn of 1647, a time when 'England was more clearly on the verge of anarchy than at any other time in the century'.[12] How to deal with the King, with the Army, with the Church – all were burning questions, none of which seemed possible of resolution between the various factions in and outside Parliament. And in some places (though not Herefordshire) the Levellers were making their society-shaking demands. But if they had no vocal adherents in Herefordshire, their ideas were known to anyone in touch with the news. Fears of warfare breaking out again were very real, and well-grounded. Under the new Puritan-led regime, the old-style celebrations of Christmas were officially forbidden, which caused riots in some towns, though not in Hereford where perhaps little effort was made to ensure that the ordinance was enforced.

At the end of 1647, the soldiers of Birch's regiment were still in Hereford, and still in dangerous mood. Edward Harley wrote to his father in London that the committee and the county treasury were in danger: '… yesterday [Major] Birch drew a commanded party of Horse and foote within a mile of the towne, & certainly resolved to make the Committee prisoners & especially my self … this place is likely to be very miserable unless you can procure a speedy order for Coll. Birch's march'.[13] Another mention of the refractory troops comes in a letter from Herefordshire read to the House of Commons on 24 January 1648. The commanding officer, Colonel Humphreys (who had replaced Samuel Birch after the mutiny), had tried to disband the infantry on the 19th, but they had again refused. It claimed that although the county had paid its levies 'to a penny', further exactions were made by the soldiers: 'And without your tender care for the preservation of this County they are utterly ruined'. The sum of £5,000 was said to be needed to disband the regiments in Herefordshire and Radnorshire.[14]

With its leading citizens known to be Presbyterians, Hereford was becoming a suspect place to those who wanted no compromise with the King. From Gloucester, Colonel Pury was keeping a beady and well-informed eye on the city, and as a result of reports from him the Committee of Both Houses (of Parliament) instructed General Fairfax on 24 January to 'take care for securing the Cities of Gloucester and Hereford, and for preventing the inconveniences mentioned in such way as you judge to be most effectual',[15] though he does not appear to have taken any particular action. Herefordshire offered less of a threat than many other places, notably Pembrokeshire, where a large force of Parliamentary troops were refusing to disband until their arrears of pay were received.

On 16 February 1648 Parliament passed an Ordinance authorising the raising of £20,000 per month 'for the Relief of Ireland'. Herefordshire was to find £289 7s 5d, in addition to other levies.[16] The 'relief' was not for the Irish people but to maintain a Parliamentary army there. Ireland was out of control; Scotland was making its own accommodation with the King; England was split three ways between the Royalists, the Presbyterians who would restore the King if he would concede at least a Presbyterian exper-imental period, and the Independents or 'sectaries' who rejected both bishops and presbytery, and whose demand for complete freedom of (Protestant only) religious expression foreshadowed further social changes. 'The bitterest division in England was no longer that between King and Parliament, Cavalier and Roundhead, but that between the sectaries and their opponents.'[17] And in south Wales a new phase of fighting, often known as the Second Civil War, began in this month when the Parliamentary forces mutinied against their former employers. The Governor of Pembroke Castle refused to hand over his command, and declared for the King. Rowland Laugharne, formerly a Parliamentary Major-General, took command of the insurgent troops. These events must have caused concern and excitement in Hereford.

John Birch was one of three Parliamentary commissioners sent to Edinburgh in February 1648 to convey a protest to the Scottish Parliament about its 'Engagement' with the King, and he appears to have remained there until May,[18] detached from events in Herefordshire. Colonel Humphreys, in command of the garrison, was no respecter of persons and one of the new preachers, Mr Woodroffe, complained to Sir Robert Harley that Humphreys and the magistrates 'have caused unruly fellows to be quartered not only upon us the city ministers, but upon our brethren of the minster'.[19] Sir Robert arranged for their exemption. He had reason to feel more confident about the way things were going. During April, dispute between different factions in the Army enabled Parliament's Presbyterian group to reassert itself. On the 27th, Sir Robert resumed attendance in the House of Commons, and on the following day negotiations with Charles I (then being held in Carisbrooke Castle on the Isle of Wight) were reopened.

Laugharne's anti-Parliament force was defeated on 7 May at St Fagans by troops from the New Model Army under Colonel Thomas Horton, and Lord General Cromwell came to south Wales to superintend the sieges of castles still held for the King. Chepstow Castle was taken by storm on 25 May. Containment of the Welsh revolt reduced the immediate threat to Parliamentary rule in Herefordshire, but its defence was strengthened. Although the revival of Presbyterian ascendancy turned out to be short-lived, one of its results was an Ordinance of 23 May 1648, for Settling the Militia in the County of Hereford,[20] achieved by Sir Robert in advance of a proposed national militia Bill. The ostensible purpose was to keep the peace against any Royalist threat, but at last the Harley group could have a force to balance the castle garrison. A Committee for the Militia in Herefordshire was formed and ordered Colonel Edward Harley to raise a regiment of foot in the hundreds of Broxash, Huntington, Wigmore, Stretford, Grimsworth and Wolphey.[21] The Militia Committee's membership in 1648 'certainly reflects a bid by the Harleys and their allies to recover control of the county – as an aspect of the opposition by the so-called Presbyterian majority in the Long Parliament to the New Model Army'.[22] In June the impeachment of Edward Harley and his ten colleagues was lifted.

It was a summer of portentous storms. Walter Powell noted a great storm of wind and rain, breaking the fruit trees, on 31 July; and torrential rain at the end of August caused floods that swept away bridges.[23] 'The summer of 1648 was the wettest for years and there was another appalling harvest.'[24] To a population with a strong sense of divine involvement in human affairs, and clinging also to still-powerful remnants of old superstitions, this was not just bad luck but retribution for the sins of the time.

The 'Second Civil War' came to a climax that August as a Scottish army led by the Duke of Hamilton advanced into England, this time on the King's behalf. Efforts had been made to organise widespread risings of English Royalists to coincide with the Scottish incursion,[25] and Herefordshire was one of the few counties to respond positively. Sir Henry Lingen, despite a huge fine and a promise not to take up arms again, was in the plot, having received a commission from the Prince of Wales to raise forces in Shropshire, Staffordshire, Worcestershire and Herefordshire. Though no other leading Royalists, apart from Robert Croft (living at Yarpole close to the ruins of Croft Castle) seem to have joined him, he rallied enough support to form a cavalry force some 400 strong, and members of such Royalist families as the Danseys, Skipps, and Unetts were with him.[26] His force might have grown larger if the plot had not been leaked, or discovered. On 21 July 1648 the Committee of Both Houses praised the very good services of Captain Yarranton, Governor of Hartpury Castle in Worcestershire, 'in discovering the designs against divers garrisons'.[27]

When Hamilton's Scottish army was routed by Cromwell at Preston, on 19-20 August, its remaining horsemen thought first of linking up with the Royalist general Lord Byron in north Wales, then 'Their next hope was to join Sir Henry Lingen, who had, as they believed, risen in Herefordshire'.[28] But they abandoned this plan. It was a long way down to Hereford, past a succession of Parliamentary garrisons. In fact, though they did not yet know, Lingen had already been defeated: 'Lingen, from whom much had been expected, had risen prematurely in Herefordshire, had been chased into Monmouthshire, and had there been routed on August 17.'[29] Despite their enthusiasm for Presbyterianism on the Scottish model, the Harleys had summoned the militia troops to resist the Royalist rising. Around 15 August, Lingen's force attacked Edward Harley's county troop near Leominster, overwhelmed it, and took 80 prisoners before withdrawing into Radnor Forest. But this victory did not bring fresh recruits, and Roundhead forces were on his trail. Two or three days later, a force of New Model veterans commanded by Colonel Horton, who had come from 'mopping up' in south-west Wales (Pembroke Castle had surrendered to Cromwell on 11 July), joined by Major Robert Harley's cavalry, took Lingen's men by surprise, not in fact in Monmouthshire but between Radnor and Montgomery, and avenged the previous defeat, regaining the prisoners and capturing Lingen himself. One writer relates a traditional tale that as Sir Henry was being led prisoner over the bridge at Lingen village, the local people threw stones at him.[30] But in fact it seems that, seriously wounded, he was taken to Powis Castle.[31] On 18 November, he was named in the abortive negotiations with the King as one of seven promoters of the Second Civil War to be banned from the country. But the ban was lifted on 13 December.[32]

While Sir Henry was a prisoner, his wife Alice petitioned for him to be liberated for six weeks in order to arrange his estate for raising money to pay the fine for compounding, and to make some provision from 'the poor remainder' for his wife and seven children, in anticipation of his being banned from the country.[33] Another Lingen child had been buried in Hereford Cathedral in 1645. In yet another example of reconciliatory behaviour, although Sir Robert Harley had been authorised to recompense his own losses from what remained of Lingen's estate, Edward Harley returned Lingen's schedule of possessions to

Alice Lingen, intact. It is not clear, though, whether Colonel Birch, awarded £500 a year from the same revenues, did the same thing.

On 16 October 1648 the Committee for Both Kingdoms ordered that 'the gentlemen in prison at Hereford be discharged upon the ordinary bail and conditions',[34] and on the 18th the House of Commons voted the full £7,500 for disbanding the Hereford troops[35] but stipulated that only two months' arrears of pay should be given as they had refused to take service in Ireland. Birch took £750 of this for his own arrears. What happened with the balance is not known. On the 24th, the Committee of Both Houses wrote to the Hereford Committee that 'We are informed that there are 100 foot in your city now to be disbanded, but who are willing to serve in Ireland'.[36] At that point, after almost two years, the majority of the troops finally dispersed from the city and county (few, if any seem to have gone to Ireland), and any who remained were absorbed into the civilian population.

Only the castle garrison of 100 or so now maintained a regular military presence, and around November 1648 Samuel More was replaced as Governor by Major Wroth Rogers.[37] Rogers, a Welsh veteran of the New Model Army and a strong Independent in religious views, was installed at the behest of Sir William Constable, Governor of Gloucester, who considered the Harley and Birch regime as insufficiently vigorous in its dealings with delinquents, as well as far too ready to see concessions made to the King. Inevitably, Rogers was soon at odds with the committee.

On 22 November the House of Commons received a humble and probably un-spontaneous petition from 'the well-affected inhabitants within the Borough and Oare of Leominster'[38] as a result of which it ordered that Colonel John Birch replace Sir Walter Pye as High Steward, taking charge of the borough's books of accounts, rolls, etc. Suspicion of the actions and intentions of Royalists was constant. In the same month, a letter from Edmund Stephens, Miles Hill and others in Herefordshire informed the Committee for the Advance of Money that the Duke of Buckingham had unsequestrated lands around Leominster and that his steward, Sir Walter Pye, 'has lately raised large sums from the estate'[39] (£2,700 in December 1647). In September 1649 the Buckingham estate would be awarded to Henry Marten, a leading regicide.

22

Sir Robert Harley in Hell

As the army presence in Hereford was melting away, within the far larger and more politically-engaged forces of the New Model Army, there was a hardening determination to bring the seemingly interminable negotiations with the King to an end. Peace seemed quite precarious, even though there was no force that could hope to oppose the army of Fairfax and Cromwell. But daily business of all kinds was still going on. On 6 December, Oliver Hughes of Kingsland signed over to Sir Robert Harley the rectory, advowson, tithes and glebe of Kingsland for an annuity of £60, to drop to £30 if Harley paid £300 within a year, or to zero if a lump payment of £600 should be made. Sir Robert was also hoping to secure Parliamentary funds for the rebuilding of Brampton Bryan church. As the debate over the King's future was coming to its peak, the Commons was considering an Ordinance relating

The rebuilt Brampton Bryan church

to the church's repair in October and November 1648.[1] With much else, this was swept aside by an abrupt constitutional crisis.

On the same day that Sir Robert's Kingsland contract was made, the military coup known as 'Pride's Purge' (Thomas Pride had replaced Edward Harley as colonel of their regiment) took place in London, when armed soldiers prevented many Members from entering Parliament. Most, including Bennet Hoskins and Walter Kyrle, were simply listed for exclusion, but 45, including John Birch, Sir Robert Harley, and Edward Harley, were arrested. Herded together by the soldiers, they were taken by coach to a 'common vict-ualling house', a drab, low-ceilinged tavern generally known as 'Hell', and kept in two dark, unlit upstairs rooms. Sir Robert's own house was nearby, and he was suffering from a bad cold. He was offered parole, but refused to appear before General Fairfax to swear it, asserting his

The hammerbeam roof of the rebuilt Brampton Bryan church which might incorporate salvaged timbers from the castle

right to appear before the House, and the offer was withdrawn.[2] Next day the prisoners were moved to confinement in two inns on the Strand where they compiled a 'Solemn Protestation' about their treatment, which the Commons condemned as 'this Obnoxious Publication'.[3] Sir Robert remained a prisoner while the King's trial was carried on, and was released on 31 January 1649, the day after Charles's execution. John Birch was also freed by the end of January. Of the other Herefordshire members, Crowther and Weaver withdrew from Parliament, and only Andrews, for Weobley, was to sit in the 'Rump' Parliament.

'The fall of the Harleys, as a result of the changes in national politics during the winter of 1648-49, led to corresponding changes in the membership of the ruling group at county level.'[4] Back in Hereford, on the news of the Purge, 'a group of malcontents seized their opportunity to overthrow the Harleys, and with the aid of mutinous supernumeraries being mustered for disbanding to arrest young Robert Harley and some of his cronies'.[5] Robert Harley with Walter Kyrle had been given leave by the House of Commons to go down to Herefordshire to help in gathering in payments of the Army Assessments.[6] His impris-onment was brief, but his role as militia head was over. 'Wroth Rogers, the local Army commander (and a fervent radical Puritan) was soon raising a force of 500 volunteers.'[7]

During the January Quarter Sessions, Rogers organised a petition from the Grand Jury, Justices and Other Gentlemen of Herefordshire to congratulate Parliament on its actions. This was duly recorded and appreciated[8] by the House. Between petition and acknowledgement the Commons repealed the Ordinance for Settling the Militia in Herefordshire.[9] Edward Harley was freed in mid-February and returned to Wigmore, while his father remained in London.

During that period, December 1648 – January 1649, events had moved with shocking speed. After four years of warfare and two of fruitless negotiations and political crises, in less than eight weeks the King had been charged, tried, and beheaded. His execution was as much of an affront to Presbyterians like Sir Robert Harley and John Birch as it was to dyed-in-the-wool Royalists like Sir Henry Lingen. For Harley and Birch, as for many others, the slogan 'Parliament and King' had been a perfectly sincere one. Wroth Rogers, promoted to colonel, had the task of ensuring that Herefordshire, its Royalist sympathies suppressed rather than forgotten, should be kept in line with the new republican regime. Opposition showed when a clerk of the Assessment Committee was attacked (presumably by or at the behest of a Royalist) and the members claimed to fear for their lives.[10] The committee protested about Rogers extorting money from its treasurer, Thomas Blayney,[11] but Rogers set about placing his own men in power. With this, the change from pre-war governance was even more marked. The Commission of the Peace and the Assessment Committee were reformed in February and April 1649, when 17 of the 31 existing members, including the Harleys and most of their friends, and also John Birch, were dropped from the latter, but Miles Hill made a reappearance, as did Sir John Bridges and Sir Richard Hopton. Only a handful of the 1646 committee were retained, including Robert Kyrle, Thomas Baskerville, John Cholmley and Thomas Rawlins, men who through principle or self-interest were willing to work in the new context. Blayney also stayed on until late in 1649.[12] It took longer to recast the Sequestration Committee, and Edward and Robert Harley remained members until it was reformed in September 1649. But by this time it had less to do.

The new members were men of relatively modest means, chosen for their political-religious views rather than for social status. Several were outsiders to the county.[13] More extensive lists of persons favourably regarded by the republican regime are seen in the collectors appointed to secure the amounts required in successive taxes raised 'for the Maintenance of the Forces in England, Scotland and Ireland' in 1649-50. Hereford's share was £2,000 a month. Apart from the newcomers, they include several men who had backed the Parliament locally from the start, including John Flackett, Ambrose Elton, Francis Pember, and John Herring. Ex-Sheriff Isaac Seward also figures in these lists.[14] Miles Hill of Weobley appears on almost all county committees from 1649. That the administrators were treading both new and old paths is shown by the petition sent by the Quarter Sessions to London in the Spring of 1650 – a dutiful plea for more religious reform, but also requesting reform of land tenure and the social system, along with familiar complaints about ironworks and the depletion of woodlands.[15]

The power of the new committee-men was backed up by Rogers's volunteer force, and ultimately by the Army. Sir William Constable at Gloucester, one of the signatories of the King's death-warrant, was also keeping himself informed of what went on in Hereford.

He had warned the Parliament that 'few of the people of Hereford are well affected to the present government and that the place is of concernment, and might prove very dangerous if it should declare against the Commonwealth, and give a beginning to new trouble'. He was requested to keep 'a watchful eye on them'.[16] Spying and informing were typical of the new Commonwealth regime, always concerned about Royalist propaganda and plots.

In the course of April 1649 the House of Commons was busy with various financial matters as well as setting up a kingless Commonwealth. Among sums transferred from other resources to the deans' and chapters' Lands were several relating to Herefordshire. From the Excise, £857 4s 8d was transferred, noted as '29 March 1647 to Col. Birch, with interest, for Ireland'. Out of 'the other Moiety of the Grand Receipt of Goldsmiths Hall' (the Sequestration funds) came £500 to Major Samuel Birch, and 'To Sir Robert Harley and the Committee of Hereford, £6,740 whereof £750 to Col. Birch'.[17] Tracing of actual cash payments is often impossible, but it seems as though these accounts were finally squared.

Sir Robert Harley, still Master of the Mint, was called to appear before the Council of State in connection with the Mint's affairs, but informed it by letter on 16 May that 'he doth decline further meddling with the Making of Money for the present'.[18] His decision was prompted by Parliament's plans for a redesigned 'republican' coinage, and the Commons voted to deprive Harley of his post. That effectively marked the end of his long public career, though he continued to live in London, sometimes finding it hard to get his rents. Still Steward of Hereford, he appointed Bennet Hoskins and Edward Freeman as his deputies in March 1649, but evidently remained active in the post as William Lowe, one of the Hereford city preachers, thanked him for obtaining exemption for him and his brethren from having to quarter soldiers,[19] and later in the year the Rev. Timothy Woodroffe and others wrote to him to propose Thomas Seaborne, apothecary, as the new Mayor. One letter to his son Edward shows a rare touch of wry humour, noting that he gave sixpence in the collection at a fast: 'I do not remember that ever I gave so little upon a like occasion, yet I never gave more, for it was all the money I had.'[20]

23

Sequestrations and Compoundings

Between April and August 1643 a succession of Parliamentary ordinances had set out to define who was delinquent and what action should be taken against them. Anyone who had served in the royal armies, or who had made voluntary contributions to the King, or had harboured or concealed Roman Catholic priests, or was bringing up children or grand-children in the Catholic religion, or had molested persons well-affected to Parliament, was included. Such persons were liable to forfeit up to two-thirds of their goods and estates. Of course many in Herefordshire fell into these categories. Furthermore, anyone who owed them money could inform the committee about the extent of their estates and be rewarded by a remission of one shilling in the pound (a twentieth) on the debt. Delinquents with wives and children were allowed to reserve one fifth of their estates from deduction, under certain conditions, including that the children should be brought up in the Protestant religion. Sequestrated estates were managed on behalf of the committee and their rents and profits delivered to the county treasurers. Confiscated property might be sold outright.

Since 30 January 1644, Parliament had offered a form of pardon to former Royalists through 'compounding': payment of a sum usually equal to two years' purchase of their estates. Composition involved providing the committee with a complete list of all posses-sions, loans, and incomes, and then being allowed to retain a percentage of these, depending on the degree of delinquency. In addition, a compounder had to affirm Protestantism by taking the Covenant, and swear not to take up arms against the Parliament. For the unfor-tunate Royalists there was the further mortification that the fruits of their inheritance or labours should go to 'the supportation of the good subjects who had borne the greatest share in the burdens of the kingdom' as well as towards the upkeep of the Parliament's army.[1] To encourage submission a series of deadlines was set, with the terms becoming stiffer each time. But while Hereford was still under Royalist control very few of Herefordshire's Royalists or neutrals, apart from isolated cases like Mr Cardiffe of The Helme at Ewyas Harold, had sought to compound. By 1646, compounding might involve the yielding of a third of one's estate. Apart from the impact on individual families, sequestration and compounding had also reduced the flow of funds and men to the King to a trickle.

The business of compounding and of arranging for the disposal of sequestrated property went on in Herefordshire from 1646 into the 1650s. Lists of delinquents were compiled and those named were summoned before the committee. Its deliberations were usually slow and interrupted by other events, and contentious matters had to be referred to London. Also, there was much to do. Some 300 sequestrations were executed in the county, and many others made composition. Fines on those who compounded amounted to £43,764 3s 8d (perhaps not all paid).[2] To this huge sum has to be added the value of sequestrated property. But the Hereford Committee was a relatively lenient one, and not only when Edward Harley was a leading member. From 1652 Silas Taylor, musician and manuscript collector, was a sequestrator, and 'had in those times great power, which power he used civilly and obligeingly, that he was beloved by all the King's party'.[3]

Some Royalists, regarded as particularly obnoxious by Parliament, were denied the opportunity of compounding (at least initially), including Fitzwilliam Coningsby, Bishop Coke, Roger Bodenham of Rotherwas, Henry Morgan of Stoke Edith, Edward Slaughter of Bishop's Frome, James Scudamore of Llangarron, Rowland Scudamore of Treworgan, Evan James of Stockton, and Robert Wigmore of Lucton. Most of these were Catholics who may have balked at taking the required oath in support of the Protestant religion.

Sir Walter Pye could not deny his affiliation to the King, but could still protest a lack of means to pay. Sir Walter listed his debts and mortgages, and claimed that, apart from some stuff at Oxford, 'all his household goods and other moveables hath bin taken from him since theis troubles, and a greate part thereof remains in the hands of divers mean persons, not disposed of to the use and benefit of the state', and asked for this to be taken into consideration.[4] Sir Walter had come to terms with the committee in 1646, being fined £2,360 in November. His fine was made payable to his cousin Sir Robert Pye Jr, a distinguished officer in the Parliament's army, 'towards satisfaction of what was due to his services to Parliament'. Whether or not this was actually paid, further fines amounted to £3,000 which he could not pay, and he was outlawed for debt in 1648. Sir Walter was ruined by his stand for the King. Others were luckier. Sir Sampson Eure, also captured at Oxford, procured a document on 28 August 1646, signed by four high constables, to attest that he 'did not execute the Commission of Array, the Commission of Impressing Souldiers for His Majestie, the Commission regarding Delinquents against his Majestie, the Commission for Subscription Money to his Majestie's aid, nor any Commission whatsoever touching the unhappy Differences between His Majestie and his Parliament'. Eure also engaged himself not to bear arms against Parliament or to do anything prejudicial. Edward Harley, Thomas Blayney and Thomas Rawlins also signed this testimonial to his good behaviour.[6] He was fined at one-tenth, £185, later reduced to £100, which, considering his role as Speaker of Charles's Oxford Parliament, seems a modest penalty.

Often, efforts were made to avoid the process altogether. In 1647 the vicars choral petitioned the Committee of Sequestration against being included in the general sequestration of property belonging to the dean and chapter, pleading their own destitution and 'having never acted anything prejudicial to the part nor being any ways under the notion of delinquency'.[7] The plea was refused and their college and cloister, valued at £20 a year, were sold to one Philip Starkey for £220.[8]

Although the properties of Hereford Cathedral had been sequestrated since early 1646, their sale did not take place until 1647-49, beginning with the disposal of the Labour in Vain tavern in London for £544 on 16 November 1647. In the course of 1648 the Manor of Whitbourne was sold for £1,348 10s 10d to Richard Salway of Worcester and two others; John Flackett acquired Bromyard Forrens (i.e. outside the borough) for £594 9s

The still extant gateway to the bishop's palace at Bosbury, acquired by Sylvanus Taylor in 1650

2d and Colwall Park (with Thomas Alderman) for £63 13s 4d. Eastnor and the Battersea properties were acquired by a Worcestershire Parliamentarian, Thomas Letchmere, on 28 November 1648 for £1,174 0s 6½d. In 1649 Sylvanus Taylor bought Bosbury for £728 10s 6¼d, James Style or Styall and John Porter bought Shelwick for £176 14s 0d, while in 1650 John Birch spent £2,475 12s 5½d on half the Bishop's Palace (Sylvanus Taylor had the other half) along with the manorial rights of Shelwick, Barton, Tupsley, Eaton Bishop, Hampton and Sugwas to add to the bishop's house at Whitbourne; and Sir Richard Hopton got the manor of Bishop's Frome for £570 16s 1d.[9] The dean's properties fetched little more than £1,000. Cathedral-owned tenements in Worcester, Lambeth and Battersea sold for £8,850 9s 3½d. These were low prices, perhaps because of a degree of fixing – the purchasers were all good Parliamentarians – and in part because there was always the possibility of a change of fortune and the Church reclaiming its property. Parliamentary supporters were most likely to be buyers because they knew those in charge of the selling, could negotiate favourable prices, had not suffered the same losses through fines as wealthy or once-wealthy Royalists, and had less compunction about acquiring Church property. But the total sums were substantial and the London Committee kept a close eye on the accounts from the counties.

Herefordshire sequestrations and fines in 1646 raised over £14,000: £4,000 from rents of sequestered private estates, £7,000 from the Church estates, £1,000 from seized personal estates, and £2,000 from the one-fifth and one-twentieth fines.[10] These very considerable sums passed through the hands of the county treasurers and were intended to be set against the costs of maintaining local garrisons and troops, and also other charges met by the committee, including schoolmasters' and preachers' salaries, bell-ringers' payments, and occasional charitable donations. The Assessment and Excise payments were sent to London.

The troubles of Viscount Scudamore at the hands of the Committee for the Advancement of Money make a seven-years' litany. In 1643 he had been assessed to contribute £1,500, and in 1644 was assessed at a further £2,000[11] with his goods at Guildhall to be sold off. On 27 February 1644 'divers goods, money and plate of Lord Scudamore were seized in the chamber of Mr Seaburne of the Inner Temple and taken to Guildhall and delivered to the Treasurers there, but no account has been given of them'.[12] In January 1645 the committee decided that he should not be molested further until the sequestration of his estate was discharged. Viscount Scudamore begged to be admitted to composition on 7 January 1647. The Committee for Compounding took a long time to consider his case, and later in the year he asked for his son James, currently 'abroad for his education', to be included.[13] Apart from knowing his estates were being raided, he had no more trouble with the committee until February 1648, when he was summoned and required to pay £2,000 as a one-twentieth part. In October he was called to appear with the money in three weeks. On 25 February 1649 he was given fourteen days to pay up, and that month he produced an account of his sufferings and losses by plunder, felling of timber, sequestrations, fines,

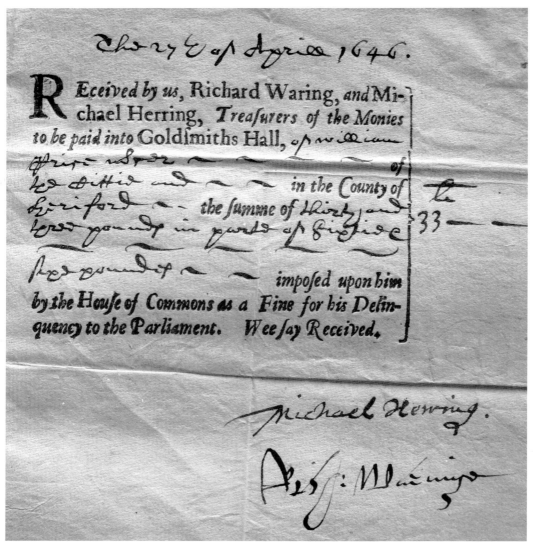

Receipt from the Treasurers at Goldsmiths Hall, Richard Waring and Michael Herring, of William Price's payment of a £33 fine for his delinquency, 27 April 1646 (HCRO CF 50/278)

law expenses, etc., a total of £29,690 besides twenty years' (*sic*) imprisonment with great sickness. He also claimed debts of £6,090 to be taken into account. The committee asked for his 'particular' to be cast up and reported on, and on 22 March respited his assessment on condition that he paid £300 within a month, 'as he is in debt'.[14] Sir Barnabas Scudamore compounded for £100, but on his death in 1652 £37 was still unpaid, and was settled by his brother.[15] Viscount Scudamore lived on prosperously, much esteemed, pursuing his agricultural and ironworking interests until his death in 1671.

Herbert Aubrey of Clehonger was fined £500. He had already lost his house, demolished by his own side.[16] John Styall of Mansel, although one of those who signed a letter advising the citizens of Hereford to surrender to the Scots in 1645, was labelled a delinquent, but made a vigorous defence, claiming he had supplied the Parliamentary garrison at Canon Frome with cheese and money.[17] Ex-Mayor Price, harried by both sides, paid £33 'for his Delinquency' to the Committee for Compounding with Delinquents and duly obtained a receipt.[18] James Barroll, Royalist major captured at Oxford, was fined at one-tenth, £77. William Scudamore of Ballingham was fined at one-fifth and one-twentieth, but kept his place on the Commission of the Peace.

Old scores and offences were raked up before the committee. One Roger Pritchard gave evidence against Mr Wingfield, one-time porter to the bishop, and keeper of his prison. It was claimed that Wingfield had spoken against Parliament, and, when asked in August 1645 to help the poor boy whose mother had been hanged for passing information to the besieging Scots, had replied that the boy should be hanged too.[19]

Well aware that delinquents and papists might give false information, the committee demanded supporting evidence of all claims. Much time was spent in searching through old deeds and records.[20] In 1646 it was given the assistance of a solicitor, George Thorne, to assist in legal wrangles. Agents and debt collectors were also used. Debts owing to delinquents were often claimed by the committee, and in a typical case, Thorne and a London debt collector, Thomas Saunders, were chasing £560 supposedly owed by William Dansey to Roger Dansey of Little Hereford, 'who now stands charged as an enemy of the state'. But William Dansey said the debt had long since been paid. Checks had to be made to establish the truth.[21] William Dansey was fined £390.[22]

Fitzwilliam Coningsby, 'though ordered beyond seas by the Articles of Worcester', petitioned to compound on 31 May 1649, affirming that his Shropshire lands were 'under extent' (seizure or claim against debt) for debts of £5,000. The Committee for Hereford reported back to London on 8 June 1650 that Coningsby's estate and those of three others were taken off sequestration, in regard of mortgages, judgements, or extents. 'Are we to re-sequestrate?' they asked, and were told: 'Seize and hold until the parties concerned make good their claims here'. In 1651 Coningsby was fined at one-third, £4,243 3s 3d, which was reduced on appeal to £3,600. In August 1653 he petitioned to be allowed to pay at a sixth, pleading the starving condition of himself and his family, but this appears to have been ignored. Like others with land in other counties, Coningsby was also having to answer to the Leicestershire Committee.[23] Hampton Court was sold in 1654, Miles Hill's brother obtaining the tenancy. The family fortunes eventually revived, but Coningbsy was another who lost everything for the King.

Another of the worthies, William Rudhall, applied for compounding in April 1649 and was fined £120. John Skipp, captured at Goodrich, his estate sequestrated, was also dealt with briskly, allowed from captivity on licence in April to plead his case, compounding for delinquency 'in both wars' and fined at one sixth, £122 6s 10d. His sequestration was suspended on 29 June when he paid half the fine and gave security for the rest. On 2 July he begged a review on account of his debts, and on 4 July his fine was reduced to £61 8s.[24] Thomas Price of Wisterton, who had been captured at Hereford in April 1643, compounded at a sixth on 27 September 1649, £1,200 less 'an abatement of £500 for settling rectories'. George Thorne certified him as 'an aged man and unfit to travel'.[25]

Some people were hauled back before the committee. In 1649 the militantly Royalist Dr Sherburn of Pembridge, who was stated to have 'ridden with sword and pistols' for the King, was fined at a third, £10, by the Committee for Compounding.[26] But someone informed against him, and John James (one of those who had been excluded from the Grand Jury in 1642, and later became a Parliamentary colonel) reviewed the case in 1651 and found that Sherburn had 'other land which he said was worth £16 a year but which was found to be above £30'. He had also made provisions for his daughters and wife in 1650 which James considered to be fraudulent against the committee.[27] Thomas Walwyn of Hellens petitioned for compounding on 28 April 1648, and was fined £10, plus one-fifth and one-sixth of his property. William Cater, vintner and ex-Mayor, owner of four tenements and shops in Hereford, was fined £12.[28]

Richard Stallard, of Ross-on-Wye, had his estate seized by the Commissioners in December 1649. He was fined £75 6s 8d, also one-sixth of the annual value of his lands and goods, rated at £44. Arthur Jones, Viscount Ranelagh, one-time member for Weobley, 'conceiving himself liable to sequestration', petitioned in February 1650 and rated his estate at a value of £31, plus 'two highway naggs' worth £14, two 'ordinary suits of apparel', £12, and two swords, £5. He was fined £5 3s 4d.[29] Few, if any, of Herefordshire's Royalists and neutrals escaped the committee's attentions. Wallop Brabazon compounded for £799, James Croft for £150, though his property was sequestrated in August 1649 for non-payment.[30] William Lochard compounded for £395, Richard Seaborne for £383, Clement Clarke for £75 6s 8d.[31] Humphrey Cornewall of Berrington Hall was assessed at £100 but discharged for £21 16s, 'it appearing that he is very much in debt'.[32]

With the Presbyterian party forced out of power in Parliament, the Committee for Taking Accounts and its local checker committees were abolished. George Thorne was scathing about the Hereford sub-committee's auditing and in March 1649 accused it of 'notorious behaviour and dishonesty'. Thomas Rawlins, who took over from Miles Hill as county treasurer from the autumn of 1646 until around November 1647, and was in charge of the cathedral funds from 1646-49, was the prime offender in Thorne's view, and he was arrested for failure to deliver up his accounts. But Rawlins, a long-time Parliamentarian, either through complicity with others or because there were few people competent to deal with complex accounts, was only off the committee for a short time before being reinstated.[33] Another long-standing committeeman, Thomas Blayney, had held back £50 of a delinquent's rental over several years, 'pretending the Parliament owes him money'.[34]

24

1649 and After

Was there any point at which the Civil War could be said to be over? There had been no truce or armistice, no formal admission of defeat. The 'Rump' Parliament and the Army were undoubtedly in control of the country, their power reflected by committees from the Council of State down to the local level. In Edinburgh, the teenage Prince of Wales had been proclaimed King Charles II of Scotland, England and Ireland, but the only way he would get the crown of England was by fighting for it. And the combination of government 'intelligencers' and the New Model Army would make it virtually impossible to raise an army on his behalf, even if anyone wanted to try.

But at least, in 1649, the English were no longer fighting one another. Neighbours, customers, colleagues, competitors were again part of a single polity even if a large proportion of them loathed and resented it. Pragmatism, patience, bad memories, a sense of making the best of a bad outcome (or the most of a good one) – all combined with the need to keep on farming, selling, trading, litigating, and doing every kind of peace-time job in order to feed families and keep the roofs over their heads. It was 'business as usual'. Royalist Joyce Jeffreys placed an order with Parliamentarian 'Good cozen Price' for some 'comodities I spake unto you for'.[1] Much of the Forest of Dean's iron-making capacity had been destroyed in the war and Lord Scudamore, on his return to Holme Lacy in 1648, set up a new forge, against which the citizens of Hereford petitioned in January 1649, claiming that the county was likely to be 'utterly ruined'.[2] The Earl of Essex had died in 1646 and his Hereford estates were now owned by his sister, the Royalist Marchioness of Hertford. On 18 February 1650 Walter Kyrle wrote to Lady Hertford, as her steward, 'Colonel Kyrle and I thank you, as for your notice of his sufferings by the foul riot in pulling down of the furnace by persons with no power by that order or otherwise to do so'.[3] Perhaps attitudes had changed. Before the war, the citizens of Hereford might have been less likely to riot against a new, wood-devouring ironworks. Their view of Viscount Scudamore and the Kyrles cannot have been quite the same as in 1642. The wool trade was reformed by the Commonwealth's Council for Trade in 1650, which observed that there was 'great abuse and deceit used in the winding and making up of fleeces of wool with lambs' wool, refuse wool, cott, tar, tail locks, hinder shanks, clay, dung, cumber and other trash'.[4] In February 1651 Parliament formed a committee to receive propositions regarding navigation of the Wye.[5] In such ways, the new regime set out to show its efficiency and that it cared for commerce as well as keeping a sharp eye for political and religious correctness. In May 1650 the Council of State wrote to Governor Wroth Rogers about certain ministers in

Herefordshire who were making difficulties about the 'engagement' oath required of them, which they would only take with 'expositions' which the Justices had allowed. Now the ministers and the Justices were called to account for this unwarranted indulgence.[6]

John Beale (1608-1683) must have been typical of many for whom the end of hostilities was a relief. He moved in 1647 from a small estate at Cobhall, Allensmore, to Stretton Grandison, in the adjacent parish to his birthplace at Yarkhill. Related to the Scudamores and Pyes, he is of interest in the Civil War context only as another example of those for whom the war was a disagreeable disruption in which they took little part. Beale was a moderate Parliamentarian and had sympathies with the Independents. In 1649 he became Master of St Catherine's Hospital in Ledbury, but the war gave him an unpleasant aftershock when he was ousted in favour of a more active and committed cleric, the Rev. John Tombes. His consuming interest was in cultivation and landscape, and his book, *Herefordshire Orchards*, published in 1657, would bring immense benefits to the county's apple and cider commerce.[7]

Through 1650 the new order ruled in Herefordshire. Increasingly, new names appear on official lists, of men picked for being 'well-affected'. In March, Wroth Rogers obtained, or perhaps arranged, a testimony to the Committee for Compounding of his 'singular vigilance' but also praising his 'modesty and integrity, abstaining from the injustice and oppression by which many others of like place have heaped up good sums', and asking for

An ironworks much as it would have appeared at the time of the Civil War, although this is of a later date, in the Downton Gorge (Hereford Library)

his official allowance to be increased.[8] The implication is of a fair administration, though Rogers would be criticised for placing excessive demands on sequestrated estates. Matters in Herefordshire were quiet enough for a troop of dragoons to be sent in March 1651 from there to Lancashire, where there were disturbances, and in the same month the garrison was required to provide fifty men for service in Ireland.[9] A new militia commission was formed in April. The Harleys and Birch had no official role in county affairs but were working to get their estates in order. Once again, rents and other incomes were flowing in. In August, at a time of high political tension, with Charles II in Scotland and Cromwell also there with an army, Edward Harley was arrested by order of Colonel Wroth Rogers and brought before the commissioners for the militia in Hereford to answer charges of being disaffected to the government. He was immediately discharged, on condition that he left the county, but his brothers Robert and Thomas were imprisoned for a time at Bristol.[10] It is not clear that a plot existed, but to the new leaders, the Presbyterians had replaced the Catholics as prime threat. Sir William Waller and some other leading Presbyterians were in prison. In the same year Sir Robert Harley, having been refused permission to live in Shrewsbury, rented a house in Ludlow.[11]

Through agents and informers, the Committee for the Advancement of Money was still pursuing Herefordshire delinquents. Sir Henry Lingen, unable to raise £1,200 pursuant to an order by the Committee for Compounding, was allowed to sell off '£100 per annum of any part of his estate' to enable him to raise money to pay the remainder of his fines.[12] Royalists who had been out with Lingen in 1648 were fined, as was Robert Wigmore of Shobdon, who had been involved in the Pembrokeshire rising that year. Colonel Thomas Mytton, of Shropshire, on the prowl for un-fined Papists, found a whole nest in Orleton, and claimed £5,000, as a share of their estates, for his information against Miles Blount and five others.[13] Mytton also unearthed evidence against Rudhall Gwyllim, of Whitchurch, one of the new members of the assessment committee, going back to the battle at Coleford in the Forest of Dean on 20 February 1643: 'When the Parliamentary forces under Colonel Berrow were routed, and fain to get over a river for safety, he commanded that their boats be sunk ... and said they were rebels against the King.'[14] Gwyllim kept his place, however.

In the late summer of 1651, the fourth Scottish army to enter England in ten years, with Charles II at its head, marched south, keeping to the west side and hoping to gather loyalist support as it went. Lord General Cromwell was close behind it. Undoubtedly this caused intense thought and heart-searching in Royalist places. By late August the royal army had reached Worcester, and any of Herefordshire's Cavaliers might have thrown off caution and gone to join them. But the conditions of 1642 could not be replicated. Of the Nine Worthies, four were dead, and the survivors had all compounded. If Lingen and Coningsby still had a fighting spirit, they had no resources, and were closely watched. The Bailiff of Ledbury proclaimed Charles II as king, but was arrested, maltreated, and forced to recant.[15] It seems that some members of the Herefordshire militia committee were against sending men to support Cromwell's army, but troops and supplies were despatched.[16] The most surprising manifestation of support for the unacknowledged king came from John Birch and his brother Samuel, who rode to Worcester to salute him (Charles II had signed the Covenant, and could at this time be regarded as a 'Presbyterian'). But they did not take part in the battle of 3 September, which ended in the defeat of the royal army and the flight of the young king, and which concluded the third phase of the Civil War. Birch's estate was sequestrated by the Herefordshire Committee, and he was briefly imprisoned at the order of the Council of State. All charges were dropped, but he continued to be a critic of the regime. This won him local popularity, and would stand him in good stead after the Stuart Restoration. A florid baroque monument in Weobley church commemorates his death in 1691.

The Civil War had cost Herefordshire, like the rest of the country, more in terms of human misery and grief than anything since the ravages of the Black Death in the 14th century. If the human cost was immense, the material cost was also great, though in an economy based on the land and its products, much could be made good in a couple of years. Herefordshire's capitalists lost no time in profiting from the destruction of the Forest of Dean's ironworks. Much wealth had simply changed hands within the county. But there had been great destruction, and one historian even writes about Hereford surrounded by a ring of ashes, referring to the numerous castles and houses demolished or burnt down. Ideals, too, perished. The tragedy for Sir Robert Harley was not the loss of his house, or even his wife's death, but the failure of his aspirations for a Presbyterian Church of England, and the execution of the King, which he had never sought. Sir Robert died in 1656 and was buried in the newly-rebuilt church at Brampton Bryan. For Fitzwilliam Coningsby and Henry Lingen, the future must also have looked dark for different reasons, but both lived to see the Stuart monarchy restored in 1660, as did Viscount Scudamore and Lord Herbert.

Between bellicosity and indifference, between engagement and detachment, lie not only a spectrum of attitudes and opinions, but also an extent of latent feeling, which can be shocked or more slowly irradiated into a sense of urgency, of commitment to a cause that must be defended at all costs. In Herefordshire, unlike many other counties, with Cheshire and Staffordshire as near examples,[17] there was no 'neutralist' movement in 1642. Sir William Croft made an effort, probably for family reasons, to 'neutralise' Sir Robert Harley, but his proposed solution was not to confront the crisis with an anti-warfare agreement but to dodge it, by uniting against the rebellious Irish. Both sides accepted the reality of the power struggle, whatever its causes, and in the summer of 1642 it seemed that in Herefordshire a strong spontaneous spirit had arisen in the King's defence. A torch might have been lit whose flames would spread to a national conflagration more intense than was actually to occur. But despite the undoubted strength of individual feelings, the sparks failed to set off a sustained fervour. Three months after the grand muster, Royalist Hereford opened its gates to Stamford's troopers. The relative passivity of the King's potential supporters was such a crucial aspect of the Civil War that it needs some examination. In Hereford, the collective spirit of July 1642 resurged during the Scottish siege of July-August 1645. Under a resolute governor, defiance to an alien army triumphed over the urgings of its Parliamentary associates to make a safe surrender. By that time, however, it was too late for the example to restore the King's declining fortunes, and within three months the fervency had faded. After the final capture of Hereford in December 1645, only a few hundred men in the entire county could be found to fight for the King.

By 1642, Charles I's 18 years on the throne had not made him generally admired or trusted, and his visits to Hereford in 1645 did not prompt new personal loyalties. In Herefordshire, the man best placed to lead his campaign chose to opt out, and the 'Nine Worthies' failed to produce a commanding figure to rally support. The most prominent Royalist in the region was Lord Herbert, who, apart from his unsuitability to military command, was a suspect figure because of his Catholicism. These were local and individual considerations, but also, to many people even the nature of the dispute may have seemed abstract and remote. Despite the fiery preachings of Dr Rogers and others, the religious dimension probably inspired more enthusiasm on the Parliamentary than the Royalist side, partly because the King's own views were somewhat veiled by his need to accommodate the Calvinist-to-Catholic range of belief among his supporters; partly because very many people disliked the direction in which he and Laud had been taking the Anglican Church. Nor did Royalism embrace any notion of social change. For people not engaged by ideology, whether political or religious, what was there to gain by active support for Charles? Many who preferred that the King should win, or at least survive in his regal position by some compromise, were not prepared to hazard their lives, their fortunes or even their convenience to help make it happen. For all who held official positions, titles, or specific rights, from the constable up, the Kingship was the ultimate guarantor of their continuance, but few people, in a secular context at least, can have seriously felt their places or privileges needed to be defended by coming out for the King. Parliament, right up to December 1648, was not proposing to do away with the King, or with monarchy. Other than to the volunteer soldier who might expect better pay (at first, anyway), a share of loot, even some excitement, the Royalist cause had nothing to offer the ordinary person beyond protection from the 'tyranny of Parliament'. By 1644-45, however, military terrorism in Royalist-controlled areas like Herefordshire was a far more real threat to security. In the course of the war years, there was a growing sense of resignation: the troubles had to be endured until God saw fit to bring an end. But by 1645 the Herefordshire clubmen were unwilling to wait humbly for that to happen. They invoked a power to which they gave more respect than to King or Parliament – the Law, by which they meant the 'known laws', not new ordinances from whatever source. Sir Barnabas Scudamore recognised this and responded with his own mention of the 'known laws'. To him and the other Royalist commanders, though, the clubmen's refusal to fight for Parliament counted for nothing against their opposition to the demands and conduct of the Royalist garrisons. By the end of the war, Herefordshire's Royalism consisted of little more than a preference for traditional forms of administration, combined with a resentment of Parliament's religious reforms, which, like the abolition of Christmas celebrations, also affected social life – and its taxes. There were few positive elements.

Uncertain and disturbing times often give rise to incidental strangenesses, noted as 'Marvels' or 'Wonders', and 17th-century people saw the hand of God, or the Devil, in many signs and portents. For the credulous, the Civil War was heralded, and the Restoration foretold, by two such events. In February 1642 a pair of monoliths, known as the Wirgens, in the Lugg watermeadows between Hereford and Sutton St Nicholas, one set upright on the other, were moved a considerable distance by some mysterious agency, making a two-foot deep furrow in the ground. 'Nine yoke of oxen' were needed to drag them back, and it was taken as a presage of disaster to come.[18] Seven years later, on 16 July 1649, an infant child, only a few months old, was said to have been discovered by workers in a field near a hamlet called The Hope, not far from Croft Castle. The child began to prophesy 'and foretell of many strange things that shall ensue in England and Ireland, within the space of three Yeares, concerning the crowning of Charles the Second King of England, Scotland and Ireland, his great Victories, with the destruction of the present Parliament and Army …'. The infant was taken to the village and fed, declaring it had never eaten so well before, after which it 'vanished away'.[19] Its prophecies were only partly correct, but the story shows that under republican control the pulse of Royalism was beating on. Like a pair of bookends, these Herefordshire marvels stand at the beginning and the end of what was – however else it may be also be described – a very English war.

Bibliography

1. Manuscript and Original Sources

Bodleian Library (Bod.)
    MS Ashmolean
    MS Tanner 303
Brampton Bryan: Harley Archives
British Library (BL)
    Additional MSS (Add.MSS)
    Harleian MSS
Hereford Public Library (HPL)
    Collectanea Herefordiensia
    Parr, F., Historical Notes of Old Ledbury
    Pilley MSS Notes
    Pilley, Notes on Hereford Castle
    Victoria County History (*VCH*)
    Hill, Miles, *A True and Impartiall Account of the Plunderings, Losses and Sufferings of the County of Hereford by the Scottish Army, During Their Siege Before the City of Hereford, Anno Dom. 1645*
Hereford County Record Office (HCRO)
    Harley bundles
    Herefordiana
    Hopton Papers
    Notes from Sequestration Papers
    'Some Passages in the Life and Character of a Lady Resident in Herefordshire and Worcestershire During the Civil War'.
    Townsend, G.F., *The Sieges in Herefordshire during the Commonwealth*.
    Transcripts of Sacks (HCRO, TS)
    Webb MSS
Historical Manuscripts Commission (HMC)
    Calendar of the Manuscripts of the Marquis of Bath (Bath MSS)
    Coke Manuscripts (Coke MSS)
    Manuscripts of the Duke of Portland (Portland MSS)
National Archives (NA)
    Calendar of the Committee for the Advance of Money (CAM)
    Calendar of the Committee for Compounding, Parts iii and iv (CCC)
    Calendars of State Papers, Domestic, Charles I, vols 462, 516 (CSPD)
    Calendars of State Papers, Domestic, Interregnum, 1649-50
    Calendar of State Papers Relating to English Affairs in the Archives of Venice, vol xxvii, 1643-47, ed. Allen B.Hinds. London, 1926
    Firth, C.H., and Rait, R.S., *Acts & Ordinances of the Interregnum, 1642-1660*. London, 1911
    State Papers (SP)
    Journals of the House of Commons (JHC)
    Journals of the House of Lords (JHL)

2. Journals

American Historical Review
English Historical Review (EHR)
Hereford Diocesan Messenger
Historical Journal
Journal of British Studies (JBS)
Midland History (MH)
Past and Present (P&P)
Transactions of the Royal Historical Society (TRHS)
Transactions of the Woolhope Naturalists' Field Club (TW)

3. Theses

McParlin, G.E., *The Hereford Gentry in County Government, 1625-61*. University of Wales, Aberystwyth.
Ref. 32/1/500 (1981)

4. Books (i): Herefordshire and The Marches

Atherton, Ian, *Ambition and Failure in Stuart England*. Manchester, 1999
Atherton, Ian (ed.), *Sir Barnabas Scudamore's Defence*. Akron, Ohio, 1992
Aylmer, G. and Tiller, J. (eds.) *Hereford Cathedral: A History*. London 2000
Bannister, A.T., *The History of Ewias Harold*. Hereford, 1902
Bannister, A.T., *Herefordshire and Its Place in English History*. Hereford, 1905
Bannister, A.T., *The Cathedral Church of Hereford: Its History & Constitution*. London, 1924
Barroll, H.H., *Barroll in Great Britain and America*. Baltimore, 1910
Bongaerts, Theo, *The Correspondence of Thomas Blount*. Amsterdam, 1978
Botzum, R. and T., *The 1675 Thomas Blount MS History of Herefordshire*. 1997
Carless, W.T., *A Short History of Hereford School*. Hereford, 1914
Coleman, Delphine, *Orcop: The Story of a Herefordshire Village*. Hanley Swan, Worcs., 1992
Collins, William, *Outlines of Old and New Hereford, Part I*. Hereford, 1911
Cooke, W.H., *Collections Towards the History and Antiquities of the County of Hereford, Continued: The Hundred of Grimsworth Part 1*. London, 1881; *The Hundred of Greytree*. London, 1882
Croft, O.G.S., *The House of Croft, of Croft Castle*. Hereford, 1949
Duncumb, John, *Collections Towards the History and Antiquities of the County of Hereford*. 1804, reprinted Cardiff, 1997
Eales, Jacqueline, *Puritans and Roundheads: The Harleys of Brampton Bryan and the Outbreak of the English Civil War*. Cambridge, 1990
Faraday, Michael, *Ludlow 1085-1660*. Chichester, 1991
Fletcher, G.W.D. (ed.) *The Registers of Hopton Castle, 1538-1812*. Shropshire Parish Register Society. London, 1901
George, R.H., *History of the Herefordshire Borderland*. Leominster, 1914
Harford, Alice, *Annals of the Harford Family*. London, 1909
Harvey, P.D.A., *Mappa Mundi*. London, 1996
Havergal, F.T., *Fasti Herefordenses*. Edinburgh, 1869
Heath-Agnew, E., *Roundhead to Royalist*. Hereford, 1979
Heath-Agnew, E., *A History of Herefordshire Cattle and Their Breeders*. London, 1993
Hughes, Pat, and Hurley, Heather, *The Story of Ross*. Logaston, 1999

Hillaby, Joe G., *The Book of Ledbury*. Buckingham, 1982

Hopkinson, C., *Herefordshire Under Arms*. Bromyard, 1985

Hopton, Madeline, *Froma Canonica: History of Canon Frome*. London, 1902

Lewis, Thomas T. (ed.), *Letters of the Lady Brilliana Harley*. London, 1854

Mason, B.H., *Coin of the Realm*. Canning, Nova Scotia, 1993

Matthews, J.H., *Collections Towards the History and Antiquities of the County of Hereford, Continued: The Hundred of Wormelow, Parts 1 & 2*. Hereford, 1913-15

Munthe, Malcolm, *Hellens: The Story of a Herefordshire Manor*. London, 1957

Parker, K., *Radnorshire from Civil War to Restoration*. Logaston, 2000

Philpott, H.W., *Diocesan Histories: Hereford*. London, 1888

Powell, Walter (ed. Joseph A. Bradney), *The Diary of Walter Powell of Llantilio Crossenny*. Bristol, 1907

Price, John, *An Historical Account of the City of Hereford*. Hereford, 1796

Rawlinson, Thomas, *The History and Antiquities of the City and Cathedral Church of Hereford*. London, 1717

Robinson, C.J., *A History of the Castles of Herefordshire and Their Lords*. London & Hereford, 1869

Robinson, C.J., *The Mansions of Herefordshire and Their Memories*. Edinburgh & London, 1882

Roe, Major (ed. John Webb), *Military Memoir of Colonel John Birch*. London, 1873

Shoesmith, Ron, *Castles and Moated Sites of Herefordshire*. Logaston, 2009

Slingsby, Sir Henry (ed. Daniel Parsons), *Diary of Sir Henry Slingsby*. London 1836

Thomas, A., and Boucher, A., *Hereford City Excavations, 4*. Logaston, 2002

Tonkin, J.W., *Herefordshire*. London, 1977

Townsend, G.F., *The Town and Borough of Leominster*. Leominster, *c*.1861

Victoria County History of Herefordshire

Watkins, Morgan G., *Collections Towards the History and Antiquities of the County of Hereford, Continued: The Hundreds of Huntington and Radlow*. Hereford, 1897

Webb, John and T.W., *Memorials of the Civil War Between King Charles I and the Parliament of England, as it Affected Herefordshire and the Adjacent Counties*. 2 vols, London, 1879

Whitehead, D., and Eisel, J., *A Herefordshire Miscellany*. Hereford, 2000

Whitehead, D., *The Castle Green at Hereford*. Logaston, 2007

Williams, W.R., *The Parliamentary History of the County of Hereford*. Brecknock, 1896

5. Books (ii). Other Books

Archer, Steven N., and Bartoy, Kevin M., *Between Dirt and Discussion: Methods, Methodology and Interpretation in Historical Archaeology*. New York, 2006

Aubrey, John, *Brief Lives*. New ed. Harmondsworth, 2000

Baxter, Richard (ed. Matthew Sylvester), *Reliquiae Baxterianae*. London, 1696

Bossy, J., *The English Catholic Community, 1570-1850*. London, 1975

Bowden, P.J., *The Wool Trade in Tudor and Stuart England*. London, 1962

Bund, J. W. Willis, *The Civil War in Worcestershire, 1642-46, and the Scottish Invasion of 1651*. Birmingham, 1905

Cary, H., *Memorials of the Great Civil War from 1642 to 1652*. 2 vols, London, 1842

Cliffe, J.T., *Puritans in Conflict*. London, 1988

Collectanea Curiosa, vol 2. Oxford, 1781

Craik, Henry, *The Life of Jonathan Swift*. London, 1882

Dore, R.N. (ed.), *The Letter-Books of Sir William Brereton*. 2 vols, Gloucester, 1984

Fletcher, A.J., *The Outbreak of the English Civil War*. London, 1981

Fletcher, A.J., *Reform in the Provinces*. London, 1986

Gardiner, Samuel, *History of the Great Civil War*. 4 vols., London, 1901

Grassby, Richard, *The Business Community of Seventeenth-Century England*. Cambridge 1995

Hill, Christopher, *Change and Continuity in Seventeenth-Century England*. London, 1975

Hughes, Ann, *The Causes of the English Civil War*. Basingstoke, 1991

Hutton, Ronald, *The Royalist War Effort, 1642-1646*. 2nd ed, London, 1996

Laslett, Peter, *The world we have lost*. London, 1965

Lehmberg, Stanford H., *Cathedrals Under Siege*. Exeter, 1996

Leslie, Michael, and Raylor, Timothy (eds.), *Culture and Cultivation in Early Modern England*. Leicester, 1992

Manning, Brian, *The English People and the English Revolution*. London, 1976

Matthews, A.G., *Walker Revised*. Oxford, 1948

McElligott, Jason, and Smith, David L. (eds.), *Royalists and Royalism during the English Civil Wars*. Cambridge, 2007

Moore-Colyer, Richard, *Welsh Cattle Drovers*. Ashbourne, 2002

Morrill, John (ed.), *Reactions to the English Civil War, 1642-49*. London, 1982

Morrill, John, *Revolt in the Provinces*. London, 1999

Newman, P.R., *Royalist Officers in England and Wales, 1642-1660*. New York & London, 1981

Oxford Dictionary of National Biography. Oxford, 2004

Powell, Anthony, *John Aubrey and His Friends*. London, 1948

Rushworth, John, *Historical Collections of Private Passages of State*, vol. 3, 1639-40, vol. 5, 1642-45, vol.6, 1645-47. London, 1722

Russell, Conrad (ed.), *The Origins of the English Civil War*. London, 1973

Russell, Conrad, *The Causes of the English Civil War*. Oxford, 1990

Russell, Conrad, *Unrevolutionary England*. London, 1990

Seaton, Rev. Preb., *History and Description of Goodrich Castle*. Hereford, 1903

Sherwood, R.E., *Civil Strife in the Midlands, 1642-51*. London & Chichester, 1974

Symonds, Richard, *Diary of the Marches of the Royal Army During the Great Civil War*. Ed. C.E. Long, London (Camden Society), 1859

Terry, C.S., *The Life and Campaigns of Alexander Leslie, Earl of Leven*. London, 1899

Thirsk, Joan, *Agrarian History of England and Wales*, Vol. 4, 1500-1640. Cambridge, 1967

Townshend, Henry (ed. J.W.W. Bund), *The Diary of Henry Townshend of Elmley Lovett, 1640-63*. 2 vols. London, 1920

Trow-Smith, Robert, *A History of British Livestock Husbandry to 1700*. London, 1957

Underdown, David, *Revel, Riot and Rebellion*. Oxford, 1985

Underdown, David, *A Freeborn People: Politics and the Nation in Seventeenth-Century England*. Oxford, 1996

Vicars, John, *Parliamentarie Chronicall*, 4 vols. London, 1644-46

Wade, Gladys I., *Thomas Traherne*. Princeton, NJ, 1944

Warburton, Eliot, *Memoirs of Prince Rupert and the Cavaliers*. 3 vols. London, 1849

Wedgwood, C.V., *The King's War*. London, 1958

Young, Peter, and Holmes, Richard, *The English Civil War: A Military History*. London, 1974

Notes and References

Foreword & Introduction

1. Brampton Bryan, Harley Archives. Funeral oration for Sir Robert Harley, 22 December 1657.
2. Fletcher, *Outbreak of the English Civil War*, 283.
3. Hutton, R., 'The Royalist War Effort', in Morrill, *Reactions to the English Civil War, 1642-49*, 51.
4. McElligott and Smith, *Royalists and Royalism*, 9f.

Chapter 1

1. Gardiner, *Civil War*, i, 337.
2. Whitehead, *The Castle Green*, 44.
3. HCRO. Pilley, 'Notes on Hereford Castle', 16; Whitehead, *op. cit*, 47.
4. Collins, *Outlines*, 100.
5. *TW* 53, 2005, Eisel, J.C., 'Hereford Market Hall and the Tolsey', 30.
6. Collins, *op. cit.*, 100.
7. Duncumb, *Collections*, i, 355ff.
8. Duncumb, *op. cit.*, 358. John Aubrey recalled seeing Alderman Wellington in 1634, 'the only person he ever saw so old-fashioned as to wear trunk-hose'; see Powell, *John Aubrey*, 33.
9. *TW*, 1994, 97-139. Shoesmith, R., and Crosskey, R., 'Go to Gaol – in Hereford'; HPL. LC942.44, Capes, W.W., 'Some Notes on Old Hereford'.
10. HCRO.TS 20.viii.ii..
11. It is not clear where this was located. In a document of 1549 the College of Vicars Choral is noted as having responsibility for the upkeep of Barr's Bridge (HMC. MSS of Rye and Hereford Corporations, App. pt iv).
12. Havergal, *Fasti*, 92.
13. Rawlinson, *History & Antiquities*, 23.
14. Russell, *Causes of the English Civil War*, 59.
15. Rawlinson, *op. cit.*, 235.
16. *ODNB*, William Marshall, 'Herbert Croft'.
17. Lehmberg, *Cathedrals Under Siege*, 160.
18. Carless, *A Short History of Hereford School*, 29.
19. McParlin, Thesis, 'The Hereford Gentry in County Government, 1625-61', 1.
20. Fletcher, *Outbreak*, 80.
21. Christopher Hill in Russell, *Origins of the English Civil War*, 67.
22. HCRO.TS 20. xxiii.ii; xxiv, ii.
23. HCRO.TS 20.xxxv.x.
24. HCRO.TS. 20.xxii.x, 13 August 1641.
25. Webb, i, 71.
26. Lewis, *Letters of Lady Brilliana*, 263.
27. *JBS*, Vol 20, No 2 (Spring 1981), 26-49. Kent, Joan, 'The English Village Constable, 1580-1642', 49.
28. McParlin, Thesis, 54.

Chapter 2

1. Atherton, *Ambition*, 146. Incidentally, this meant that Scudamore could sit in the Irish, but not the English, Parliament (assuming either were summoned).
2. McParlin, Thesis, 21.
3. Atherton, *op. cit.*, 228.
4. Webb, i, 20.
5. Lewis, *Letters of Lady Brilliana*, 152. Letter to Edward Harley, 19 March 1641.
6. HMC. De l'Isle MSS, vol vi, Sidney Papers, 1626-98, 70.
7. Newman, *Royalist Officers*, 83.
8. Williams, *Parliamentary History*, 44, wrongly says Fitzwilliam Coningsby was High Steward of Leominster; the post was held by Sir Walter Pye.
9. The story of the Westminster Soap Company is given briefly in Manning, *The English People*, 152.
10. HCRO.AA17/89. 'Some Passages', 217.
11. JHC, 28 May 1641.
12. Eales, *Puritans*, 20.
13. HCRO. Harley bundle 78, 2.
14. Webb, i, 69. Sir Walter was enough of a courtier to have his portrait painted by Van Dyck. See *Burlington Magazine,* vol 124, no. 949, April 1982, 235.
15. Cooke, *Collection*, 73.
16. Symonds, *Diary*, 196.
17. McParlin, Thesis, 58, 70.
18. *TW, * xl, 1972, 373-387. Aylmer, G.E., 'Who Was Ruling in Herefordshire from 1645 to 1661', 375.
19. 'The Vale Royal of England', 1656, quoted in Laslett, *The World we have lost*, 186.
20. HCRO. CF 50/100, 'Herefordiana', vol. 5, 210.
21. *TW*, xl, 1972. Aylmer, *op. cit.*
22. Hill, *Change and Continuity*, 223ff.
23. Gardiner, *Civil War,* iii, 193, 196.
24. A point made in Underdown, *Revel, Riot & Rebellion*, 165.
25. *JBS*, Vol 19 No. 2, Spring 1980, 54-73, Holmes, C., 'The County Community in Stuart Historiography', 72.
26. Lewis, *Letters of Lady Brilliana*, 3, 182, 263n.
27. HCRO. AA17/89, 'Some Passages in the Life and Character of a Lady Resident in Herefordshire and Worcestershire During the Civil War'. Joyce Jeffreys died in 1650 and is buried in the church at Clifton on Teme.
28. HMC. Portland MSS, iii, 85.

29. Quoted in McParlin, Thesis, 51; CSPD 1637, 37.
30. Hill, *Change & Continuity*, 12.
31. Quoted in Cliffe, *Puritans in Conflict,* 1.
32. Eales, *Puritans*, 157; Fletcher, *Outbreak*, 109.
33. Eales, *op. cit.*, 56.
34. Hillaby, *Book of Ledbury*, 96.
35. *TW*, xl, 1972. Aylmer, *op. cit.,* 380.
36. Botzum, *The 1675 Thomas Blount MS*, 5.
37. George, *History of the Herefordshire Borderland*, 45.
38. Matthews, *Collections: Hundred of Wormelow*, i, 35f.
39. McParlin, Thesis, 10.
40. Bossy, *The English Catholic Community*, 405.
41. Eales, *Puritans*, 16, 40.
42. Matthews, *op. cit.*, ii, 33.
43. Fletcher, *Outbreak*, 63, 69.
44. Gardiner, *Civil War*, iii, 200, wrote 'The country gentlemen … were Calvinists almost to a man', but this excludes the numerous Catholics and Catholic sympathisers.
45. Hughes, *Causes*, 107.
46. Eales, *Puritans*, 90, 97f.
47. Fletcher, *Outbreak*, 328.
48. Munthe, *Hellens*, 89.

Chapter 3
1. Laslett, *The World we have lost*, 147.
2. Noted in Morrill, *Revolt in the Provinces*, 46.
3. HCRO. Miscellaneous Papers, iv, 85.
4. Symonds, *Diary*, 203.
5. *TW*, 54, 2006, 71-100, Grundy, J.E., 'Herefordshire farmsteads in their agrarian context', 74.
6. Trow-Smith, *History of British Livestock Husbandry*, 208.
7. Bowden, *The Wool Trade*, 29.
8. Trow-Smith, *op. cit.*, 164.
9. Quoted in Hughes and Hurley, *The Story of Ross*, 50; see also Mason, *Coin of the Realm*, 56; Trow-Smith, *op. cit.*, 256.
10. Thirsk, *Agrarian History*, iv, 108f.
11. *TW*, 1937, Rhys Jenkins, 'Industries of Herefordshire in Bygone Times,' 70-75.
12. Illustrated in Hillaby, *The Book of Ledbury*, 100.
13. Bowden, *The Wool Trade*, 58.
14. See 'Presentment by the Grand Jury', 1640, and the 'Petition' of 1642, reprinted in Webb, ii, 335f, 338.
15. Foster, *Alumni Oxonienses, 1500-1714*.
16. Harford, *Annals*, 14. Harford got his D.Med. in 1639, aged 32 (Foster, *Alumni Oxonienses*).
17. HCRO. AA 17/89. 'Some Passages,' 197.
18. *TW*, 1958-60. Leeds, Winifred, 'Early Postal History of Herefordshire', 160-167.]

19. CSPD, Charles I, 437: Undated 1639. Items 21, 22.
20. *TW*, 1958-60, Leeds, *Ibid.*, 161.
21. Lewis, *Letters of Lady Brilliana*, 125, 147.
22. Moore-Colyer, *Welsh Cattle-Drovers*, 155.
23. HCRO. AA17/89, 'SomePassages', 200.
24. Hillaby, *The Book of Ledbury*, 105.
25. HCRO. TS, xxxix. xi (1642).
26. *TW*, xlvi,1986, Taylor, Elizabeth, 'The 17th Century Iron Forge at Carey Mill,' 450-467.
27. *TW*, xlvi, 1986, Taylor, *op. cit.*, 451.
28. Tonkin, *Herefordshire*, 197; Faraday, *Ludlow*, 173.
29. HCRO. Harley bundle 54. 4.
30. *TW*, xlv, 1985, 721-9. Bayliss, D.G., 'The Effects of Bringewood Forge and Furnace on the Landscape of Part of North Herefordshire'.
31. 'Presentment by the Grand Jury, see Webb, ii, 335.
32. *Economic History Review*, Vol 26 No 4 (1973), 593-613. Hammersley, G., 'The Charcoal Iron Industry and Its Fuel', 609.
33. *TW*, vol xxxv part 2 (1956). Morgan, F.C., 'Herefordshire Potteries', 133; vol 57, 2009, 127-131, Harrison, M., 'A Kiln at New House, Brilley'.
34. Archer & Bartoy, *Between Dirt and Discussion*, 18ff. Endogamy within the craft community was helpful in preserving trade secrets. Coplestone-Crow's *Herefordshire Place Names* finds no early evidence for 'Pipe' here, unlike the not-far-off Pipe and Lyde.
35. Cooke, *Collections: Hundred of Grimsworth*, i, 5.

Chapter 4
1. Webb, i, 36.
2. McParlin, Thesis, 33, 99; *VCH*, 'Political History,' 382-3. Duncumb, iv, 96, records him as only having been imprisoned in Hereford Castle gatehouse.
3. Cooke, *Collections: Hundred of Grimsworth*, i, 96.
4. *VCH*, 'Political History', 385f.
5. CSPD, Charles I, 462, April-July 1640, 544.
6. Full text reprinted in Webb, ii, 335f.
7. JHC, vol. 5, 1646-48, 397-401.
8. Williams, *Parliamentary History*, 156f.
9. Hill, *Change & Continuity*, 9.
10. Eales, *Puritans*, 115.
11. Eales, *op. cit.*, 106.
12. Fletcher, *Outbreak*, 27.
13. Lewis, *Letters of the Lady Brilliana,* 130. Letter to Edward Harley, 21 May 1641.
14. Rushworth, *Historical Collections*, iv, 101.

15. HMC. Portland MSS, iii, 79, Letter to Sir Robert Harley, 9 August, 1641.
16. Rushworth, *Historical Collections*, iv, 144. 'Delinquent' became a catch-word of the time for anyone offending against Parliament's Acts or Ordinances.
17. Fletcher, *Outbreak*, 140.
18. HMC. Coke, 305, 'A Great Discovery of a Damnable Plot at Raglan Castle'.
19. HMC. 10th Report 1885, Corporation of Bridgnorth MSS, 433-4.
20. Webb, i, 52.
21. *ODNB*, J. Eales, 'Sir Robert Harley'; Webb, i, 42.
22. Fletcher, *Outbreak*, 183.
23. *ODNB*, I. Atherton, 'George Coke'.
24. Webb, i, 45.
25. Full text reproduced in Webb, ii, 337f.
26. *VCH*, 'Political History', 368f
27. McParlin, Thesis, 60.
28. Eales, *Puritans*, 132f.
29. BL. Portland MSS Loan 29/173 ff.207r, 222v, 'Isaac Seward to Harley, 7 and 19 February 1642.
30. Fletcher, *Outbreak*, 208.
31. BL.Portland MSS Loan 29/173 ff.228r-229v, 239r-240r, 'Herefordshire JPs to Harley and Humphrey Coningsby'.
32. Cliffe, *Puritans in Conflict*, 13.
33. BL. Portland MSS Loan 29/173 ff.239r-240r, 'Herefordshire JPs to Harley and Humphrey Coningsby'.
34. Text in Webb, ii, 338.
35. Cliffe, *Puritans in Conflict,* 7.
36. BL. Portland MSS Loan 29/173, f.226r. 'John Tombes to Harley, 5 March 1642.
37. Lewis, *Letters of Lady Brilliana*, 159. Letter to Edward Harley, May 7, 1642.

Chapter 5

1. Webb, i, 66. Pye's mission, often referred to (see for example Lovell, C., and Pikes, P.J., in Archenfield Archaeology project AA_57, 'Pool Farm, Much Dewchurch', 2004) is not noted in Albion's *Charles I and the Court of Rome* (London, 1935). It is likely his role was that of a courier rather than a diplomat.
2. Lewis, *Letters of Lady Brilliana*, 167. Letter to Edward Harley, June 4, 1642.
3. Eales, *Puritans*, 161. Powell, *John Aubrey*, 57, 109, notes that Elizabeth Broughton was said to have been first seduced by the parish clerk of Canon Pyon, 'one Weaver'. A ditty of the times went:
'From the watch at twelve a clock

And from Bess Broughton's buttond smock, Libera nos, Domine.'
4. Lewis, *Letters of Lady Brilliana*, 170. Letter to Edward Harley, 20 June, 1642.
5. Morrill, *Revolt in the Provinces*, 54.
6. Fletcher, *Outbreak*, 305.
7. Full text in Webb, ii, 343-4. This is the document in which Lady Harley saw the hand of Mary Tomkins.
8. Webb, i, 86.
9. Fletcher, *Outbreak*, 305.
10. Fletcher, *op. cit..*, 250.
11. HMC. Portland MSS, iii, 88. Hutton suggests that 'Drs Rogers, Mason and Sherburn raised the county for the King by fiery preaching' (*The Royalist War Effort*,13).
12. HMC. Portland MSS, iii, 93. Letter to Sir Robert Harley, 17 July 1642.
13. Atherton, *Ambition*, 224f.
14. Webb, i, 81.
15. Lewis, *Letters of Lady Brilliana*, 176.
16. Atherton, *op. cit.*, 225.
17. McParlin, Thesis, 62.
18. *VCH*, 'Political History', 388.
19. The commissioners would have given the captaincy to Edward Harley, if he took the King's side; see Lewis, *Letters of Lady Brilliana*, 176, 8 July 1642.
20. Lady Harley to Harley, 5 July 1642, quoted in Eales, *Puritans*, 155.
21. Bod. MS Tanner, 303. Coningsby, 'A true Accompt', 2f.
22. Atherton, *op. cit.*, 230.
23. Atherton, *op. cit.,* 154.
24. Webb, i, 106f.
25. *ODNB*, Louis A. Knafla, 'John Egerton, 1st Earl of Bridgewater'.
26. Atherton, *op. cit.*, 228.
27. HMC. Portland MSS, iii, 94.
28. HMC. Portland MSS, iii, 92-3. Letter to Sir Robert Harley, July 15, 1642.
29. HMC. Portland MSS, iii, 93.
30. Bod. MS Tanner, 303, Coningsby, 'A true Accompt', 2f.
31. BL. Harleian MS 7189, 'Certain Observations', f241v.
32. Eales, *Puritans*, 152.
33. Lewis, *Letters of the Lady Brilliana,* 167.
34. Lewis, *op. cit.,* Letter to Edward Harley, July 19, 1642, 182.
35. BL. Harleian MS 7189, 'Certain Observations', f241v.
36. BL. Harleian MS 7189, 'Certain Observations', f242r.
37. HMC. Portland MSS, iii, 95; McParlin, Thesis, 62.

Chapter 6
1. Webb i, 71; Thomas & Boucher, *Hereford City Excavations*, 182.
2. Baxter, *Reliquiae*, 41.
3. McParlin, Thesis, 64.
4. McParlin, Thesis, 81f.
5. BL. Portland MSS. Loan 29/72.
6. Hughes, *Causes of the English Civil War*, 177.
7. BL. Harleian MS 7189, 'Certain Observations', f242r.
8. Webb, i, 96. Davies is probably the same person who was a relative of the Harleys and later one of the defenders of Brampton Bryan.
9. See Eales, *Puritans*, 35f for the Harley family's inter-county ramifications.
10. Eales, *op. cit.*, 150.
11. BL. Portland MSS Loan 29/27, i, 'Lady Brilliana to Harley in Harley's hand'.
12. Symonds, *Diary*, 262: 'Harley ruined it at the beginning of the Parliament'.
13. Quoted in Webb, i, 124.
14. *TRHS*, 4th series, Vol 9 (1920), 135-8, Skeel, Caroline, 'The Cattle Trade Between Wales and England from the 15th to the 19th Centuries', 140.
15. Rushworth, *Historical Collections*, v, 77-102, 341-387; 8 December 1642, 17 July and 17 October 1643.
16. *TRHS*, Skeel, *op. cit.*, 140.
17. CSPD, 1641-43, 398ff. Nehemiah Wharton's letters.
18. Webb, i, 154, 162.
19. McParlin, Thesis, 63.
20. Fletcher, *Outbreak*, 395, quoting *Perfect Diurnal*, 26 Sept-3 Oct, sub 26 Sept; Phillips, *Civil War in Wales* ii, 24-5.
21. CSPD, 1641-43, 398ff. Nehemiah Wharton's letters.
22. Webb, i, 154.

Chapter 7
1. Thomas & Boucher, *Hereford City Excavations*, vol. 4, 178.
2. CSPD, 1641-43, 398ff.
3. Atherton, *Ambition*, 233.
4. Atherton, *op. cit.,* 233.
5. BL. Harleian MS 7189, 'Certain Observations', f242v.
6. Webb, i, 163.
7. CSPD, 1641-43, 398ff.
8. Gardiner i, 12.
9. Webb, i, 188; ii, 354.
10. Webb, i, 177f.
11. HCRO. CF50/275D.
12. HPL. LC. PC 2306, Pamphlets.

13. Croft, *The House of Croft*, 88; though Newman, *Royalist Officers*, 93, was unable to trace any record of a commission for Sir William.
14. Webb, ii, 408n.
15. HCRO. AA17/89. 'Some Passages,' 207. Geers' son John, a Fellow of New College, Oxford, was turned out of his Fellowship in 1648 and reinstated in 1660.
16. Craik, *Life of Jonathan Swift*, 4; Duncumb, Collections: Wormelow Hundred i, 62; Matthews, *Collections*, vi, 75.
17. JHL, vol 5, 1 November 1642. 'Earl of Stamford's Letter, 1 November 1642, 424-9.
18. JHL, vol 5, 1 November 1642, *ibid.*.
19. Webb, i, 195.
20. JHL, vol 5, 1642-43: 21 November 1642, 452-3, 'Earl of Stamford's Letter'.
21. Webb, i, 197.
22. HPL. Parr, 'Historical Notes of Old Ledbury', 27. Letter of 13 December 1642 from Hu Elliott to Sir Richard Leveson, reprinted in *Hereford Times*, 3 May 1884.
23. Quoted in Webb, i, 195.
24. JHL, vol 5, 1642-43: 21 November 1642, 452-3, 'Earl of Stamford's Letter'.
25. Powell, *Diary*, 13 November 1642.
26. Webb, i, 200.
27. This was a frequent gambit, as old friends were often on the other side.
28. Webb, i, 203.
29. HMC. Portland MSS, iii, 102.
30. BL. Harleian MS 7189, 'Certain Observations', f243r.
31. HPL. Parr, 'Historical Notes of Old Ledbury,' 27. Letter of 13 December 1642 from Hu Elliott to Sir Richard Leveson, reprinted in *Hereford Times*, 3 May 1884.
32. HCRO. CF50/263. 'Civil War Assessments'.
33. HCRO. BC63/1, 'All Saints Parish'.
34. BL. Harleian MS 7189, 'Certain Observations', f243r.
35. *Ibid.*
36. HCRO. AA17/90, G.F. Townsend, 'The Sieges in Hereford During the Commonwealth'.
37. BL. Harleian MS 7189, 'Certain Observations', f 243r,v. Price had a certificate, signed by Stamford and Edward Massey, stating that he 'freely showed his love and affection towards us in the Parliament's cause' (HCRO. CF/50.275D).

Chapter 8
1. Bod. MS Tanner, 303, Coningsby, 'A true Accompt', 16.
2. Webb, i, 206ff.

3. In *TW*, 1994, 97-139, Shoesmith R. and Crosskey R., 'Go to Gaol – in Hereford', 101, suggest it was in disuse by the 16th century. CCC, vol. 1, 651. 1 August 1646.

4. Webb, i, 208.

5. NA. C.231/3/22, 106; BL Add. MSS 11043, ff14v-18.

6. *Perfect Diurnall*, 2 February 1643, quoted in Webb, i, 218.

7. Firth & Rait, *Acts & Ordinances*, 85-100.

8. Bod. MS Tanner, 303, Coningsby, 'A true Accompt', 2f.

9. Atherton, *Ambition*, 236.

10. Grassby, *The Business Community,* 100.

11. HCRO. AA17/89, 'Some Passages', 209.

12. Bod. MS Tanner, 303. Coningsby, *op. cit.*, 3, 4.

13. Atherton, *Ambition*, 237.

14. Bod. MS Tanner, 303. Coningsby, *op. cit.*, 4.

15. HCRO. TS 21.i.xv.

16. Bod. MS Tanner, 303. Coningsby, *op. cit.*, 5.

17. CAM, ii, 1052-63, 3 April 1651.

18. 'A Coppy of a Letter', quoted in Webb, ii, 349-353.

19. Corbet, *Biographical and Historical Memoir*, 27.

20. Webb, i, 237.

21. Clarendon, *History of the Great Rebellion*, iii, 465.

22. Warburton, *Memoirs of Prince Rupert*, iii, 533ff. 'Marquess of Worcester's Statement'.

23. Quoted in Cooke, *Collections: Hundred of Grimsworth*, i, 120.

24. Warburton, *op. cit.*, iii, 533ff. 'Marquess of Worcester's Statement'.

25. Quoted in Webb i, 238.

26. Bod. MS Tanner, 303, Coningsby, *op. cit.*, 6.

27. Bod. MS Tanner, 303, Coningsby, *op. cit.*, 5.

28. See Webb, i, 274ff. Hutton, *The Royalist War Effort*, 57, suggests Coningsby had actually resigned and Price was acting in his place, as 'unofficial governor', but there is no evidence for this.

29. Webb, i, 240; Bod. MS Tanner, 303, Coningsby, *op. cit.,* 7.

30. See Atherton, *Ambition*, 234ff.

31. Webb, i, 241.

32. Webb, i, 243.

33. Rushworth, *Historical Collections*, v, 102ff.

34. Webb, i, 247.

35. HCRO. CF50/275D.

36. See *ODNB*, U. Lotz-Heumann, 'St John, Oliver'.

37. NA. C115/N2/8521. Letter from Lady Brilliana to Viscount Scudamore, 27 December, 1642.

38. Quoted in Eales, *Puritans*, 164.

39. HMC. Portland MSS, iii, 105.

40. BL. Portland MSS Loan 29/174ff.18-19, Marquess of Hertford to Lady Brilliana; 29/174 f17r, Lady Brilliana to Harley, 8 March 1643.

41. Eales, *Puritans*, 167.

42. Webb, i, 253.

43. Young & Holmes, *The English Civil War*, 121.

Chapter 9

1. Webb, i, 254.

2. Cave's testimony, quoted in Webb, i, 275.

3. Hutton, *The Royalist War Effort*, 58.

4. Cave's testimony, Webb, i, 276.

5. Bod. MS Tanner, 303. Coningsby, 'A true Accompt', 11.

6. Bod. MS Tanner, 303. Coningsby, *op. cit.*, 10.

7. Cave's testimony, Webb, i, 277.

8. Bod. MS Tanner, 303, Coningsby, *op. cit.*, 12.

9. Bod. MS Tanner, 303, Coningsby, *op. cit.*, 13, 16.

10. Bod., MS Tanner, 303, Coningsby, *op. cit.*, 22-23.

11. Col. Price's evidence at Cave's court-martial, quoted in Duncumb, *Collections,* 260.

12. Bod. MS Tanner, 303, Coningsby, *op. cit.*, 14.

13. Bod. MS Tanner, 303, Coningsby, *op. cit.*, 18.

14. Bod. MS Tanner, 303, Coningsby, *op. cit.*, 9

15. Bod. MS Tanner, 303, Coningsby, *op. cit.,* 22.

16. Terms reprinted in Webb, i, 257f.

17. Apart from Herbert Price, among the garrison officers was also Lt- Col. Thomas Price, of Wisterton (Newman, *Royalist Officers*, 306).

18. Atherton, *Ambition*, 114.

19. Bod. MS Tanner, 303, Coningsby, *op. cit.*, 15.

20. Cave's testimony, Webb, i, 283.

21. Bod. MS Tanner, 303, Coningsby, *op. cit.*, 26.

22. Bod. MS Tanner, 303, Coningsby, *op. cit.*, 18, 23.

23. Had Price been acting as Governor, it is most unlikely that he would have escaped trial.

24. Bod. MS Tanner, 303, Coningsby *op. cit.*, 24f.

25. Webb, i, 286.

26. HPL. LC942.44. PC 2306, 'The Welchman's Lamentation for the Losse of her creat Town, and City of Hereford'.

27. Quoted in Webb, i, 263f.

28. Webb, i, 266.

29. HCRO. AA17/89, 'Some Passages', 210. She also had to pay 'for mending the tiles over my new closet, which Sir William Waller's soldiers brake down to shoot at Widemarsh Gate'.

30. Vicar's *Parliamentary Chronicle*, 318, quoted in Townsend, *Town and Borough of Leominster*, 103.

31. George, *History of the Herefordshire Borderland*, 55.

32. Quoted in Webb, i, 261.

33. HMC. Portland MSS, iii, 87, Letter of 9 May 1643.

34. Webb, i, 288.
35. Webb, i, 289.
36. BL. Harleian MS 7189, 'Certain Observations', f 244r,v.
37. Webb, i, 265.
38. Cliffe, *Puritans in Conflict*, 181, 184, 193.
39. Webb, i, 292.

Chapter 10

1. Quoted in Townshend, *Diary of Henry Townshend,* ii, 120f.
2. HMC. Portland MSS, iii, 111, Lady Brilliana to Sir Robert Harley, 9 May 1643.
3. Symonds, *Diary*, 263.
4. McParlin, Thesis, 81.
5. Rushworth, *Historical Collections*, vol 5: 1642-45, May 1643, 154-164.
6. Lewis, *Letters of the Lady Brilliana*, 205, No. CCI, 30 June 1643.
7. Hutton, *The Royalist War Effort,* 113.
8. Eales, *Puritans*, 150.
9. Webb, i, 318.
10. Lewis, *Letters of Lady Brilliana*, 186. Letter to Edward Harley, December 25, 1642.
11. HMC. Portland MSS, i, 1.
12. HMC. Portland MSS, iii, 111.
13. HMC. Bath MSS, i, 8.
14. Warburton, *Memoirs of Prince Rupert*, ii, 273.
15. Clarendon, *History*, iv, 181.
16. HCRO. CF50/263, document dated 5 August 1643.
17. BL. Harleian MS 7189, 'Certain Observations', f245r.
18. HMC. Bath MSS, i, 2.
19. Kenyon, *The Civil Wars of England*, 86.
20. HMC. Bath MSS, i, 26-27.
21. HMC. Bath MSS, i, 6, 14.
22. Eales, *op. cit.*, 172.
23. HCRO. CF50/263. 'Civil War Assessments'.
24. BL. Portland Mss Loan, 29/72, 'Lady Brilliana to Sir Robert Harley'.
25. HMC. Bath MSS, i, 26-27.
26. HMC. Bath MSS, *ibid.*
27. Lewis, *Letters of Lady Brilliana*, 209. Letter to Edward Harley.
28. HMC. Bath MSS. Davies, *op. cit.*, 27; Introduction, iv.
29. HMC. Bath MSS, i., 33; HPL.PLC 920.
30. BL. Portland MSS Loan, 29/174 f.64r, 'Harley to Nathaniel Wright and Samuel More'.
31. Rait, *Acts and Ordinances of the Interregnum, 1642-60,* 274-283, 8 September 1643.
32. Matthews, *Walker Revised*, 195.
33. Webb, i, 363; Warburton, *Memoirs of Prince Rupert*, i, 524.

34. Corbet, *Biographical and Historical Memoir*, 85; Bund, *Civil War in Worcestershire,* 104ff; Webb, i, 360f .

Chapter 11

1. Williams, *Parliamentary History*, 127.
2. Eales, *Puritans*, 180.
3. McParlin, Thesis, 80, quoting HCRO, City Records, iv, 55-57.
4. Webb, ii, 6.
5. Letter of 10 February 1644, quoted in Webb, i, 354.
6. *TW*, 1936, 27-29. Eisel, J., 'Hopton Castle'.
7. Fletcher, *Outbreak*, 350, and *ODNB,* J.T. Peacey, 'Robert Wallop'.
8. Warburton, *Memoirs of Prince Rupert*, i, 511.
9. HMC. Bath MSS, i, Account of Col. Samuel More, 39.
10. HMC. Bath MSS, i. Account of Capt. Priamus Davies, 29; Account of Col. Samuel More, 37-38.
11. HMC. Bath MSS, i, Account of Col. Samuel More, 37-38.
12. Fletcher, *Registers of Hopton Castle.*
13. South-West Shropshire Hist. & Arch. Soc., *The Gale of Life*: Bigglestone, Peter, 'The Civil War', 163.
14. Webb, i, 389.
15. See *American History Review*, Vol 99, No 4, Donagan, *op. cit.* 1137; also *Historical Journal*, 44,2 (2001), 368-389. Donagan, 'The Web of Honour: Soldiers, Christians and Gentlemen in the English Civil War.'
16. HMC. Bath MSS, i, Account of Capt. Priamus Davies, 30f.
17. Webb, ii, 359f., quoting *Rupert Correspondence*, ii, 135, 146, 151-2.
18. HMC. Bath MSS, i, 29-33. Account of Capt. Priamus Davies.
19. HMC. Bath MSS, i, 33. Account of Capt. Priamus Davies.
20. HMC. Portland MSS, iii, Letter of 3 June 1644.
21. HMC. Bath MSS, i, 35. Letter from Thomas Harley to his father.
22. Brampton Bryan Harley Archives, Document from Samuel Shilton, brought to Westminster on 23 July 1647.
23. Quoted in Cliffe, *Puritans in Conflict*, 85.
24. *ODNB*, Andrew Warmington, 'Sir William Vavasour'.
25. Warburton, *Memoirs of Prince Rupert*, i, 514.
26. BL. Harleian MSS 6802.169.
27. HMC. Bath MSS, i, 34.
28. Webb, i, 380n.; Hutton, *The Royalist War Effort*, 118.
29. HMC. Bath MSS, i, 27.

30. Webb, ii, 10n.
31. Munthe, *Hellens*, 91.
32. *Mercurius Aulicus*, 6 May 1644.
33. Quoted in Webb, ii, 21.
34. Bund, *Civil War in Worcestershire*, 125ff.
35. HCRO.AA17/89. 'Some Passages', 213.
36. Cooke, *Collection*, 164.

Chapter 12
1. Webb, ii, 46, quoting SP2, v. 837, 839.
2. Webb, ii, 66.
3. Young & Holmes, *The English Civil War*, 46.
4. CSPD. Charles I, vol. 502, August 1644, 387-465. Massey's Report to the Committee of Both Kingdoms.
5. CSPD. Charles I, vol 502: August 1644, pp 387-465, ibid.
6. See Webb, ii, 80; reference to 'Rupert Correspondence'.
7. Warburton, *Memoirs of Prince Rupert*, i, 524.
8. Bod.MS. Firth, c.8,f328r.
9. Newman, *Royalist Officers*, 17.
10. Atherton (ed.), *Sir Barnabas Scudamore's Defence*, 9.
11. Webb, ii, 79, quoting 'official papers'.
12. Bannister, *History of Ewyas Harold*, 91.
13. Corbet, *Biographical and Historical Memoir*, 119.
14. Webb, ii, 115ff.
15. Morris, Alan, 'Numismatic Activities', in Whitehead and Eisel, *A Herefordshire Miscellany*, 186f.
16. *ODNB*, William Marshall, 'Herbert Croft'; see also Wedgwood, *The King's War*, 530, quoting Walker, *Sufferings of the Clergy*, ii, 34.
17. Webb, ii, 112.
18. John Webb had 'reason to believe that Colonel Barnard took possession of it of it as Governor on the tenth of September 1644' (HCRO. Hopton Papers, 11). It is possible that the house was garrisoned by Mynne during his time as governor.
19. Webb, ii, 73.
20. Webb, ii, 121; HCRO. Hopton Papers, 11, 32.
21. Webb, ii, 123.
22. Corbet, *Biographical and Historical Memoir*, 136; Atherton (ed.), 'Sir Barnabas Scudamore's Defence', 12; Webb ii, 123.
23. Barroll, *Barroll*, 20. John Barnold, or Barnard, is something of a mystery man. If he was also temporary Governor of Hereford and of Cwm Hîr, as Webb suggests (ii, 134), it might be expected that he would have significant family connections with Herefordshire or the Marches, but none are traceable, though Webb notes 'Ap Arnold, a Herefordshire name' (ii, 160n). He has been identified with James Barroll, Mayor of Hereford in 1639, a combative royalist: see Robinson, *History of the Mansions and Manors*, 61-62; Watkins, *Collections: Hundred of Radlow*, 38; Barroll, *Barroll*, 20. But a contemporary puritan source, the 'Certain Observations', refers separately and disapprovingly to Barroll, 'a city captain' and Colonel Barnard, 'a foul monster … as his life was wicked his death was suitable'. No record has been found of John Barnold's earlier career, nor of James Barroll's later life. His son, also James Barroll, a major in the royalist army, was at Oxford when it capitulated. In 1646 he compounded for the family lands at Byford and was fined for delinquency at one-tenth, £77 (SP Series II, vol xvi, 105; Barroll, *Barroll*, 25).
24. *Weekly Account*, March 19-25, 1645, quoted in Webb, ii, 142n.
25. Brereton's estimate; Webb, ii, 142.

Chapter 13
1. Warburton, *Memoirs of Prince Rupert*, i, 524.
2. Atherton (ed.), 'Sir Barnabas Scudamore's Defence', 11.
3. BL. Harleian MS 7, f245v.
4. Quoted in Townshend, *Diary of Henry Townshend*, ii, 192ff. Local resistance had already begun in southern Shropshire, led by the parson of Bishop's Castle, Gervase Needham.
5. Warburton, *Memoirs of Prince Rupert*, iii, 53, letter from Maurice to Rupert, undated, January 1645.
6. Warburton, *op. cit.*, 54, letter from Maurice to Rupert, 29 January 1645.
7. Dore, *Letter Books*, i, 62.
8. In *Midland History*, 1985, vol x, 63, Paul Gladwish, 'The Herefordshire Clubmen: A Reassessment', 63, says that the 600 men were intended for the King's field army, though the Association's aim was to raise a local force which would make the garrisons redundant.
9. Dore, *Letter Books*, i, 62.
10. Dore, *op. cit.*, 65.
11. Morrill, *Revolt in the Provinces*, 126.
12. *Midland History*, Gladwish, *op. cit.*, 66, quoting Faraday, *Military Assessments, 1663*, 17.
13. Gladwish, *op. cit.*, 66.
14. P&P, No. 85 (November 1979), 25-48. Underdown, D., 'The Chalk and the Cheese: Contrasts Among the English Clubmen', 47.
15. BL.Harleian MS 7189, 'Certain Observations', f246r.
16. *Ibid*.

17. BL. Harleian MS 7189, *op. cit.*, fol.246r.
18. BL. Harleian MS 7189, *op. cit.*, f246v.
19. Dore, *Letter Books*, i, 62.
20. Hutton, *The Royalist War Effort*, 163.
21. Webb, ii, 159; Symonds, *Diary*, 263.
22. Full text quoted in Webb, ii, Appendix xx, 369f.
23. Letter from Gloucester, 22 March, 1645, quoted in Webb, ii, 154f.
24. HMC. Portland MSS iii, 138. Letter from Gloucester, 4 July 1645.
25. Dore, *op. cit.*, 132.
26. Dore, *op. cit.*, i, 141.
27. *Midland History*, Gladwish, *op. cit.*, 67; Hutton, *Royalist War Effort*, 170, agrees.
28. HCRO. CF50/97, 'Herefordiana', transcribed letters from King Charles to Barnabas Scudamore, No. 14, 25 March 1645.
29. Hutton, *The Royalist War Effort*, 170.
30. BL. Harleian MS 7189, 'Certain Observations' f247r.
31. BL. Harleian MS 7189, 'Certain Observations', f247r; Dore, *Letter Books*, i, 141-3, No. 142.
32. HPL. PC 180, Pilley, MSS Notes, 297.
33. Hutton, *op. cit.*, 170f.
34. Warburton, *Memoirs of Prince Rupert*, ii, 82n, notes a letter sent by him to Lord Jermyn in Paris on 1 April.
35. Atherton, 'Sir Barnabas Scudamore's Defence', 14f.
36. *VCH*, 'Political History', 394.
37. *P&P*, No. 85 (Nov. 1979), 25-48. Underdown, D., 'The Chalk and the Cheese: Contrasts among the English Clubmen', 47.
38. See *Midland History*, 1994, vol 19, Osborne, S., 'The War, the People, and the Absence of Clubmen in the Midlands, 1642-1646.'

Chapter 14

1. Webb, ii, 171. Astley was the son of Sir Jacob, later Lord, Astley, the royalist general.
2. *Perfect Occurrences*, April 26, 1645, quoted in Webb, ii, 172f.
3. *EHR*, Vol 13 No. 52 (Oct 1898), 729-741. The *Journal of Prince Rupert's Marches in England from September 5 1642 to July 4, 1646.*
4. *Mercurius Aulicus*, Friday 25 April, quoted in Webb, ii, 178f.
5. Massey's despatch to the Speaker, quoted in Webb, ii, 181.
6. JHC, Vol 4, 1644-46, pp 127-8.
7. Powell, *Diary*, 24 May 1645.
8. See Symons, *Diary*, 167,9.
9. Duncumb, *Collections*, 1, 266.
10. HCRO. AA17/89. 'Some Passages,' 215.

11. Quoted in Vicars, *Parliamentarie Chronicall*, iv, 178.
12. Walker, *Iter Carolinum*, 20, quoted in Atherton (ed.), 'Sir Barnabas Scudamore's Defence', 16.
13. From Barksdale, *The Cotswold Muse*, quoted in Webb, ii, 196.
14. Walker, *ibid.*
15. Warburton, *Memoirs of Prince Rupert*, ii, 113.
16. BL. Harleian MS. 6988. 68, letter of 23 June 1645.
17. Warburton, *op. cit.*, 122.
18. Warburton, *op. cit.,* 119f.
19. HCRO. CF50/97, 'Herefordiana', transcribed letter from King Charles to Barnabas Scudamore, No. 3, 2 July 1645.
20. Webb, ii, Appendix xxiii, 374f.
21. *VCH.* 'Political History', 394. Webb ii, 197.
22. Matthews, *Collections*, vi, 75. The garment was sent to Charles at Raglan.
23. Webb, ii, 198n.

Chapter 15

1. Rushworth, *Historical Collections*, v, 556ff.
2. Symonds, *Diary*, 203.
3. HCRO. Report from the Earl of Leven, from Ledbury, July 23, 1645.
4. *Ibid.*
5. Terry, *Leven,* 371.
6. CSPD 1645-47, 151.
7. Scudamore's letter to Lord Digby, quoted in Webb, ii, 385f.
8. HPL. PC 151, Pilley, MS Notes, 17f. The *posse comitatus*, 'county force, was an emergency assembly of all able-bodied and armed men.
9. Miles Hill, see Webb, ii, 398.
10. Quoted in Rushworth, *Historical Collections,* v, 556ff.
11. Letter from Corbet to Speaker of the House of Commons, 31 July, 1645, quoted in Bund, *Civil War in Worcestershire*, 165.
12. Webb, ii, 216, 398.
13. Leven's Declaration, in Rushworth, *op. cit.,* vi, 116-141.
14. JHC, vol. 4, 1644-46, 9 July 1645.
15. SP 24/75, quoted in Sherwood, *Civil Strife in the Midlands.*
16. McParlin, Thesis, 115.
17. Hill, quoted in Webb, ii, 397.
18. HPL. PC180, Pilley, MSS Notes, 306f, quoting *A Perfect Diurnall*, 11 August 1645.
19. Warburton, *Rupert*, iii, 115.
20. Symonds, *Diary*, 218.
21. Terry, *Leven*, 375.
22. Terry, *op. cit.*, 376.
23. Webb, ii, 393.

24. Webb, ii, 396.
25. Leven's Declaration, quoted in Rushworth, *op. cit.*, vi, 116-141.
26. Bod. MS Tanner, 303. Coningsby, 'A true Accompt', 15.
27. Letter to Lord Digby from Sir Barnabas Scudamore, quoted in Webb, ii, 385ff.
28. Scudamore in Webb, ii, 387.
29. *TW*, 1912, Watkins, A., 'Supposed Subterraneous Passages near Hereford', 26.
30. Leven's Declaration, quoted in Webb, ii, 385.
31. Johnson, *Ancient Customs of Hereford*, 121n.
32. *TW*, Watkins, *op. cit.*, 27.
33. HPL. PC180. Pilley. MSS Notes, 252-3.
34. Provisionally noted findings of 2009-10, still to be published.
35. Letter reprinted in Webb, ii, 389f.
36. HMC. Portland MSS, iii, 139.
37. Leven to the House of Lords, 12 August 1645, quoted in Webb, ii, 392.
38. Scudamore, Webb, ii, 386.
39. See Webb, ii, 218, referring to Slingsby, *Diary*, 163.
40. SP xcvii, quoted in Webb, ii, 219.
41. Scudamore's Letter to Digby quoted in Webb, ii, 387.
42. Webb, ii, 218.
43. Scudamore's Letter to Digby, quoted in Webb, ii, 388.
44. Botzum, *The 1675 Thomas Blount MS*, 56.
45. Webb, ii, 218.
46. Philpott, *Diocesan Histories*, 220; Lehmberg, *Cathedrals Under Siege*, 231.
47. Scudamore's Letter to Digby, Webb, ii, 387.
48. Leven's Declaration, Rushworth, *op. cit.*, vi, 116-141.
49. Letter from Col. Purefoy MP to the Speaker, 3 September 1645, quoted in Bund, *Civil War in Worcestershire*, 168.
50. Leven's Declaration, Rushworth, *op. cit.*, vi, 116-141
51. Bod. Ashmolean MSS. xxxvi, No. 226.
52. Terry, *Leven*, 377.
53. Matthews, *Collections, Hundred of Wormelow*, ii, 44, from Portland MSS, i, 362. See also Webb, ii, 381f, for Major Smith's account.
54. Terry, *Leven*, 372, Letter from Leven to Callendar, from Ledbury, 23 July 1645.
55. HPL. LC942.44. PC 2306, 'A True and Impartiall Account of the Plunderings... by the Scottish Army, During their Siege Before the City of Hereford, Anno Dom. 1645'.
56. *TW* 53, 2005, 25-40, Eisel, J.C., 'Notes on the Former Hereford Market Hall and the Tolsey', 30; 38.

Chapter 16
1. HCRO. BC63/1.
2. HPL. PC 180, Pilley, MSS Notes, 301.
3. Webb, ii, 240.
4. Warburton, *Memoirs of Prince Rupert*, ii, 117.
5. HPL. PC 151, Pilley, MS Notes, 2.
6. Symonds, *Diary*, 233, 238. Clark, *Raglan Castle*, 49.
7. BL. Bibl. Harl. 944. Richard Symons, 'A continuation of the marchings and action of the royall army'.
8. Walker, *Iter Carolinum*, in 'Collectanea Curiosa', 446.
9. HMC. 13th Report, Appendix, iv, 1662.
10. BL. Harleian MS 7189, 'Certain Observations', f248v.
11. Cooke, *Collections, Hundred of Grimsworth*, 1, 11. The Marshal was an officer of the Sheriff's, responsible for prisons and prisoners.
12. Webb, ii, 247.
13. See Ian Roy, 'Royalist reputations, the Cavalier ideal and the reality', in McElligott & Smith, *Royalists and Royalism*, 89-111.
14. Symonds, *Diary*, 276.
15. HCRO. CF50/97, 'Herefordiana', transcribed letters from King Charles to Barnabas Scudamore, No. 6, 1st October 1645.
16. Webb, ii, 242.
17. Dore, *Letter Books*, ii, 162. Letter from Col. Samuel More to General Brereton, 28 October 1645.
18. Webb, ii, 244.
19. Ian Roy, 'The Cavalier ideal and the reality', in McElligott & Smith, *Royalists and Royalism*, 110. Vaughan was an energetic commander, but his sobriquet perhaps is owed to his breaking parole when he regained Shrawardine Castle after surrendering to Mytton.
20. HCRO. CF50/97, 'Herefordiana', vol. 5, transcribed letters from King Charles to Barnabas Scudamore, No. 15, 11 October 1645.
21. HMC. Portland MSS, iii, 139.
22. Vicars, *Parliamentarie Chronicall*, iv, 318.
23. Vicars, *ibid*.
24. *True Informer*, 7 November 1645.
25. Webb, ii, 246.
26. Symonds, *Diary*, 263.
27. Webb, ii, 247.
28. *Mercurius Veridicus*, quoted in Webb, ii, 430.

Chapter 17
1. Roe, *Military Memoir*, 23.
2. Atherton (ed.), 'Sir Barnabas Scudamore's Defence', 44.
3. Atherton, *Ambition*, 95, 126.

4. BL. Harleian MS 6868. Silas Taylor, f100.
5. 'Sir Barnabas Scudamore's Defence' quoted in Roe, *op. cit.*, 117.
6. Quoted in Roe, *op. cit.,* 116n.
7. Paper to the House of Lords from the Committee for Both Kingdoms, quoted as Appendix XV in Roe, *op. cit.*, 218f.
8. Roe, *op. cit.*, 24.
9. Reproduced in Webb, ii, 401.
10. *Perfect Diurnall*, 11 August 1645 notes that Col. Morgan is put in command of all Garrisons of Cities of Gloucester, Monmouth, Glamorgan and Hereford; Dore, *Letter Books*, ii, 446. Letter from the Committee of Worcestershire to General Bereton.
11. Roe, *op. cit.*, 24.
12. Roe, *op. cit.*, 26.
13. Roe, *op. cit.*, 29.
14. Roe, *op. cit.*, 27.
15. Roe, *op. cit.*, 28.
16. Roe, *op. cit.*, 28.
17. 'A New Tricke to Take Townes', quoted in Webb, ii, 402.
18. *Ibid.*
19. Quoted in Vicars, *Parliamentarie Chronicall*, iv, 331.
20. Atherton (ed.), 'Sir Barnabas Scudamore's Defence', 47.
21. Atherton, *op. cit.*, 47.
22. Roe, *op. cit.*, 30.
23. 'A New Tricke', quoted in Webb, ii, 403.
24. Roe, *op. cit.*, 30.
25. Roe, *op. cit.*, 30.
26. 'Sir Barnabas Scudamore's Defence', Webb, ii, 405.
27. *Ibid.*
28. Atherton (ed.), 'Sir Barnabas Scudamore's Defence', 49.
29. *True Informer*, 30 October 1845.
30. HCRO. AA17/90. Townsend, G.F., 'The Sieges in Hereford During the Commonwealth', 52.
31. See Dore, *Letter Books*, ii, 420, note.
32. JHL. Letter from Colonels Birch and Morgan to the House of Lords, 22 December 1645.
33. Roe, *op. cit.*, 118.
34. See list of ransoms in Roe, *op. cit.*, Appendix xvii, 225. Perhaps Harford's 'contribution' of silver for the mint counted against him.
35. *ODNB*, Julia Smith, 'Thomas Traherne'.
36. Traherne, 'Innocence'.
37. Traherne, 'That Childish Thoughts Such Joys Inspire'.
38. Traherne, 'Solitude'.
39. Including Nehemiah Wharton, in 1642

40. CSPD, December 1645, 251, 258.
41. Dore, *Letter Books*, ii, 399.
42. Dore, *op. cit.*, ii, 395.
43. JHC. 3 January 1646.
44. *Ibid.*
45. CSPD, 1645-47, 276, 298f. Letters from the Committeee to Sir John Bridges, and to Bridges, Morgan and Birch, 24 December 1645, 7 January 1646.
46. CSPD, 1645-47, 413; JHC 18 March 1647; JHL, vol 9, 1646, 30 March 1647.
47. Dore, *Letter Books*, ii, 446. Letter of 28 December 1645 from Sir William Brereton to Col. Bowyer.
48. Dore, *op. cit.*, 1420f. Letter from Committee of Salop to Brereton, 23 December 1645.

Chapter 18
1. CSP Venice, vol xxvii, 1643-47. ed. Allen B.Hinds. London, 1926. 328: 'Advices from London, the 4th January, 1646.
2. See Heath-Agnew, *Roundhead to Royalist*; *ODNB*, Newton E. Key, 'John Birch'.
3. McParlin, Thesis, 111ff.
4. JHC, 18 March 1647.
5. HPL. 942.44, Allen J., 'Collectanea Herefordiensia', 15. Webb points out, in ii, 307, that the list is not comprehensive.
6. HCRO.F.76/iv/9.
7. BL. Harleian MS7. f249v.
8. Quoted in Collins, *Outlines of Old & New Hereford*, 109.
9. Noted in Cooke, *Collections*, 53, from BL.Add MS 16, 178.
10. See BL.Add.MS16178. 'Orders and Graunts Made by the Commytee … at Hereford', with documents and orders from March 1646 to May 1647.
11. *TW*, xl, Aylmer, G.E., 'Who Was Ruling in Herefordshire from 1645 to 1661', 379.
12. BL.Add.MS16178, 141.
13. Whitehead, *The Castle Green*, 49.
14. Price, *An Historical Account*, 134.
15. *ODNB*, William Marshall, 'Herbert Croft'.
16. See Lehmberg, S., with Aylmer, G.E., 'Reformation to Restoration, 1535-1660' in Aylmer & Tiller, *Hereford Cathedral*, 87-109.
17. Quoted in Carless, *A Short History of Hereford School*, 29.
18. Rawlinson, *History and Antiquities*, viii.
19. Williams, Joan, 'The Library', in Aylmer & Tiller, *Hereford Cathedral*, 521.
20. Harvey, *Mappa Mundi*, 14; Lehmberg, *Cathedrals Under Siege*, 48. The earliest direct

reference to it is from 1680, when it was noted as a 'curiosity' in the Library.

21. Massey, Roy, 'The Organs' in Aylmer & Tiller, *Hereford Cathedral*, 470.
22. HCRO. BC63/1.
23. Matthews, *Walker Revised*, 194, 192.
24. Matthews, *op, cit.*, 196.
25. HCRO. CF50/275D. Receipt signed by Miles Hill.
26. McParlin, Thesis, 57.
27. HMC. Portland MSS, iii, 137. Col. Edward Massey to Col. Edward Harley, 17 March 1645.

Chapter 19

1. Townsend, *The Town and Borough of Leominster*, 109.
2. *TW,* xl, Aylmer, G.E., 'Who Was Ruling in Herefordshire from 1645 to 1661', 377.
3. Quoted in Collins, *Outlines of Old and New Hereford*, i, 109.
4. HMC. Portland MSS, iii, 142.
5. Webb, ii, 263, 410ff.
6. Roe, *Military Memoir*, 33.
7. CSPD, Charles I, 1645-47, 361-396, March 2, 1646; Roe, *Military Memoir*, 34.
8. JHC, vol 4, 18 March 1646.
9. Roe, *Military Memoir*, 35.
10. SP 1, xlii, 255, quoted in Webb, ii, 277.
11. Rushworth, *Historical Collections*, v, 584.
12. Hughes and Hurley, *The Story of Ross*, 39.
13. CSPD Charles I, vol 514, April 1646, 397-430; 431.
14. CSPD Charles I, vol 514, 430-439, Committee of Both Kingdoms to Col. Birch, 4 May, 1646.
15. HCRO. CF50/86, transcribed letter.
16. Webb, ii, 268, quoting *Perfect Occurrences.*
17. Bund, *The Civil War in Worcestershire*, 188.
18. See Atherton (ed.), 'Sir Barnabas Scudamore's Defence'.
19. Letter to Speaker of the House of Commons, 18 June, 1646, reprinted in Webb, ii, 414.
20. *TW*, 1919, 172-4. Watkins, A., 'Roaring Meg'. The mortar is now displayed at Goodrich Castle.
21. Letter of 14 June 1646, reprinted in Webb, ii, 415.
22. Letter of 14 June, *ibid*.
23. Most accounts say the breach was in the north-western, or Ladies', tower, but Seaton, *History & Description of Goodrich Castle*, 8, considers that guns of the period could not have been brought to bear on this tower, and places the breach in the opposite, southern, wall.
24. Robinson, *History of the Castles of Herefordshire*, 68ff.

25. Roe, *Military Memoir*, 138.
26. HCRO. LC Deeds 8580, 'Hopton Papers', item 11.

Chapter 20

1. Collins, *Outlines of Old and New Hereford*, 109.
2. HPL. PC151, Pilley, 'Notes on Hereford Castle, 32f. Ravenhill is not mentioned in the conveyance from Page to Birch.
3. Cary, *Memorials*, i, 142, letter dated 7 August 1646. Birch sent a number of petitions, or requests for payment, of sums he considered as owed to him by Parliament.
4. JHC, 1 March 1647: 'Resolved that Goodrich Castle be disgarrisoned and slighted'.
5. HMC. Portland MSS, iii, 145.
6. Webb, ii, 291.
7. Noted in Roe, *Military Memoir*, 226.
8. CSPD, Charles I, 1645-47. Letter of 3 July 1646 from Derby House.
9. HMC. Portland MSS, iii, 144.
10. HMC. Portland MSS, iii, Letter from Eardisley, 29 July 1646.
11. JHC, 4 August 1646.
12. Brampton Bryan Harley Papers, A23. 'Transcripts and Notes', Winton's Account.
13. HMC. Portland MSS, iii, 134f, 137; viii, 4.
14. Brampton Bryan Harley Papers, A23. 'Transcripts and Notes', Winton's Account.
15. BL.Add.MS16178, f110.
16. HCRO. CF61/6. Letters from James Scudamore to William Scudamore, 24 October, 14 November, 19 December 1646.
17. JHC, 5, 702, 708; Roe, *Military Memoir,* 144, 148.
18. HCRO. CF61/6. Scudamore MSS, 67.
19. HMC.Portland MSS iii, 146.
20. McParlin, Thesis, 128.
21. BL.Add.MS16178, f182; CCAM, 3, 613.
22. BL.Add.MS16178, f47v.
23. McParlin, Thesis, 128.
24. Hughes and Hurley, *The Story of Ross*, 32.
25. JHC, 4, 694-5, 15 October 1646.
26. Listed in Rushworth, *Historical Collections*, v, 559-603, in 'Subscribers to a Declaration of Charles I, 19 March 1643'.
27. HMC. Portland MSS, iii, 147.
28. Collins, *Outlines of Old & New Hereford*, 109.
29. Williams, *Parliamentary History*, 158.
30. NA. SP 28/154, 28/2098; 28/256-8.
31. Matthew, *Walker Revised*, 192. Quotation noted in Fletcher, *Outbreak*, 106.
32. Matthew, *op. cit.*, 192ff.
33. HMC. Portland MSS, iii, 148. Letter of I January 1647.

34. HMC. Portland MSS, iii, 148, letter of 28 December 1646.
35. HCRO. CF50/86. Documents dated 26-30 January 1647.
36. HMC. Portland MSS, iii, 148, 149, 1 and 23 January 1647.
37. NA. SP28/257. Letter of the subcommittee at Hereford, 18 April 1647.
38. BL. Add.MS16178, ff117v, 136, and 112v, 130v, 148. Flackett Jr bought the land in 1647.
39. HMC. Portland MSS, iii, 148.
40. HMC. Portland MSS iii, 151. Letter to Edward Harley, 16 January 1647.
41. HMC. Portland MSS, iii, 151, letter of 22 January 1647 to Major Richard Hopton and others.
42. HMC. Portland MSS iii, 151, 154.
43. HMC. Portland MSS, iii, 154, 3 March 1647.
44. *Ibid.*
45. JHC, 1 March, 1647.
46. Bund, *Civil War in Worcestershire*, 201; Hopton, *History of Canon Frome*, quoting an unsigned letter sent from Hereford, 24 March 1647. The regiment, formed at the end of 1645, was made up of local men. See Hopton's proposal for its formation, HMC. Portland MSS, iii, 140f
47. HMC. Portland MSS, iii, 158; Robinson, *Mansions*, 165.
48. CCC, i, 62. 5 April, 1647.

Chapter 21
1. *VCH*, 'Political History', 396.
2. JHL, 5, 1646-48, 210-12, 15 June 1647.
3. Cary, *Memorials*, i, 183; JHC,V, 130-1, quoted in Eales, 187.
4. BL. Loan 29/122, Draft Letter of 22 June 1647 addressed to 'M.M.'.
5. Firth & Rait, *Acts and Ordinances of the Interregnum*, 958-984, 23 June 1647.
6. Rushworth, *Historical Collections*, iv, I, 482.
7. JHC vol 5, 19 July 1647, pp 249-51.
8. Rushworth, *op. cit.,* iv. I, 482.
9. *TW,* xl, Aylmer, G.E., 'Who Was Ruling in Herefordshire from 1645 to 1661', 377.
10. HCRO. CF54/56. Item 55PC, letter of 9 October 1647.
11. Eales, *Puritans*, 189.
12. Morrill, *Revolt in the Provinces*, 169.
13. HCRO. CF50/86. Webb MSS I, transcript of a letter of 12 January 1648.
14. Bell, 'Fairfax Correspondence', quoted in Webb/Roe, 233.
15. Firth & Rait, *Acts & Ordinances of the Interregnum,* 1072-1105.
16. Wedgwood, *The King's War*, 575.

17. CSPD, Charles I, vol. 516, January 1648, 7f.
18. HMC. Portland MSS, iii, 157-8.
19. HMC. Portland MSS, iii, 160f, 162.
20. JHL, x, 276-7.
21. HMC. Portland MSS, iii, 163.
22. *TW*, xl, Aylmer, *op. cit.*, 380.
23. Powell, *Diary*, 31 July, 29 August 1648.
24. Underdown, *Somerset in the Civil War*, 152.
25. Morrill, *Revolt in the Provinces*, 205.
26. Webb, ii, 301ff.
27. CSPD, 1648-49, 206.
28. Gardiner, *Civil War,* iv, 194.
29. Gardiner, *ibid.*
30. Heath-Agnew, *Roundhead to Royalist*, 77.
31. *ODNB*, Gordon Goodwin and David Whitehead, 'Sir Henry Lingen'.
32. Gardiner, *Civil War*, iv, 26; *ODNB*, *ibid.*
33. JHL, quoted in Webb, ii, 430.
34. CSPD 1648-49, 308.
35. Roe, *Military Memoir,* 93f .
37. McParlin, Thesis, 133, 144ff.
38. JHC. vol 6, 82-84. 22 November 1648.
39. CAM, I, 1642-45, 525-547.

Chapter 22
1. JHC, vol 6, 16 October, 28 November 1648.
2. Underdown, *Pride's Purge*, 148.
3. JHC, vol 6, 15 December 1648.
4. *TW* xl, Aylmer, G.E., 'Who Was Ruling in Herefordshire from 1645 to 1661', 378.
5. Underdown, *op. cit.*, 179.
6. JHC, vol 6, 25 November 1648.
7. Underdown, *ibid.*
8. JHC, vol 6, 3 February 1649.
9. JHC, vol 6, 17 January 1649.
10. CSPD, 1649-50, 119; NA. SP28/229, Letter of the Committee at Hereford, 2 January 1649.
11. CCC, I, 140-1, 21 April 1649.
12. McParlin, Thesis, 151; *TW*, Aylmer, *op. cit.*, 381ff.
13. McParlin, Thesis, 151. Their personal abilities may of course have been equal to anyone's, but religio-political correctness took precedence.
14. Firth & Rait, *Acts & Ordinances of the In terregnum,* April 1649, 29-57; November 1650, 456-490.
15. BL.Add.MSS. 11053, ff110-111.
16. CSPD, Commonwealth, 1649-50, vol i, May 1649, 119.
17. JHC, vol. 6, 21 April 1649.
18. JHC, vol 6, 10 May, 16 May 1649.
19. HMC. Portland MSS, iii, 162, letter of 24 April 1649.
20. HMC. Portland MSS, iii, 169, letter of 10 August 1649.

Chapter 23
1. Gardiner, *Civil War*, iii, 197f; Webb, ii, 89.
2. *Hereford Diocesan Magazine*, June 1911. Capes, W.W., 'The Cathedral During the Civil War', 138; *VCH*, 396.
3. Aubrey, *Brief Lives*, 308ff.
4. SPO Series ii, xix, 151, 26 November 1646, noted in Webb transcripts.
5. HCRO. CF61/4. Notes from Sequestration Papers, xlix.485.
6. HCRO. F.76/iv/9.
7. Matthews, *Walker Revised*, 8f.
8. *HDM*, June 1911, Capes, W.W., 'The Cathedral During the Civil War',138.
9. Rawlinson, *History & Antiquities,* 1ff; Capes, W.W., 'The Cathedral During the Civil War' in *Hereford Diocesan Messenger*, June 1911, 137-9.
10. BL.Add.MS5494, ff 125-134; Add.MS 16178, f139v; NA. SP 28/154 and SP28/209B.
11. CAM, vol 1, 193. 10 July 1643, 1 November 1644.
12. CAM, *ibid.*, 18 March 1650.
13. CCC, iii, January 1647, 1637-57.
14. CAM, i, 193f.
15. HPL. PC180, Pilley MS Notes, 351; CCC, iv, 2861-7.
16. SPO Series ii, xxx, 349.
17. *Ibid.*, xvii, 625.
18. HCRO. CF50/275D. It is not clear which of the three Mansel locations is referred to.
19. CCC, i, 651. 1 August, 9 September 1653.
20. CCC, i, 46.
21. CCC, i, 52. 23 December 1646.
22. HCRO. CF61/4. Notes from Sequestration Papers, Series II, xxxviii, 491.
23. CCC, i, 111. 21; iii, 2064-71.
24. CCC, iii, 2000.
25. HCRO. CF61/4. Notes from Sequestration Papers, xlix. 667.
26. CCC, vol. 3, 2035. 4 May, 11 June 1649; Matthews, *Walker Revised*, 195.
27. CCC, vol. 1, 391. 10 January 1651.
28. HCRO. CF61/4. Notes from Sequestration Papers, Series II, xliii, 199.
29. HCRO. CF61/4. Notes from Sequestration Papers, Series II, xlviii, 7, 61.
30. CAM, ii. 1052-63, 3 August 1649.
31. HPL. PC180, Pilley, MSS Notes, 351. *A Catalogue of the Lords, Knights & Gentlemen who have Compounded for their Estates* (1655).
32. CAM, xi, 1052-63, 11 April 1649.
33. McParlin, Thesis, 120; NA. SP24/4, ff25v, 41; 24/71. Petition of Thomas Rawlins, 8 March 1649.
34. CCC, i, 391.

Chapter 24
1. HCRO. CF50/275D, 14 February 1649.
2. *TW*, Taylor, Elizabeth, 'The 17th Century Iron Forge at Carey Mill, 464.
3. HMC Bath MSS, iv, Seymour Papers, 242.
4. CSPD, Interregnum, 228-276. June 1650.
5. CSPD, Interregnum, 26 February 1651.
6. CSPD, Interregnum, 135-185. May 1650.
7. See Leslie & Raylor, *Culture & Cultivation*, 139f.
8. CCC. 1, 183, 9 March 1650.
9. CSPD, 4 March, 21 March 1651.
10. BL. Portland MSS, Loan 29/119, and 176, ff.185-90, 192, 202.
11. Cliffe, *Puritans in Conflict*, 181.
12. CCC, xi, 181, 7 March 1850.
13. CAM, ii, 1052-63, 3 April 1651.
14. CAM, *ibid.*
15. Webb, ii, 430f.
16. McParlin, Thesis, 159.
17. Hutton, *The Royalist War Effort*, 9ff.
18. Botzum, *The 1675 Thomas Blount M*S, 111; Webb, i, 17; ii, 333f. Webb attributes the moving to the wind, but the event remains obscure.
19. HPL. LC942.44. PC2306, 'Vox Infantis, or the Prophetical Child'. Very similar stories come from other places, e.g. Burslem, Staffordshire.

Index

189